The Florida Lawn Handbook

Florida A&M University, Tallahassee
Florida Atlantic University, Boca Raton
Florida Gulf Coast University, Ft. Myers
Florida International University, Miami
Florida State University, Tallahassee
New College of Florida, Sarasota
University of Central Florida, Orlando
University of Florida, Gainesville
University of North Florida, Jacksonville
University of South Florida, Tampa
University of West Florida, Pensacola

The Florida Lawn Handbook

Best Management Practices for Your Home Lawn in Florida

Third Edition

Edited by Laurie E. Trenholm and J. Bryan Unruh

University Press of Florida

Gainesville · Tallahassee · Tampa · Boca Raton
Pensacola · Orlando · Miami · Jacksonville · Ft. Myers · Sarasota

Published in cooperation with Cooperative Extension Service,
University of Florida, Institute of Food and Agricultural Sciences

16 15 14 13 12 11   8 7 6 5 4 3

A record of cataloging-in-publication data is available from
the Library of Congress.
ISBN 978-0-8130-2802-6

The University Press of Florida is the scholarly publishing agency
for the State University System of Florida, comprising Florida A&M
University, Florida Atlantic University, Florida Gulf Coast University,
Florida International University, Florida State University, New
College of Florida, University of Central Florida, University of Florida,
University of North Florida, University of South Florida, and University
of West Florida.

University Press of Florida
15 Northwest 15th Street
Gainesville, FL 32611-2079
http://www.upf.com

Cooperative Extension Service, University of Florida, Institute
of Food and Agricultural Sciences, Larry Arrington, Director,
in cooperation with the United States Department of Agriculture,
publishes this information to further the purpose of the May 8 and
June 30, 1914, Acts of Congress; and is authorized to provide research,
educational information and other services only to individuals and
institutions that function without regard to race, color, age, sex,
disability, or national origin. The information in this publication
is available in alternate formats. Information on copies for purchase
is available from IFAS-Extension Bookstore, University of Florida,
PO Box 110011, Gainesville, FL 32611-0011 or visit our Web site
at ifasbooks.ufl.edu. Information about alternate formats is available
from IFAS Communication Services, University of Florida, PO Box
110810, Gainesville, FL 32611-0810. This information was published
December 1990 as SP 45, Florida Cooperative Extension Service.
Revised 1997, 1998, February 2003.

Contents

Preface

This book is intended to provide information for homeowners on the Best Management Practices for residential lawns. Following the information contained within this book will help to ensure the future quality of Florida's ground and surface waters. As we make continual advances in turfgrass research and as chemical product availability changes, some of the recommendations may change over time. Contact your local Extension Service office or go to http://turf.ufl.edu for the latest in recommendations.

The use of trade names in this publication is solely for the purpose of providing specific information. It is not a guarantee or warranty of the products mentioned and does not imply that they are the only products available for use.

The pesticide recommendations in this publication are current with state and federal regulations at the time of publication. The user is responsible for determining that the intended pesticide use is consistent with directions on the label of the product being used. Always read and follow the label when applying fertilizer or pesticides!

Acknowledgments

The editors wish to extend their gratitude to the many people who have contributed to this book. We especially thank Eileen Buss, John Cisar, Billy Crow, Monica Elliott, and Jerry Sartain, all of whom have written excellent, up-to-date articles on their areas of expertise. We thank Shirley Anderson and Bart Schutzman for editing and technical help and Chana Bird and Carol Church at IFAS Communications for their editing help.

Introduction

What Is Extension?

The Cooperative Extension Service is a partnership among county, state, and federal governments that serves the citizens of Florida by providing information and education in a variety of areas. In Florida, extension is part of the Institute of Food and Agricultural Sciences at the University of Florida and is included in selected programs at Florida A&M University. Extension provides information to homeowners and industries alike in agriculture, horticulture, gardening, food safety, child and family development, energy conservation, food and resource economics, pest control, and natural resource conservation.

What Is a Master Gardener?

Master Gardeners are adult volunteers recruited and trained by county extension agents and University of Florida specialists to provide assistance in extension home horticultural programs. Through this program, enthusiastic gardeners study in such fields as botany, horticulture, soil science, and plant and insect identification and management. After successfully completing the training program, Master Gardeners teach and promote environmental action—awareness and wise use of resources as well as reduced chemical, water, and energy usage. They conduct gardening clinics at malls, write about gardening for local newspapers, speak in clubs, libraries, and schools, answer phone questions, and conduct demonstration gardens at fairs. The Florida Master Gardener Program is administered by the Extension Service at the University of Florida, Institute of Food and Agricultural Sciences.

Why Are Best Management Practices for Home Lawns Important in Florida?

There are approximately 5 million acres of home lawns in the state of Florida, of which about 1 million are managed by professional lawn care services. Whether you take care of your own yard or hire someone to do the job, the management of this acreage is critical to the future of Florida's ground and surface waters. By following the practices outlined in the *Florida Lawn Handbook*, you can grow an attractive, healthy, stress-tolerant lawn that can help absorb impacts from stormwater runoff and actually reduce potential pollution. For more information on residential lawn management and the turfgrass science program at the University of Florida, refer to http://turf.ufl.edu.

Grasses

Selection of a Turfgrass for Florida Lawns

The lawn is an integral part of the landscape. A beautiful lawn will enhance any landscape, while a poor lawn will detract from the overall appearance (plate 1). Lawns not only increase the aesthetic and economic value of the landscape, they also provide recreational surfaces for outdoor activities, aid in erosion control, filter pollutants, and provide oxygen to our environment. Because many of the grasses used in Florida vary widely in their adaptation, consideration should be given to choice of the proper grass for a particular environment. Table 1.1 provides information to assist in selecting the proper grass for a location.

Some of the following questions may serve as guidelines to grass selection:

What type of lawn is desired or expected and what level of maintenance can you provide? It is important to have an idea of the type of yard you want to maintain. Do you want a lawn that is highly manicured and carefully tended, or are you looking for an average lawn, which will require medium inputs in terms of fertility and maintenance? Or perhaps you're looking for something more natural, with less grass and more plantings of other types. Since maintenance levels differ among the lawngrasses commonly used in Florida, it is important that the correct grass be selected for the type of yard you desire. Most turfgrasses will respond to a range of maintenance levels; however, there is an optimum level for each grass. Levels of maintenance are closely related to cost and time, with high-maintenance turf costing the most and taking the most time to maintain. It is important to realistically assess your ability to maintain your lawn, whether you do the work yourself or pay to have it done. For example, a bermudagrass or St. Augustinegrass lawn will not perform well in a site that does not provide supplemental irrigation during dry times. And while bahiagrass may be able to survive without supplemental irrigation, it may never form a dense, lush, dark green lawn as some of the other grass species will.

Are there any physical or environmental limitations to the planting site? Quality turf requires irrigation, so water quantity and quality requirements are selection factors. Can the area be easily mowed? Soil type, pH, drainage, and other soil characteristics are important. The amount of shade the turf will re-

Table 1.1. Comparison of lawngrasses available for use throughout Florida

Environment	Bahiagrass	Bermudagrass	Carpetgrass	Centipedegrass	Seashore Paspalum	St. Augustinegrass	Zoysiagrass
Adapted to	Statewide	Statewide	Wet areas	N. Florida, Panhandle	Statewide	Statewide	Statewide
Mowing Ht. (in.)	3–4	0.5–1.5	1.5–2	1.5–2	1.5–2	2.5–4	1–2
Soil	Acid, sandy	Wide range	Acid, wet	Acid, infertile	Wide range	Wide range	Wide range
Leaf	Coarse-medium	Fine-medium	Medium	Medium	Fine-medium	Coarse-medium	Fine-medium
Drought Tolerance	Excellent	Good	Poor	Medium	Good	Poor	Medium
Salt Tolerance	Very poor	Good	Poor	Poor	Excellent	Poor	Good
Shade Tolerance	Poor	Poor	Fair	Fair	Fair	Good	Good
Wear Tolerance	Poor	Good-excellent	Poor	Poor	Good-excellent	Poor	Good-excellent
Nematode Tolerance	Very good	Poor	Poor	Poor	Good	Good	Poor
Maintenance Level	Low	Medium-high	Low	Low	Medium	Medium	High
Uses	Lawns, roadsides	Athletic fields, golf courses	Wet areas	Lawns	Lawns, athletic fields, golf courses	Lawns	Lawns
Establishment	Seed, sod	Sod, sprigs, plugs, some seed	Seed, sprigs	Seed, sod, sprigs, plugs	Sod, plugs, sprigs	Sod, plugs, sprigs	Sod, plugs, sprigs

ceive can limit the selection of suitable grasses (plate 2). With answers to these questions in mind, use table 1.1 and the following descriptions to select the proper turfgrass for your Florida lawn.

What does your budget allow for installation and establishment of a lawn? It is important to follow the procedures outlined in chapter 2 for best long-term response of your lawn. A lawn should be considered a long-term property investment and your choice of a grass should reflect what you desire and can adequately maintain.

Region of Adaptation

Environmental and soil conditions vary throughout the state, and certain turfgrasses grow better in some locations than others. There are several turfgrass species and cultivars within those species from which to choose. Some turfgrasses can be planted statewide, while others perform best in the panhandle and north Florida. *Note:* Grasses grown in Florida are maintained in a completely different way from those grown in the northern regions of the United States. Northern-grown grasses (e.g., fescue, bluegrass, ryegrass) will grow in Florida only during fall, winter, and early spring months, and will *not* survive year-round.

Soil Conditions

Several turfgrasses can grow in a wide range of soil conditions, including pH values of 5.0 to 8.5. Most Florida soil types for turfgrass growth include sand, clay, marl, or muck-type soils. For example, centipedegrass and carpetgrass grow best in acid soils. Iron chlorosis is a problem if these grasses are grown in high pH (alkaline) soils. Carpetgrass grows best in wet soils, whereas an established planting of bahiagrass is more tolerant of drought and grows better in sandy soil than most other lawngrasses.

Environmental Stress Tolerances

Turfgrasses vary in their ability to withstand stresses. Drought tolerance is a measure of how well the turf will survive extended dry periods without irrigation or rainfall. For example, bahiagrass and centipedegrass have good drought tolerance, while St. Augustinegrass does not. In many coastal areas, turf can be subjected to salt stress from irrigation water, saltwater intrusion, or salt spray from the ocean. Most grasses will not grow well in this type of environment, but seashore paspalum will grow in a salt-affected site. Although shade from trees or buildings is common in most landscapes, turfgrasses vary widely in their shade tolerance. Both St. Augustinegrass and zoysiagrass have good shade tolerance compared to other warm-season grasses (plate 3). Wear tolerance is a measure of how well a grass continues to grow after being walked or played upon and can determine whether or not a grass will be able to survive in an area of moderate traffic. Seashore paspalum, zoysiagrass, and bermudagrass all have good wear tolerance.

Major Pest Problems

Each turfgrass has some major pest problem that could limit its use in certain locations. Major insect pests are chinch bugs, mole crickets, ground pearls, webworms, spittlebugs, and billbugs. Major disease problems are brown patch, dollar spot, *Pythium, Helminthosporium,* and gray leaf spot. Nematodes can limit use of some species in home lawn locations. Other pest problems can occur and cause severe damage. Proper management practices can help keep most pest problems to a minimum.

Leaf Texture

Leaf textures may be coarse, medium, or fine. This is a relative measure of the leaf blade width. The choice of texture is merely a visual preference unless the grass is important for a sport such as golf. Most southern lawn grasses are coarser in leaf texture than those grown further north (e.g., fescue, bluegrass, and ryegrass). This is especially true of the three most used lawn grasses in Florida: St. Augustinegrass, bahiagrass, and centipedegrass.

Turf Density

The number of leaves or shoots per area is a measure of turf density. Species with a high density and finer leaf texture generally produce better-quality lawns. Turf with a lower density and coarser leaf texture often requires a higher mowing height to produce an acceptable quality of lawn. Higher-density varieties include hybrid bermudagrasses and zoysiagrass. Bahiagrass has a low stand density while other warm-season grasses have a medium density.

Maintenance Level

Each turfgrass grows at a different rate and has optimum levels of fertility, mowing, and irrigation that produce a quality turf. Generally, as more water and fertilizer are applied to the turf, mowing and pest control needs are increased. Turf at a low level of maintenance is fertilized two to three times a year, mowed as needed (often just to remove seedheads), and may or may not be irrigated. High-maintenance turfgrasses receive more frequent fertilization and mowing. More fertilizer applications, particularly during the summer months, result in more shoot growth (more mowing needed), and increase the incidence of some insect or disease problems.

Mowing Height

The growth habit of each turfgrass determines the mowing height for the best quality turf. Mowing turf below the recommended height can stress the grass and subject it to invasion by weeds, insects, and diseases. Mowing at higher heights results in increased leaf surface for more photosynthesis, deeper root systems, better drought tolerance, and healthier turf.

Mowing Frequency

Turfgrass species and level of management determine how often a lawn needs to be mowed. The frequency of mowing can be reduced somewhat by moderating amounts of fertilizer and water applied. Grass clippings should be left on the lawn to provide organic matter and return nutrients to the lawn.

Establishment Methods

Some turf species (e.g., St. Augustinegrass) are limited to vegetative propagation by sod, sprigs, or plugs because seed is not available or does not germinate true to type. Other turf species produce seed in sufficient quantity and trueness to type to allow establishment by seed (e.g., bahiagrass, centipedegrass, carpet-grass, and common bermudagrass). A quality lawn can be established by either method if the site is properly prepared and maintained.

Bahiagrass for Florida Lawns

Bahiagrass (*Paspalum notatum* Flugge) was introduced from Brazil in 1914. It was originally used as a pasture grass on the sandy soils of the southeastern United States. Additional varieties have been introduced since that time for use as lawngrasses. Bahiagrass is a popular low-maintenance lawngrass for infertile soils. Although bahiagrass does not produce a high-quality, dense, dark green lawn like some other warm-season lawngrasses, it does provide a good low-maintenance lawn where slightly reduced visual quality is acceptable (plate 4).

Advantages

Bahiagrass forms an extensive root system, which makes it one of our most drought-tolerant grasses. It performs well in infertile, sandy soils and does not require high inputs of fertilizers. It does not form excessive thatch. It may be grown from seed, which is abundant and relatively cheap, or it may be established from sod, sprigs, or plugs. It has relatively few disease problems, and mole crickets are the only primary insect problem.

Disadvantages

Bahiagrass forms tall, unsightly seedheads throughout the spring, summer, and fall months. This necessitates mowing on a regular schedule. Because the seed stems are tough, it is also more difficult to mow than some other grass species. Bahiagrass does not perform well in high-pH soils and is susceptible to mole crickets. It does not have good tolerance to shade, traffic, or saltwater. With the exception of Pensacola bahiagrass, there is little tolerance for cold temperatures in this species. Leaves of bahiagrass may tend to turn yellow as a result of iron deficiency. This deficiency can be alleviated by modification of soil pH or application of iron fertilizer. For more information on iron deficiency, please refer to "Fertilization" in this section.

Bahiagrass displays an open growth habit, which can allow encroachment of weeds into sparse areas. In addition, bahiagrass has a low tolerance for many herbicides, making chemical weed control difficult. It has a coarse leaf texture and provides less cushioning for recreational activities than some other species (plate 5).

Cultivars

There are four cultivars of bahiagrass available for home lawn or utility use. These may all be established by seed or sod.

'Common'

Common bahiagrass is a coarse-textured, light-colored bahiagrass. It has an open and sparse growth habit and is very susceptible to cold temperatures. It is not normally recommended for use as a lawngrass.

'Argentine'

Argentine forms a relatively dense sod and has a dark green color, making it acceptable for lawn use in many situations. It has wider leaf blades than Pensacola bahiagrass. It has good insect and disease resistance and tolerates cold temperatures well.

'Pensacola'

Pensacola bahiagrass was selected in Pensacola, Florida, in 1935 and is the most widely grown bahiagrass today. It has an extensive root system that imparts excellent drought tolerance. It also tolerates either hot or cold temperatures well. It produces an abundance of seedheads, which reduces its desirability for use as a lawngrass, but makes it suitable for roadside plantings. It has longer and narrower leaf blades than Argentine.

'Paraguay'

This cultivar is also known as Texas bahiagrass. It has short, tough, hairy leaves that have a grayish tint to them. It does not have good cold tolerance and is susceptible to dollar spot disease. It does not perform as well in the lawn as Argentine or Pensacola.

Maintenance of Bahiagrass

Establishment

Bahiagrass can be established as sod or seed. Advantages of planting a bahiagrass lawn from sod are rapid establishment of the lawn and fewer opportunities for weed pressure or other stresses to cause problems. The primary disadvantages of this method are the expense and the labor required to lay the sod. In contrast, bahiagrass seed is not expensive and requires less labor than sodding. Scarified seed, which has been chemically treated to enable faster germination, should be used when available.

Plugging or sprigging bahiagrass is not typically recommended. Because of the slow growth habit of bahiagrass, the plugging method will leave open areas of soil that can be taken over by fast-growing weed species. Diligent weed control measures are needed if this method of planting is used.

The best time to establish bahiagrass is during the spring or early summer months. This enables the grass to grow in before cooler weather begins, when growth is reduced. Seed may safely be sown until later in the year, but growth will again be greatly reduced in the fall. When establishing any grass, it is important to irrigate more frequently than usual. Until a viable root system is established, turf demands for irrigation are greater. It is also important not to mow a newly established lawn until the roots have had a chance to work down into the soil and establish themselves.

Proper site preparation before planting is critical to ensure successful establishment. Refer to "Preparing to Plant a Florida Lawn" in chapter 2 for complete information on site preparation.

Fertilization

Proper fertilization of any lawngrass is an important component of the best management practices for your home lawn. Fertilization and other cultural practices influence the overall health and quality of your lawn and will reduce its vulnerability to numerous stresses, including weeds, insects, and disease.

It is advisable for homeowners to have soil tests done. Your local Extension Service office has instructions and supplies for taking soil samples and submitting them to the UF/IFAS Extension Soil Testing Laboratory for analysis. In particular, phosphorus levels should be determined by soil testing. Since many Florida soils are high in phosphorus, little or no phosphorus may be needed for satisfactory lawn growth after establishment.

Established bahiagrass lawns have relatively low fertility requirements. As with any lawngrass, do not apply more than ½ pound of water-soluble nitrogen per 1000 square feet at any one time. If using a fertilizer that has at least 50 percent of the nitrogen in slow-release form, up to 1 pound of nitrogen per 1000 square feet may be applied at one time.

Table 1.2. Bahiagrass: recommended ranges of nitrogen rates

Location	Pounds N per 1000 sq ft
North Florida	2–3
Central Florida	2–4
South Florida	2–4

In general, two weeks following spring regrowth, apply a complete fertilizer at the rate of ½ (water-soluble) to 1 (slow-release) pound of nitrogen per 1000 square feet. Look for a fertilizer with 2 percent or less phosphorus such as a 15-2-15. The three numbers on the fertilizer bag refer to the percentages of nitrogen, phosphorus, and potassium, respectively. For example, a 50-pound bag of 15-2-15 contains 15 percent nitrogen or 7.5 pounds total nitrogen. This bag will fertilize 7500 square feet at the rate of 1 pound of nitrogen per 1000 square feet.

University of Florida guidelines for lawngrass fertility show a range of fertilizer rates over which a particular species may be successfully grown for various areas of the state. These ranges are included to account for individual homeowner preferences for low-, medium-, or high-input grass. Additionally, localized microclimate conditions can have a tremendous effect on turfgrass growth, and a range of rates allows for these environmental variations. An example of this would be a typical home lawn that is partially shaded and partially sunny. The grass growing in the shade should receive lower rates of fertilizer than that growing in full sun. The guidelines are also separated into three geographical locations statewide, as indicated in table 1.2 above. All rates are in pounds of nitrogen per 1000 square feet. For questions on how and when to apply these amounts, refer to "Fertilizer Recommendations for Your Florida Lawn" in chapter 3.

Fertilizer should be applied to bahiagrass in two to four applications from spring green-up through fall (table 1.3). Do not apply nitrogen too early in the growing season, particularly in north Florida, or subsequent frosts may damage the grass. Likewise, don't fertilize too late in the year, as this can slow regrowth the following spring. If applying water-soluble forms at the lower application rate, it will take more applications to apply the total amount of fertilizer needed for the year than if applying a slow-release fertilizer form.

One of the disadvantages of bahiagrass is its tendency to yellow because of iron deficiency. This problem can be overcome by using a complete fertilizer that contains iron, or by addition of a separate iron material. Soluble iron sources that can be used include ferrous ammonium sulfate, ferrous sulfate, and various iron chelates. Avoid oxide forms of iron, as they will be much less effective than sulfates or chelated forms in alleviating iron deficiency. Apply ferrous sulfate at the rate of 2 ounces in 3–5 gallons of water per 1000 square feet. This can be applied evenly and easily with a hose-end applicator. Follow chelated iron label directions if using one of these materials. Iron applications every six weeks will help maintain green color and, unlike nitrogen, will not promote excessive top growth. Many cases of iron deficiency occur in soils with pH greater than 7.0. An alternative method of alleviating iron deficiency is to lower the soil pH to

Table 1.3. Calendar guide to annual bahiagrass fertilization, by region[a,b]

Region[c] and Maintenance Level	J	F	M	A	M	J	J	A	S	O	N
North Florida											
Basic			C					C			
Moderate			C		SRN			C			
High			C		SRN		Fe	C			
Central Florida											
Basic			C		Fe			C			
Moderate			C			N	Fe		C		
High			C	N		SRN	Fe		C		
South Florida											
Basic		C				Fe				C	
Moderate		C		N		Fe				C	
High		C		N		SRN		Fe		C	

a. For initial spring application, particularly in North Florida, the recommended time to fertilize is after the last frost rather than on a specific calendar date.

b. C = complete fertilizer application (NPK), N = nitrogen application only, SRN = nitrogen only in a slow-release form, Fe = iron application only.

c. For purposes of this table, North Florida = north of Ocala, Central Florida = south of Ocala to a line extending from Vero Beach to Tampa, South Florida = the remaining southern portion of the state.

6.0. This can be done by use of ammonium nitrogen fertilizer sources (e.g., ammonium nitrate or ammonium sulfate) or by application of elemental sulfur *prior* to bahiagrass establishment. Elemental sulfur applied at 10 pounds per 1000 square feet will provide a short-term pH reduction. Once the grass is established, up to 5 pounds of elemental sulfur may be added per 1000 square feet if it is immediately irrigated in to prevent burn.

Mowing

Proper mowing practices are necessary to keep any lawn healthy and attractive. During times of active growth, bahiagrass should be mowed every seven to fourteen days at 3–4 inches of height. Higher mowing heights promote a deeper, more extensive root system that enables the grass to better withstand drought stress. Remove no more than one-third of the height of the leaf blades with any mowing (e.g., for a lawn to be maintained at 3 inches in height, mow when the turf reaches 4–4½ inches). It is important not to mow bahiagrass at lower heights, as that will reduce the tolerance of the grass to heat, drought, and other stresses. It will also suppress root growth. As bahiagrass does not grow extremely tall, mowing cycles are often dictated by seedhead production. Clippings should be left on the ground after mowing. They do not contribute to thatch buildup, as is often assumed, but are actually readily degraded by microorganisms. They also provide a source of nutrients for the lawn and can reduce fertility requirements if left on the lawn on a regular basis.

A sharp, heavy-duty rotary mower blade is needed to cut bahiagrass. Because bahiagrass leaves are very tough, the mower blade will have to be sharpened frequently to ensure a good, clean cut. If this is not done, the leaves may be torn by the mower blades, which can compromise both the health and the appearance of the lawn.

Watering

Irrigating as needed is the best way to water any established, mature grass, as long as the proper amount of water is applied when needed. Irrigation is needed when leaf blades begin to fold up, to actually wilt, or to turn blue gray in color, or when footprints remain visible after walking on the grass. Apply ½–¾ inch of water per application. This will apply water to roughly the top 8 inches of soil, where the majority of the roots are. To determine the amount of irrigation supplied by a sprinkler system, place several coffee cans throughout the irrigation zones to find out how long it takes to apply the recommended amount of water. During prolonged droughts, irrigation may be needed more often. Bahiagrass has the best drought tolerance of all lawngrasses grown in Florida and will usually recover from severe drought injury soon after rain or irrigation. It is very important not to overwater bahiagrass lawns as this weakens the turf and encourages weeds. During extended periods of drought, bahiagrass may go dormant if left without irrigation. The grass will turn brown and stop growing during this dormant period, but will revive and resume growth upon regular application of water. Refer to "Watering Your Florida Lawn" in chapter 4 for additional information.

Pest Problems

Although bahiagrass is generally less troubled by insects, diseases, and nematodes than other Florida lawngrasses, it is still not completely pest free. Following are some of the major problems encountered in a bahiagrass lawn. For more information on turfgrass pests and their control, refer to chapter 5 of this book.

Weed Control

The best method of weed control is to maintain a healthy, vigorous turf. Following UF/IFAS recommendations for fertility, irrigation, and mowing will ensure a healthy lawn that is able to outcompete most weeds. Nevertheless, the following chemical treatments may be used on bahiagrass for weed control when needed.

Preemergence herbicides are used before a weed germinates and grows. Preemergence chemicals inhibit germination or form a barrier at the soil line to inhibit weed growth after germination. To effectively use preemergence chemicals, knowledge of weed problems from the previous year is needed. To control areas where crabgrass, sandbur, annual bluegrass, goosegrass, or crowfootgrass have been problems in previous years, apply benefin, bensulide, prodiamine, dithiopyr, pendimethalin, oryzalin, or dacthal prior to their germination. Timing of application is important for successful control. As a general rule of thumb, apply February 1 in south Florida, February 15 in central Florida, and March 1 in north Florida.

Apply postemergence herbicides (e.g., 2,4-D, dicamba, and/or MCPP) in May as needed for control of annual and perennial broadleaf weeds such as knotweed, spurge, and lespedeza. Selective control of emerged grass weeds such as goosegrass, crabgrass, or alexandergrass is only by hand pulling. Bahiagrass is severely damaged by postemergence grass herbicides such as DSMA or MSMA. Check with your county Extension Service office for positive identification of weeds and exact herbicide recommendations. Apply herbicides only when adequate soil moisture is present, air temperatures are between 60°F and 85°F, and the turf is not suffering from water or mowing stress. Failure to follow these precautionary statements will result in damaged turf.

Note: Many popular "weed-n-feed" type fertilizers for home lawns contain the herbicide atrazine. Atrazine will result in some damage to bahiagrass; therefore, it is not recommended for use on this grass.

Insects

The most serious insect threat to bahiagrass is the mole cricket. These insects burrow though the soil and damage roots, causing rapid wilting of the grass. Check for mole crickets by (1) looking for their tunneling and mounds; or (2) applying 2 gallons of water with 1–2 ounces of detergent soap per 2 square feet of turf in suspected damaged areas. If present, the mole crickets will surface in a few minutes.

Recently, several bait-type insecticides have been introduced and show real promise as a control measure. However, insecticides available for mole crickets are constantly changing. Check with your county Extension Service office for the latest control recommendations.

Diseases

The only serious disease of bahiagrass is dollar spot. This is expressed as spots several inches in diameter scattered across the turf. A light application of nitrogen (½ pound nitrogen per 1000 square feet) should encourage the grass to outgrow these symptoms. If nitrogen application does not provide satisfactory results, refer to "Disease Management" in chapter 5.

Nematodes

Nematodes are not typically as damaging to bahiagrass as to other species. Because of bahiagrass's deep, extensive root system, nematode damage seldom becomes noticeable. However, if grass becomes thin and less vigorous in growth and develops a weak root system, nematode presence should be suspected. Take a representative soil sample to your county Extension Service office to be analyzed, and if nematodes are found, ask for control recommendations. Proper cultural factors to encourage bahiagrass root growth will lessen nematode stress. These include not applying excess fertilizer, providing less frequent but deep watering, and ensuring ample soil potassium and phosphorus. Please refer to "Nematode Management" in chapter 5 for additional information.

Bermudagrass for Florida Lawns

Bermudagrasses (*Cynodon* spp.) are among the most widely used warm-season grasses. Improved, fine-textured bermudagrasses are used throughout the south on golf courses, athletic fields, and in high-profile residential and commercial landscapes where a fine-textured, dense ground cover is desired (plate 6). Because of the high maintenance requirements of the improved bermudagrasses, however, they are not generally recommended for use as a home lawngrass. Common bermudagrass varieties are often found as pasture and roadside grasses; these coarse-leaved varieties do not provide the high quality nor do they require the high maintenance of the fine-textured types.

Advantages

Bermudagrass produces a vigorous, medium green, dense turf that is well adapted to most soils and climates found in Florida. Bermudagrass has excellent wear, drought, and salt tolerance. It establishes rapidly and is able to outcompete most weed species. It is readily available as sod or plugs, and some improved cultivars are available as seeded varieties. Common varieties are available as seed, sod, or plugs.

Disadvantages

Improved bermudagrasses require high levels of maintenance. They have poor tolerance to many insect, disease, and nematode pests, which limits their use in home lawn sites. They grow very aggressively from stolons (aboveground stems) and rhizomes (belowground stems) and can rapidly invade flower and landscape beds. This aggressive growth also fosters thatch buildup. Bermudagrasses generally have poor to medium cold tolerance and relatively poor shade tolerance. Since bermudagrass performs best with higher levels of fertilizers and chemicals than other Florida lawngrasses, a professional lawn care company may best handle maintenance of this species.

Cultivars

'Common'

Common bermudagrass is a coarse-textured, low-density cultivar often found in pastures or on roadsides. It has a lighter green color and overall lower visual quality than the improved cultivars. It is available by seed or as sod, and is often mixed with bahiagrass for low-utility usage.

Other seeded varieties include 'Cheyenne,' 'Sahara,' 'Sundevil,' 'Jackpot.'

These newer seeded varieties have a darker green color, deeper roots, more shoot density, and a less coarse leaf texture than common bermudagrasses. While these varieties are suited for lawns, sports turf, parks, or roadsides, their performance and overall quality are comparable to common bermudagrass.

'FloraTex™'

FloraTex™ was a joint release from the University of Florida and Texas A&M University in 1993. It is generally of intermediate quality and maintenance between the seeded varieties and the improved cultivars. It has lower fertility and water requirements than other hybrid varieties and remains green for more of the year. It is medium in leaf texture and shoot density. It produces numerous seedheads but is less susceptible to dollar spot disease and bermudagrass stunt mite.

Maintenance of Bermudagrass

Establishment

Bermudagrasses are established vegetatively by planting sprigs, sod, or plugs. Each of these methods can be equally successful if the site is properly prepared before planting and if correct establishment practices are followed. For detailed information on lawn establishment, refer to "Establishing Your Florida Lawn" in chapter 2. The best time to plant bermudagrass is when plants are actively growing, normally April through September. Other times may be suitable if sufficient care is given to prevent desiccation and cold damage in north or central Florida.

Sprigging

The most common method of planting bermudagrass is by sprigging. This is done mechanically over large areas or by hand in small areas. Fresh sprigs are rhizomes and stolons that have at least 2 nodes or joints. Sprigs are usually broadcast over an area at a rate of 200–400 bushels per acre, or 5–10 bushels per 1000 square feet, then pressed into the soil. Sprigging is less expensive than sodding, but does not produce an instant lawn as does sodding. An alternative method of establishment is to plant sprigs end-to-end in furrows 6–12 inches apart, but this will take longer to establish.

Sodding

Establishment of bermudagrass by sodding produces an instant turf surface. Sod should be laid over only bare moist soil, with pieces laid in a staggered bricklike pattern and the edges fitted tightly together to avoid any open cracks. Rolling and watering thoroughly will ensure good contact with the soil for fast rooting. Sodded areas should be watered two or more times per day with ¼ inch of water until the sod is held fast to the soil by roots (usually two to three weeks). After the root system has established itself, watering should be reduced to longer, less frequent waterings on an as-needed basis.

Plugging

Sod can be cut into round plugs with a golf green cup cutter or into small squares with a machete. Spacing of plugs varies from 12 to 24 inches, with the closer spacing covering in three to six months and the farther spacing covering in six to nine months.

Seeding

Only common-type bermudagrasses can be established from seed. Bermuda-grass seed should be planted at a rate of 1–2 pounds of hulled seed per 1000 square feet.

Fertilization

Proper fertilization of any lawngrass is an important component of the best management practices for your home lawn. Fertilization and other cultural practices can influence the overall health and quality of your lawn and will reduce its vulnerability to numerous stresses, including weeds, insects, and disease.

It is advisable for homeowners to have soil tests done. Your local Extension Service office has recommendations and bags for taking soil samples and submitting them to the UF/IFAS Extension Soil Testing Laboratory for analysis. In particular, phosphorus levels are best determined by soil testing. Since many Florida soils are high in phosphorus, little or no phosphorus may be needed for satisfactory lawn growth.

Maintaining a good-quality bermudagrass turf requires a properly planned fertilization program. Fertilizer timing and amounts for bermudagrass are based largely on the turf use. Generally, bermudagrasses require higher levels of fertilizer than other warm-season grasses for acceptable growth, durability, and appearance. Bermudagrasses can be maintained at moderate maintenance levels in areas such as lawns, athletic fields, or golf course fairways.

In general, two weeks following spring regrowth, apply a complete fertilizer at the rate of ½ (water-soluble) to 1 (slow-release) pound of nitrogen per 1000 square feet. Look for a fertilizer with 2 percent or less phosphorus such as 15-2-15. The three numbers refer to the percentages of nitrogen, phosphorus, and potassium, respectively. For example, a 50-pound bag of 16-4-8 contains 16 percent nitrogen or 8 pounds total nitrogen. This bag will fertilize 8000 square feet at the rate of 1 pound of nitrogen per 1000 square feet.

University of Florida guidelines for lawngrass fertility show a range of fertilizer application rates for various areas of the state that enable different species to grow successfully. These ranges are included to account for individual homeowner preferences for low-, medium-, or high-input grass. Additionally, localized microclimates can have a tremendous effect on turfgrass growth, and a range of rates allows for these environmental variations. An example of this would be a typical home lawn that is partially shaded and partially sunny. The grass growing in the shade should receive lower rates of fertilizer than that

Table 1.4. Bermudagrass: recommended ranges of nitrogen rates

Location	Pounds N per 1000 sq ft
North Florida	3–5
Central Florida	4–6
South Florida	5–7

Table 1.5. Calendar guide to annual bermudagrass fertilization, by region[a,b]

Region[c] and Maintenance Level	J	F	M	A	M	J	J	A	S	O	N
North Florida											
Basic			C		SRN				C		
Moderate			C		SRN		SRN		C		
High			C	SRN	C		SRN	Fe	C		
Central Florida											
Basic			C		N		SRN		C		
Moderate		C		N		SRN		SRN		C	
High		C	N	SRN		C	Fe	SRN		C	
South Florida											
Basic		C		N		SRN			C		C
Moderate		C	N		C		SRN		SRN		C
High		C	N	SRN	C	SRN	Fe		SRN		C

a. For initial spring application, particularly in North Florida, the recommended time to fertilize is after the last frost rather than on a specific calendar date. FloraTex Bermudagrass requires less nitrogen annually.
b. C = complete fertilizer application (NPK), N = nitrogen application only, SRN = nitrogen only in a slow release form, Fe = iron application only.
c. For purposes of this table, North Florida = north of Ocala, Central Florida = south of Ocala to a line extending from Vero Beach to Tampa, South Florida = the remaining southern portion of the state.

growing in full sun. The guidelines are also separated into three geographical locations statewide as indicated in table 1.4. All rates are in pounds of nitrogen per 1000 square feet. For questions on how and when to apply these amounts, refer to "Fertilizer Recommendations for Your Florida Lawn" in chapter 3.

Fertilizer should be applied to bermudagrass in three to seven applications from spring green-up through fall (table 1.5). Do not apply nitrogen too early in the growing season, particularly in north Florida, or subsequent frosts may damage the grass. Likewise, don't fertilize too late in the year, as this can slow regrowth the following spring. If applying water-soluble forms at the lower application rate, it will take more applications to apply the total amount of fertilizer needed for the year than if applying a slow-release fertilizer form.

Mowing

Proper mowing practices are necessary to keep any lawn healthy and attractive. Both height and frequency of cut need to be adjusted for the level of turf management and season of the year. Under low to moderate levels of management, bermudagrass should be cut at a height of ¾–1½ inches, which may require mowing one to three times per week. Common bermudagrass should be mowed at the highest recommended heights. This will help the grass develop a deep root system and give it a better appearance. Under higher levels of management, bermudagrass can be maintained at a height of ½ inch if the turf is mowed every other day during the growing season. Mowing at this height and frequency requires more fertilizer and water to maintain an attractive and durable turf. It should be noted that low cutting heights and high maintenance levels predispose the turf to many weed and pest problems. Under low to moderate management practices, mowing frequency should be adjusted to the amount of growth. Remove no more than one-third of the total leaf blade with any mowing.

A reel mower is preferred for cutting bermudagrass. This gives a cleaner cut, and these mowers can also be more accurately adjusted to low heights. In a home lawn situation, a rotary mower may be used if the blades are sharp and well-adjusted enough to get a clean, smooth cut and if the cutting height is high enough for the mower. Grass clippings can be left on turf maintained with low to moderate fertility levels if mowed at the proper height and frequency. The clippings do not contribute to thatch, and they provide supplemental sources of nutrients. Remove the clippings only if the amount is so excessive that clumps form, or if appearance is important.

Watering

An established bermudagrass turf should be watered as needed. Irrigation is needed when leaf blades begin to fold up, to actually wilt, or to turn blue gray in color, or when footprints remain visible on the grass. Apply ½–¾ inch of water per application. This will apply water to roughly the top 8 inches of soil, where the majority of the roots are. To determine how much water a sprinkler system is providing, place several coffee cans throughout the irrigation zones to find out how long it takes to apply this amount of water. This is how long your irrigation system should run for each application.

During prolonged droughts, bermudagrass may go dormant if it does not receive irrigation. The grass will turn brown and stop growing during this dormant period, but it will revive and resume growth upon irrigation with sufficient amounts of water.

Pest Problems

Several severe pest problems can affect bermudagrass. Diagnosis and recommendations for treatment of pest problems are available from your county Extension Service office. Refer to chapter 5, "Pest Management," for additional information.

Nematodes

One of the most serious pests of bermudagrasses in Florida are nematodes. Nematodes cause yellowing and general thinning of older turf, especially during hot, dry periods. These pests cause extensive turf damage, particularly to turf grown on sandy soils or under high-maintenance regimes. Although some cultivars tolerate nematodes better than others, no cultivar is resistant to nematode infestation. Chemical nematode control is extremely limited for home lawns and usually requires commercial applicators. Following the cultural and fertilization recommendations in the *Florida Lawn Handbook* can help to alleviate some nematode damage.

Insects

Mole crickets are a major insect pest of bermudagrass. Other insects that cause damage in bermudagrass are sod webworms, armyworms, cutworms, grass loopers, and bermudagrass mites. High levels of nitrogen fertilizer encourage insect problems. There are several chemical controls available to treat insect pests, but these should be used only when necessary in conjunction with sound cultural and fertility practices.

Diseases

Bermudagrass is subject to many diseases, including dollar spot, brown patch, and *Helminthosporium*. A sound cultural program can minimize most disease problems, and fungicides can be used to cure major disease outbreaks.

Weeds

Weed problems in bermudagrass turf are a sign that the turf has become weakened by improper management practices or damage from pests. Refer to "Weed Management" in chapter 5 for more information. Proper management practices can eliminate most weed problems. If weeds are a persistent problem, herbicides labeled specifically for bermudagrass can be used for preemergent or postemergent weed control.

Carpetgrass for Florida Lawns

Carpetgrass (*Axonopus affinis* or *Axonopus compressus*) is a creeping, warm-season grass that is native to the West Indies. It was introduced into the United States in the early 1800s and has become naturalized in the southeastern states, especially on poorly drained soils. Carpetgrass physically resembles centipedegrass in terms of leaf density and shape.

Advantages

Carpetgrass grows on wet, low-pH soils where few other grasses persist, and has moderate shade tolerance. It is low growing and produces a dense turf with good color if moderate fertilization rates are applied. It is a low-maintenance grass that does not require excessive amounts of fertilizer. Carpetgrass also can be grown from seed.

Disadvantages

Carpetgrass will not survive on very dry soils unless irrigated frequently. It has shallow roots that impart poor drought tolerance. During the summer, carpetgrass produces numerous tall, thin seedheads that require frequent mowing for removal. It has poor cold tolerance, turning brown with the first cold spell. It is also slow to green up in the spring. Carpetgrass has poor salt tolerance and a medium leaf texture. It is subject to insect, nematode, and disease problems. It does not grow well outside of acidic (pH: 5.0–5.5) soils. Carpetgrass is not recommended for a high-quality lawn; however, it can be used in wet, shady areas where ease of maintenance is more important than quality.

Cultivars

No named varieties of carpetgrass are available. The species *A. affinis* is sold as carpetgrass for lawn purposes.

Maintenance of Carpetgrass

Establishment

Carpetgrass may be established from seeds or sprigs. Sod is not commonly available. Success with either propagation method is highly dependent on proper soil preparation. Refer to "Preparing to Plant a Florida Lawn" in chapter 2 for information on seedbed preparation.

Seeding

Seeding is easier and less expensive than sprigging. Use fresh, weed-free seed. Broadcast at the rate of 5 pounds per 1000 square feet. For best results, plant from April to July. It is advisable to kill any existing weeds with a nonselective herbicide such as glyphosate before planting.

Sprigging

Planting carpetgrass by sprigs is as effective as seeding but more laborious. Fresh vigorous stolons (runners) with at least 2 nodes or joints should be planted in rows 12 inches apart, spacing the sprigs end-to-end or 6–12 inches apart in the row. Cover sprigs about 1–2 inches deep, leaving a portion of the sprig exposed to light. Rolling will press sprigs into close contact with the soil. Soil must be kept continually moist until the plants initiate new growth.

Fertilization

Proper fertilization of carpetgrass is an important practice in a good maintenance program. Carpetgrass does not tolerate excessive use of fertilizer, especially nitrogen. For a low-fertility regime, a complete fertilizer can be applied at 1 pound of N per 1000 square feet annually. For a slightly higher-quality lawn, up to 2 pounds of N can be applied annually.

Mowing

If fertilized as recommended, carpetgrass will require mowing every ten to fourteen days at a height of 1–2 inches. Weekly mowing with a rotary mower may be necessary during the summer to remove the unsightly seedheads.

Watering

Carpetgrass thrives in wet soil and will require irrigation if grown on well-drained soils. Irrigating as needed is an excellent way to water any grass, provided the proper amount of water is applied when needed and not at a later or more convenient time. When using this approach, water at the first sign of wilt and apply ¾ inch of water per application. During prolonged droughts, it may be necessary to water carpetgrass every other day. If carpetgrass is grown on naturally wet soils where it is best adapted, irrigation may not be necessary.

Pest Problems

Carpetgrass is damaged by nematodes and several insects and diseases. Refer to chapter 5, "Pest Management," for additional information.

Insects

Lawn caterpillars, mole crickets, and spittlebugs cause damage. Caterpillars are especially damaging on well-fertilized carpetgrass.

Diseases

The principal disease affecting carpetgrass is brown patch.

Nematodes

If carpetgrass is grown on poorly drained, wet soils, nematodes should not be a major problem. However, on well-drained soils, nematodes can cause very serious damage to carpetgrass. These soilborne, microscopic worms attack the grass roots and, if not controlled, can weaken or ultimately kill the entire lawn.

Centipedegrass for Florida Lawns

Centipedegrass (*Eremochloa ophiuroides* [Munro] Hack.) was introduced into the United States from southeastern Asia. It is well adapted to the climate and soils of central and northern Florida and is the most common home lawngrass in the Florida Panhandle. It is a slow-growing grass with low fertility requirements when compared to other lawn grasses. It grows close to the ground, is medium textured, and is naturally yellow green in color. Overfertilizing to obtain an unnaturally dark green color reduces its cold tolerance, increases long-term maintenance problems, and is believed to contribute to centipedegrass decline, a disease complex that produces dead patches of turf in the spring.

Advantages

Centipedegrass does very well in acidic and infertile soils. It has fair shade tolerance and survives drought conditions. It can be established from seed, sod, or plugs, and it spreads by aboveground stems called stolons. Maintenance and fertility requirements are low compared to other turfgrasses.

Disadvantages

Centipedegrass is highly susceptible to damage from nematodes (especially ring nematodes) and ground pearls. Historically, nematode damage limits the use of centipedegrass in south Florida's sandy soils. It has a naturally pale yellow green color and is prone to iron chlorosis (yellowing of leaf blades). It has poor salt, wear, and freezing tolerance. Stolons from centipedegrass have a high lignin content and contribute to a heavy thatch layer, particularly when high fertilization rates are applied. The grass is often subject to centipedegrass decline, caused by *Gaeumannomyces graminis* var. *graminis*. The decline is influenced by improper management practices, particularly high fertility. Intensive management over a period of four to five years results in root dieback in the spring. This root dieback then reduces shoot growth and results in the death of large patches of the lawn. This condition is aggravated by thatch accumulation, which results in new stolons growing several inches above the soil surface. Proper management, with an emphasis on maintenance of a viable root system, is the best solution to this condition. This includes irrigation during prolonged drought stress, maintaining a mowing height of 1½ inches, prevention of thatch accumulation, and adherence to low fertility rates.

Cultivars

Because of a relatively small region of use, few centipedegrass varieties have been developed. Here is a list of those varieties that have been released.

'Common'

This is a low-maintenance variety that can be established by seed or vegetative means. It grows slowly and in a prostrate manner.

'Oklawn'

Oklawn is an improved cultivar that has better cold tolerance than Common. It must be established vegetatively.

'Centennial'

Centennial was also selected for cold tolerance. Like Oklawn, it requires vegetative establishment, but it is more tolerant of alkaline soils than Oklawn or Common.

'TifBlair'

TifBlair was released by the University of Georgia in 1997. It has good cold and freezing tolerance and can be propagated by seed or vegetative means. It reportedly has a slightly faster rate of growth than other centipedegrass cultivars.

'TennTurf'

Released by Tennessee in 1999, this cultivar has good cold tolerance. It is currently available only as sod, sprigs, or plugs. TennTurf prefers full sun but will tolerate some shade.

Maintenance of Centipedegrass

Establishment

Centipedegrass can be established by seed, plugs, sprigs, or sod. Planting centipedegrass as sod will produce an instant lawn that will establish more rapidly and be less susceptible to various stresses. Lay the sod on a well-prepared seedbed, fitting the pieces tightly together to avoid gaps in the turf. Wet the soil surface thoroughly prior to laying the sod. After the sod is in place, roll with a lightweight roller to ensure firm contact between the sod and soil, and then water thoroughly. The entire area should be watered daily with ½ inch of water per application. Once the sod has rooted into the soil, irrigation frequency can be reduced to an as-needed basis. Although sodding is more expensive than seeding or plugging, good-quality, weed-free sod will produce the best quality lawn.

Seed of centipedegrass is expensive, but the seeding rate is low. The suggested seeding rate is 4 ounces per 1000 square feet. The best time to seed is during the period from April to July, since this permits a full growing season before winter weather. Fall seeding is undesirable because the young seedlings may not become sufficiently established to withstand cold injury during the winter. While centipedegrass seed is less expensive than sod, it is slow to germinate and establish. It may take up to eight weeks for the lawn to establish. During this establishment period, it is necessary to monitor carefully for weeds and to manage irrigation correctly. Lightly mulching the seeded area can help control weeds and will also aid in keeping seeds from washing away by rain or irrigation. Seed quality should be considered when purchasing seed for planting. Insist on seed with a purity of 90 percent or better and a minimum of 85 percent germination.

Plugging or sprigging centipedegrass will leave open areas of soil that are subject to invasion by fast-growing, opportunistic weed species. Because of the slow growth of centipedegrass, weeds will dominate and the area should be mowed on a weekly basis to minimize weed competition.

The best time to establish centipedegrass is during the spring or early summer months. This will enable the grass to grow in before cooler weather begins, when growth will be reduced. Seed may safely be sown until later in the year, but growth will again be greatly reduced in the fall. When establishing any grass, it is important to irrigate it more frequently than is normally recommended. Until a viable root system is established, turf demands for irrigation are greater. It is also important not to mow until the roots have had a chance to work down into the soil and establish themselves there.

Proper site preparation before planting is critical to ensure successful establishment. Refer to "Preparing to Plant a Florida Lawn" in chapter 2 for complete information.

Centipedegrass is best adapted to a soil pH of 5.0–5.5. Severe iron chlorosis may occur if pH is above 6.5–7.0. *Preplant* application of wettable sulfur at the rate of 430 pounds per acre (10 pounds per 1000 square feet) can be used to lower the pH of some Florida soils 1 pH unit. Do not apply more than 10 pounds per 1000 square feet of wettable sulfur per application. Where more is required, allow sixty days between applications. Irrigate with 1 inch of water after each application to activate the sulfur. Lime is seldom required for centipedegrass.

Fertilization

Proper fertilization of any lawngrass is an important component of the best management practices for a lawn. Fertilization and other cultural practices can influence the overall health of a lawn, and can reduce its vulnerability to numerous stresses, including weeds, insects, and disease.

It is advisable for homeowners to have soil tests done. Your local Extension Service office has recommendations and bags for taking soil samples and submitting them to the UF/IFAS Extension Soil Testing Laboratory for analysis. In particular, phosphorus levels should be determined by soil testing. Since many Florida soils are high in phosphorus, little or no additional phosphorus may be needed for satisfactory lawn growth.

Established centipedegrass lawns have low fertility requirements. Centipedegrass is a low-maintenance turfgrass and does not respond well to excessive use of fertilizer, especially nitrogen. *Do not overfertilize centipedegrass with nitrogen to equal the color of St. Augustinegrass.* Overfertilization of centipedegrass can result in centipedegrass decline, increased insect pressure, and thatch accumulation. As with any lawngrass, do not apply more than ½ pound of water-soluble nitrogen per 1000 square feet at any one time. If using a fertilizer with at least 50 percent of the nigrogen in slow-release form, up to 1 pound of nitrogen per 1000 square feet may be applied at one time.

In general, two weeks following spring regrowth (after the last frost), apply a fertilizer at the rate of ½ (water-soluble) to 1 (slow-release) pound of nitrogen

Table 1.6. Centipedegrass: recommended ranges of nitrogen rates

Location	Pounds N per 1000 sq ft
North Florida	1–2
Central Florida	2–3
South Florida	2–3

Table 1.7. Calendar guide to annual centipedegrass fertilization, by region[a,b]

Region[c] and Maintenance Level	J	F	M	A	M	J	J	A	S	O	N
North Florida											
Basic				C							
Moderate				C		Fe					
High				C		SRN	Fe				
Central Florida											
Basic			C			SRN					
Moderate			C			SRN	Fe				
High			C			SRN		C			
South Florida											
Basic			C			Fe				C	
Moderate		C	SRN							C	
High		C	SRN			Fe				C	

a. For initial spring application, particularly in North Florida, the recommended time to fertilize is after the last frost rather than on a specific calendar date.
b. C = complete fertilizer application (NPK), N = nitrogen application only, SRN = nitrogen only in a slow-release form, Fe = iron application only.
c. For purposes of this table, North Florida = north of Ocala, Central Florida = south of Ocala to a line extending from Vero Beach to Tampa, South Florida = the remaining southern portion of the state.

per 1000 square feet. Look for a fertilizer with 2 percent or less phosphorus, such as a 15-2-15. The three numbers refer to the percentages of nitrogen, phosphorus, and potassium, respectively. For example, a 50-pound bag of 15-0-15 contains 15 percent nitrogen or 7.5 pounds total nitrogen. This bag will fertilize 7500 square feet at the rate of 1 pound of nitrogen per 1000 square feet. If applying water-soluble forms at the lower application rate, it will take more fertilizer applications to apply the total amount of fertilizer needed for the year than if applying a slow-release fertilizer form.

University of Florida guidelines for lawngrass fertility show a range of fertilizer application rates for various areas of the state that enable a particular species to grow successfully. These ranges are included to account for individual homeowner preferences for low-, medium-, or high-input grass. Additionally, localized microclimate conditions can have a tremendous effect on turfgrass growth, and a range of rates allows for these environmental variations. An example of this would be a typical home lawn that is partially shaded and partially sunny. The grass growing in the shade should receive lower rates of fertilizer than that growing in full sun. The guidelines are also separated into three geographical locations statewide, as indicated in table 1.6. All rates are in pounds of nitrogen per 1000 square feet. For questions on how and when to apply these amounts, refer to "Fertilizer Recommendations for Your Florida Lawn" in chapter 3.

Fertilizer should be applied to centipedegrass in one to three applications from spring green-up through fall. Do not apply nitrogen too early in the growing season, particularly in north Florida, or subsequent frosts may damage the grass. Likewise, don't fertilize too late in the year, as this can slow regrowth the following spring. A general guideline for the last fertilizer application is mid-September for north Florida, early October for central Florida, and late October for south Florida. If applying water-soluble forms at the lower application rate, it will take more applications to apply the total amount of fertilizer needed for the year than if utilizing a slow-release fertilizer form.

As mentioned previously, one of the common problems of centipedegrass is leaf yellowing called chlorosis, which is usually caused by iron deficiency. This condition is most severe where soil pH is high (above 6.5) or where the soil contains large quantities of calcium or phosphorus. This yellowing is generally worst in early spring, when daytime temperatures are warm but nighttime temperatures are still cool. Warm daytime air temperatures promote leaf and stolon growth, but cool nighttime temperatures limit root growth. The roots cannot take up enough nutrients to supply the growing leaves, causing the leaves to turn yellow. As soils become warmer, this temporary nutrient deficiency disappears. Avoid using excessive phosphorus fertilizers unless soil test results indicate the need to do so. Iron chlorosis can be controlled by several methods. Soil pH can be lowered by regular use of acid-forming fertilizers such as ammonium nitrate or ammonium sulfate. These will render the iron more available to the grass. If the soil is naturally iron-deficient, iron fertilization is necessary. Centipedegrass usually responds well to supplemental applications of iron. Chelated or ferrous sulfate iron can be applied evenly and easily with a hose-end applicator. Apply the ferrous sulfate at the rate of 2 ounces in 3–5 gallons of water per 1000 square feet. Consult the label for chelated iron rates. Fertilizers containing iron and a combination material of ammonium sulfate and ferrous sulfate are also available.

Mowing

Proper mowing practices are necessary to keep any lawn healthy and attractive. Centipedegrass that is actively growing should be mowed every seven to fourteen days at 1½–2 inches in height. Mowing at this height promotes a deeper, more extensive root system that enables the grass to better withstand drought and nematode stress. Remove no more than one-third of the height of the leaf blades with any mowing (e.g., for a lawn to be maintained at 2 inches in height, mow when the turf reaches 3 inches).

Clippings should be left on the ground after mowing. They do not contribute to thatch buildup, as is often assumed, but are actually readily degraded by microorganisms. They also provide a source of nutrients to the lawn and can reduce fertility requirements if left on the lawn on a regular basis. A sharp and well-adjusted rotary or reel mower should be used.

Watering

Irrigating as needed is an excellent way to water any grass, provided the proper amount of water is applied when needed. Irrigation is needed when leaf blades begin to fold up and wilt or turn blue gray in color, or when footprints remain visible on the grass. Apply ½–¾ inch of water per application, which will wet the top 8 inches of soil, where the majority of the roots are. To determine application rates of a sprinkler system, place several coffee cans throughout the irrigation zones to find out how long it takes to apply this amount of water. During prolonged droughts, irrigation may be needed more often. Centipedegrass, however, has good drought tolerance and will usually recover from severe drought injury soon after rain or irrigation. Do not overwater centipedegrass lawns as this weakens the turf and encourages weeds. Refer to "Watering Your Florida Lawn" in chapter 4 for additional information.

Pest Problems

Centipedegrass is damaged by nematodes, insects, and diseases. You can obtain help in identification of pest problems and current control recommendations from your county Extension Service office.

Weeds

Weeds easily invade newly established or poorly maintained lawns. Grass weeds include crabgrass, goosegrass, dallisgrass, annual bluegrass, and torpedograss. Broadleaf weeds include dandelions, clover, pennywort, betony, oxalis, henbit, and others. Refer to "Weed Management" in chapter 5 for more information.

Insects

Several insects may damage centipedegrass, but hardest to control are scale insects called ground pearls, for which there are no effective chemicals for control. Lawn caterpillars, grubs, mole crickets, spittlebugs, and sod webworms also damage centipedegrass. For more information, refer to "Insect Management" in chapter 5.

Diseases

As previously mentioned, the principal disease affecting centipedegrass is centipedegrass decline, which can be minimized by following the proper cultural practices. Brown patch and dollar spot can be a sporadic problem and both can be controlled with fungicides. Refer to "Disease Management" in chapter 5 for additional information.

Nematodes

Nematodes can be a very serious threat to centipedegrass. These are microscopic worms that attack grass roots and cause the lawn to thin and eventually die. Areas of heavy infestation will show symptoms of severe wilt, even when well-watered. The Cooperative Extension Service nematode assay laboratory in Gainesville can diagnose whether nematodes are a problem by looking at a soil sample taken from the margin of the affected area. Proper cultural factors to encourage centipedegrass root growth will lessen nematode stress. These include applying less nitrogen, providing less frequent but deep watering, and ensuring ample soil potassium and phosphorus. Refer to "Nematode Management" in chapter 5 for more information.

Centipedegrass Decline

After a few years, established centipedegrass may develop yellowing (chlorosis) and/or dead spots as spring growth resumes. Numerous conditions contribute to the problem, including:

- High pH (greater than 6.5).
- Excessive nitrogen fertilization in prior years.
- Uneven soil surface resulting from stolons being suspended above the soil and over a mat of thatch. (Such stolons never sufficiently develop roots and are killed by freezing weather. Alternating freezing or cool temperatures and thawing conditions exacerbate the problem.)
- Root dieback or any environmental conditions that may stress roots, such as soil compaction, very low mowing heights, overirrigation.
- Nematodes and/or other disease organisms such as *Gaeumannomyces, Rhizoctonia,* or *Pythium* species, which weaken the grass, making it susceptible to injury from otherwise normal conditions.

To remedy this condition:

- Check soil pH and adjust it if too high.
- Do not overfertilize with nitrogen or phosphorus.
- Follow recommended mowing heights and frequencies to avoid scalping or excessive thatch buildup.
- Spray with 2 oz. ferrous sulfate per 1000 square feet, or use chelated iron as directed if excessive yellowing occurs.
- Consult with your Extension Service agent to send samples for identification of nematodes and diseases.

Seashore Paspalum for Florida Lawns

Seashore paspalum (*Paspalum vaginatum* Swartz) is a warm-season grass that is native to tropical and subtropical regions worldwide. Seashore paspalum grows naturally in coastal environments, often in brackish marsh water or in close proximity to ocean waters. It also grows in areas that receive extended periods of heavy rains and low light intensity. Its best growth occurs in response to warm temperatures and long day lengths.

Seashore paspalum is believed to have been introduced into the United States from around the world through maritime travel. It was reputedly used as bedding in the hulls of slave ships. As the ships came into southern U.S. ports, bedding would be discarded on the shore, leaving the grass to regrow and establish on the banks in these coastal towns. It has since spread along coastal areas of the southeastern United States, thriving in the salt-affected waters and environments of these areas.

Seashore paspalum does not produce viable seed and therefore must be planted as sod or sprigs. The fine-textured types are similar in appearance to hybrid bermudagrass (*Cynodon* spp.). They produce a dense, dark green turf. Although the species has been in existence for hundreds of years, selection of cultivars for commercial, residential, and sports turf use has been taking place only since the mid- to late 1990s. The largest collection of seashore paspalum can be found at the University of Georgia's turfgrass breeding program in Griffin, which has gathered and tested more than 300 ecotypes of this species.

Advantages

Seashore paspalum produces a dense, dark green turfgrass with relatively low fertility inputs (plate 7). While it has initially been marketed for golf course and athletic field use, it has good potential for use in the home lawn market as well. However, it is important that homeowners realize that this is not a miracle grass and that it will not perform better than currently available grasses in all environments. Although you may see it touted as being extremely drought tolerant, it still requires water to remain green, just like any other turfgrass. It does have characteristics that make it tolerant to a wide range of stresses and it does have the ability to survive in harsh environmental conditions, but for best growth and performance, it should be grown under optimal conditions. Some of the advantages for use of seashore paspalum in a home lawn situation include:

- Excellent tolerance to saline or recycled water
- Excellent wear tolerance
- Good tolerance to reduced water input, but does require water to remain green
- Relatively low fertility inputs needed to produce a dense, dark green lawn
- Tolerance to a wide pH range
- Grows well with potable (drinking) water as well as poor quality water
- Tolerance to extended periods of low light intensity, such as from prolonged cloudy or rainy periods

- Dense growth habit that discourages weed competition
- Production of a dense root system, which is important in giving turfgrass good tolerance to most stresses

Disadvantages

Some of the disadvantages include:
- Poor shade tolerance
- Low mowing requirements: this grass performs best when mowed at 2 inches or less. Also requires mowing weekly or more frequently to avoid scalping.
- Weed control: seashore paspalum is sensitive to many common herbicides and may be injured or killed by their use. In addition, most herbicides currently on the market are not labeled for use on this species yet, although the chemical companies will be expanding those labels to comply with increased use of seashore paspalum.
- Seashore paspalum tends to become thatchy, particularly when overfertilized and overirrigated. This may mean increased verticutting needs for homeowners.
- Limited data on nematode resistance and tolerance of seashore paspalum.

Cultivars

The species *Paspalum vaginatum* encompasses a wide range of types and much diversity may be found within the species. For example, seashore paspalum types may be fine textured, with small, narrow leaf blades, or they may be coarse-textured types that grow in a less dense, more open style. Generally, we think of these coarser types as being preferred for roadside utility or soil stabilization uses, while the finer-textured types are better suited for landscape or athletic use. Since most of the university research done on seashore paspalum to date has been conducted in northeast Georgia, we do not have all the information at this time to answer all questions on best management of this grass in Florida. The following are some of the cultivars currently available for homeowner use.

'Salam'

Salam is a proprietary cultivar grown by Southern Turf Nurseries. It was released in the 1990s and is suited for athletic, golf course, and landscape use. It has many qualities similar to Sea Isle 1.

'Sea Isle 1'

At the present time, this is the cultivar with the most university testing. This cultivar was released by the University of Georgia in 1999. It is a fine-leaved, dense-growing selection from Argentina, intended for use in commercial or residential landscapes or athletic use in fairways or sports fields. It produces a dark green, dense grass with excellent salinity tolerance and good tolerance to drought and wear. Problems have been reported with diseases in Sea Isle 1, particularly *Helminthosporium, Fusarium,* and take-all. Fungicides can control these diseases after the disease has been diagnosed. The primary insect problems of Sea Isle 1 are caterpillars, including sod webworms and fall armyworms.

'Sea Lawn'

Sea Lawn is a proprietary cultivar produced in Florida by Environmental Turf Solutions. There are other seashore paspalum cultivars available that are intended primarily for golf courses, athletic fields, or roadside utilization.

Maintenance of Seashore Paspalum

Establishment

Seashore paspalum must be established vegetatively by sod or sprigs. Sprigging rates should range from 5 to 10 bushels per 1000 square feet. Plugs should be spaced no more than 12 inches on center (plate 8). The closer together plugs are planted, the more quickly they will provide full ground cover. The best time for establishment is during periods of most active growth, when temperatures exceed 70°F. When you first plant seashore paspalum, you most likely won't see any shoot growth for the first ten to fourteen days. This is very typical of seashore paspalum—it initially concentrates on root establishment. Once it has a root system capable of supporting itself, it will divert growth to the shoot system. This is when it will start to spread and fill in rapidly.

Be sure to irrigate frequently during establishment to ensure that the roots stay moist and make contact with the soil. For newly sprigged areas, irrigate several times daily for short periods of time for the first ten days. After the sprigs have rooted, irrigation frequency can be decreased to every other day for another seven to ten days. At this time the grass should have a well-established root system and can withstand irrigation twice weekly. After the first thirty to forty days, you will need to irrigate only on an as-needed basis.

Before you begin planting, make sure that you have properly prepared the site. For information on this, refer to the section titled "Preparing to Plant a Florida Lawn" in chapter 2.

Fertilization

Proper fertilization of any lawn grass is an important component of the best management practices of your home lawn. Fertilization and other cultural practices influence the overall health of your lawn, and can reduce or increase its vulnerability to numerous stresses, including weeds, insects, and disease.

It is advisable for homeowners to do an initial soil test on their property. Your local Extension Service office has instructions and kits for taking and submitting soil samples to the UF/IFAS Extension Soil Testing Laboratory for analysis. These tests form the basis for your home lawn fertility program. In particular, phosphorus levels should be determined by soil testing. Since many Florida soils are high in phosphorus, little or no phosphorus may be needed for satisfactory lawn growth after initial establishment.

Seashore paspalum will grow a dense, dark green lawn with moderate fertility. As with any lawn, the fertility regime will determine not only the rate of growth and curb appeal of your lawn, it will also determine the amount of maintenance required to keep it in optimal condition.

During establishment of a seashore paspalum lawn, small amounts of fertilizer should be applied on a regular basis to hasten growth and ground cover. "Spoon-feeding" ¼–½ pound of nitrogen per 1000 square feet in two applications during a three- to four-week period will stimulate growth. To encourage root development, phosphorus should be applied during establishment at rates equal to or greater than the nitrogen. More potassium is also needed during establishment. A 1:2:3 fertilizer ratio of N:P:K applied every other week for the first two months will provide a good fertility program for establishing seashore paspalum. If sodding seashore paspalum, ground cover will be immediate, but at least two weeks will be needed to insure that the root system is functional and capable of supporting the shoot system. If sprigging, coverage will take longer, and establishment fertility requirements will need to be in place until both root and shoot systems have grown in.

Following this establishment period, the fertility regime should be reduced. Since seashore paspalum responds very readily to fertilizer and will grow rapidly following nitrogen application, it is best to apply fertilizer in small increments (at least two to four applications) from late March or early April through August. For north Florida, application of 2–3 pounds of nitrogen per 1000 square feet per year will produce a healthy, attractive lawn. In south Florida, 3–5 pounds of nitrogen per 1000 square feet can be applied yearly. Never apply more than ½ pound of water-soluble nitrogen per 1000 square feet at any one time. If using a fertilizer that has at least 50 percent of the nitrogen in slow-release form, up to 1 pound of nitrogen per 1000 square feet may be applied. Phosphorus should be applied depending upon results of soil tests. As some Florida soils contain ample amounts of phosphorus, little or none may be required. Apply equal amounts of potassium to nitrogen for best performance of seashore paspalum. A 1-0-1 fertilizer blend or something similar would be a good choice.

Mowing

Seashore paspalum used in home lawns should be mowed at 1½–2 inches in height. Higher mowing heights will reduce turfgrass density and increase weed problems. Mower blades should be kept sharp to avoid tearing leaf tissue. Seashore paspalum develops problems when too much leaf material is removed at any one time (scalping), so frequency of mowing needs to be watched carefully. During active times of growth in the summer months, particularly under higher nitrogen, mowing more frequently than once a week would be preferred if possible. When mowing, never remove more than one-third of the leaf blade at any one time. If the grass takes on a scalped appearance, too much leaf material is being removed at one time. If the lawn is under stress from drought, shade, nutrient deficiencies, insects, or disease, it is best to maintain a higher cutting height until the stress is relieved. Do not mow when the grass is wet or the soil is soggy. Seashore paspalum may be mowed with a rotary mower, but better results will be obtained if a reel mower is used.

Grass clippings should be left on the lawn. These do not contribute to thatch buildup and are readily decomposed by microbial action. Clippings also serve as a nutrient source and can actually reduce the fertilizer requirements when returned to the lawn.

Irrigation

Irrigation of any lawngrass is recommended on an as-needed basis. Signs that water is needed include rolling of leaf blades, wilting, and foot imprints that remain on the lawn. At these signs of water deficit, apply ½–¾ inch of irrigation to the entire lawn. This will supply water to a depth of approximately 6–9 inches in most Florida soils and should provide adequate water. Do not apply smaller volumes of water more frequently, as this will not encourage deep root growth. To avoid overwatering when rainfall is adequate, reduce the frequency of irrigation. Overwatering lawn grasses not only wastes water, but may result in weakened root systems, increased nutrient leaching through the soil, and poor stress tolerance.

How frequently your lawn will need water will vary depending on time of year, your soil type, and how much shade you have. For more information on proper watering, refer to "Watering Your Florida Lawn" in chapter 4.

Because seashore paspalum is very tolerant of poor water quality, it can be irrigated with recycled or saline water. It is important to realize, however, that even this grass can develop salt toxicity problems with repeated use of saline water over extended periods, particularly in areas receiving little rainfall. Ample rainfall will flush out accumulated salts in the soil and minimize salt toxicities. Seashore paspalum may also be grown with good-quality, potable water.

Thatch Control

Thatch is the layer of dead and decomposing leaf blades, stems, and roots on top of the soil surface. Thatch occurs as a result of excessive nitrogen application, overwatering, or poor mowing practices. Vertical mowing is the most efficient remedy for excessive (greater than 1 inch) thatch. Vertical mowing uses vertical knifelike blades to thin out thatch by slicing into it. While this process can alleviate buildup by removing thatch, it also removes portions of the grass and will cause temporary damage to the turf. It is best to have this job done by experienced professionals who are familiar with the specialized equipment as well as the needs of your lawn. For seashore paspalum, vertical blades should be spaced 2–3 inches apart for successful verticutting. It is important to perform this procedure only during times of active grass growth, and only on healthy, nonstressed grass (i.e., no drought, shade, insect, or disease problems). Verticutting should be followed by an application of ½ pound per 1000 square feet of a quick-release nitrogen source to help the grass recover from the injury. Mulching mowers are also quite effective in minimizing thatch buildup and can be used by homeowners.

Shade Tolerance

Seashore paspalum does not have good shade tolerance, particularly when the shade is due to trees or vegetative canopies rather than to buildings. It can tolerate a few hours of shade daily, but would not be a good choice for a heavily treed area. For more information on how to best manage your lawn in shade, refer to "Shade Stress" in chapter 6.

Pests

Weeds

Current herbicides available to homeowners are generally not labeled for seashore paspalum, which means that it is not legal to use them on this species, but this is only because the label does not cover this species yet. However, many of the herbicides commonly used on lawn grasses will injure seashore paspalum and should not be used. Preemergence herbicides for homeowner use that do not injure seashore paspalum include pendimethalin (Pre-M and other trade names) and oryzalin (Surflan). Postemergence herbicides that are safe on seashore paspalum include three-way mixtures of 2,4-D + MCPP + dicamba such as Trimec Southern and Weed-B-Gone, halosulfuron (Manage), and Dicamba (Vanquish). Licensed pest control operators have a wider array of products available for use than homeowners, some of which are also safe on seashore paspalum. Consult your county Extension Service office for proper identification of weeds and a prescription for environmentally friendly control of the problem.

Insects

Seashore paspalum is subject to problems from sod webworms and fall armyworms. It may also experience some problems with mole crickets or spittlebugs. For more information on chemical and cultural control of insects in turf, please refer to chapter 5, "Pest Management."

Disease

Seashore paspalum can have problems with disease organisms, particularly when under stress. Problems can be seen in response to the following stresses: scalping, or removal of too much shoot tissue at one time; underirrigation, particularly during establishment; or overfertilization with nitrogen. Organisms that may cause problems include *Fusarium* blight, which may be found under hot, humid conditions, or when the grass is under drought stress. When infected, the entire turfgrass plant will change color from green to reddish brown to dark brown. *Helminthosporium* disease may also occur under conditions of high humidity or soil compaction. This disease is seen as small purple leaf spots with brown centers and light tan halos. There are also reports of take-all organisms damaging seashore paspalum. Seashore paspalum can outgrow disease problems following treatment with the proper fungicide to arrest disease development. Once regrowth begins, the grass will fill in to again provide a green lawn. For more information on chemical and cultural control of disease in turf, please refer to chapter 5, "Pest Management."

To summarize, seashore paspalum has both benefits and drawbacks for use in the home lawn. It will at least initially be viewed primarily as a good choice for coastal or salt-affected areas, or anywhere reclaimed water might be used for irrigation. It will produce a dense, dark green lawn without excess fertilization. It will tolerate foot or vehicle traffic well but will not perform well in shaded areas. Weed control may also be difficult for homeowners, and it may require periodic verticutting to reduce thatch.

St. Augustinegrass for Florida Lawns

St. Augustinegrass (*Stenotaphrum secundatum* [Walt.] Kuntze.) is widely adapted to the warm, humid (subtropical) regions of the world. It is believed to be native to the coastal regions of both the Gulf of Mexico and the Mediterranean. In Florida, St. Augustinegrass is the most commonly planted turfgrass in urban, coastal areas. It performs best in well-drained, fertile soils but can grow satisfactorily in a wide variety of soils. To produce a lawn of acceptable quality, St. Augustinegrass requires irrigation and moderate fertility (plate 9).

Advantages

St. Augustinegrass produces a green to blue green dense turf that is well adapted to most soils and climatic regions in Florida. It has relatively good salt tolerance and certain cultivars possess good shade tolerance (plate 10). Establishment of St. Augustinegrass from sod is quick and easy. Several different cultivars of St. Augustinegrass sod and plugs are available from garden centers and custom sod installers throughout Florida.

Disadvantages

St. Augustinegrass, like most turfgrasses, has certain cultural and pest problems. It does not remain green during drought conditions and may die without supplemental irrigation. It produces excessive thatch when moderate to high fertilization rates and frequent irrigation are applied. It has poor wear tolerance and some varieties are susceptible to cold damage. The coarse leaf texture is objectionable to some people. The major insect pest of St. Augustinegrass is the chinch bug, although resistance to chinch bugs varies somewhat among cultivars. For example, Floratam and Floralawn have traditionally been considered chinch-resistant, but over time the insect has overcome this resistance and is now considered a pest to these cultivars as well. St. Augustine Decline Virus (SADV) is a major disease problem in some parts of the United States but has not been identified as a problem in Florida. Most cultivars are also susceptible to gray leaf spot disease.

Cultivars

There are several cultivars of St. Augustinegrass available for lawn use in Florida. The different cultivars vary in their tolerances to environmental stresses and their susceptibility to pests, so it is advisable to check with your county Cooperative Extension Service office for the best grass for your location and needs. Table 1.10 lists some relative growth characteristics for currently available cultivars.

'Bitterblue'

Bitterblue was an improved variety selected in the 1930s. Although Bitterblue is marketed as a certified cultivar, there is no certified Bitterblue germplasm maintained at this time. What is typically sold as Bitterblue has a fine, dense texture and dark blue green color. It has improved cold tolerance and good shade tolerance, but is not resistant to chinch bugs or gray leaf spot disease.

'Common' and 'Roselawn'

These are pasture types of St. Augustinegrass that evolved in the 1800s. They produce a coarse, open turf that is susceptible to chinch bugs, herbicide damage, shade, and cold damage. They also have a light leaf color and do not respond well to fertilization. Avoid planting these cultivars if lawn appearance is important.

'Delmar'

Delmar is a semidwarf cultivar that is often sold as sod or plugs. It has improved shade tolerance, short internodes, dark green color, and good cold tolerance. It should be mowed at 1½–2½ inches. Delmar is susceptible to chinch bugs, sod webworms, and brown patch disease. It has slow lateral runner growth; thus, grow-in from plugs or recovery from damage may take longer. Delmar performs well in sun or shade.

'Floralawn'

This cultivar was released in 1986 by the Florida Agricultural Experiment Station. It is resistant to chinch bugs, sod webworms, and brown patch. Like Floratam, it has poor shade and cold tolerance. It is also coarse textured. Floralawn should be grown in mild environments in full sun to moderate shade and receive low to moderate fertilization.

'Floratam'

Floratam is an improved St. Augustinegrass that was released jointly in 1973 by the University of Florida and Texas A&M. Floratam is the most widely produced and used St. Augustinegrass in Florida. It is a coarse-textured cultivar that has poor cold and shade tolerance. It will thin in direct relation to the amount of shade received. It grows vigorously in warm weather, but has a relatively long period of dormancy in north Florida and greens up more slowly in the spring than some cultivars. It has some degree of chinch bug resistance, although new strains of chinch bugs that can damage Floratam have been identified. Floratam is tolerant of atrazine herbicides when temperatures are below 85°F.

'Floratine'

This is an improved selection from Bitterblue that was released in 1962 by the Florida Agricultural Experiment Station. It has a finer leaf texture and a denser and shorter growth habit that allows closer mowing than common St. Augustinegrass. It is not resistant to chinch bugs but tolerates light to moderate shade. Floratine is similar to Bitterblue in many characteristics and the two are difficult to distinguish.

'Palmetto'

Palmetto was a selection found by a Florida sod grower in 1988. It is of intermediate growth, with shorter leaf blades and internodes than many other cultivars, but is slightly larger than the dwarf St. Augustinegrass cultivars such as Seville and Delmar. It has a nice growth habit and does well in full sun or partial shade. It is sometimes referred to as drought tolerant, but research has not shown that it has any greater degree of drought tolerance than other St. Augustinegrasses. It sometimes has problems with disease, particularly in humid, damp summer months.

'Raleigh'

Raleigh is a cold-hardy cultivar released by North Carolina State University in 1980. It has a medium green color with a coarse texture. It is susceptible to chinch bugs, but can be planted in northern Florida because of its tolerance to lower temperatures. It is also susceptible to brown patch disease. During peak summertime heat, Raleigh has been noted to yellow and to not grow as aggressively as during cooler temperatures. Supplemental iron applications can reduce this yellowing tendency. Raleigh is best adapted to the heavier, organic, clayey soils with medium to low soil pH in central and north Florida.

'Seville'

Seville is a semidwarf, fine-leaved variety with a dark green color and a low growth habit. It is susceptible to chinch bug and webworm damage. Due to its compact growth habit, Seville tends to be thatch prone and shallow rooting. Seville performs well in both shade and full sun, but is cold sensitive. Its cold tolerance is similar to Floratine's. Being a semidwarf variety, Seville's maintenance is different than that of taller-growing varieties.

Other Varieties

Several other lesser-known and available St. Augustinegrass varieties have been released. These include 'FX-33,' 'Sunclipse,' 'Mercedes,' 'Gulf Star,' and others. Research performed on these varieties has been limited, and generally they have not proven superior to older varieties that are currently available.

Maintenance of St. Augustinegrass

It is advisable to check with your local county Extension Service office for cultivars best adapted to your geographical area and uses. As emphasized throughout the *Florida Lawn Handbook*, proper lawn maintenance practices are the best means for avoiding pest problems and obtaining a high-quality lawn.

Establishment

The best time to establish St. Augustinegrass is during the spring or early summer months. This enables the grass to grow in before cooler weather begins, when growth will be reduced. In south Florida, establish St. Augustinegrass during winter or spring. When establishing any grass, it is important to provide irrigation more frequently than normal recommendations call for. Frequent, short irrigations throughout the course of the day will help the root system to become established in the soil and become viable. Mowing should not be done until the roots have had a chance to peg down into the soil. For more information on preparing the site and establishment, see "Establishing Your Florida Lawn" in chapter 2.

St. Augustinegrass is established by vegetative propagation rather than by seeds. Vegetative propagation means that plant parts with growing points are used for planting rather than seeds. St. Augustinegrass has stolons (aboveground stems) that have areas of actively dividing cells at the nodes. These areas are capable of generating new shoot growth and are responsible for lateral growth of St. Augustinegrass along the ground.

Sodding

Sodding will produce an instant lawn, as you cover virtually the entire area with grass growing in squares of sod. Sod should be laid over bare moist soil with pieces laid in a staggered bricklike pattern with the edges fitted tightly together to avoid any open cracks. Rolling and watering thoroughly will ensure good contact with the soil for fast rooting. Sodded areas should be watered at least twice per day with ¼ inch of water until the sod is held fast (usually ten to fourteen days) to the soil by roots; then watering should be reduced to an as-needed basis.

Sprigging

Sprigging is less expensive than sodding, but does not produce an instant lawn as does sodding. It is a labor-intensive way to cover a large area. Sprigs contain nodes on stolons, which are planted end-to-end in furrows 6–12 inches apart. Stolons should be covered with soil, but leaf blades should be left exposed. The soil should be tamped and thoroughly saturated. Soil should be kept moist until new stolons appear.

Plugging

A number of St. Augustinegrass cultivars are available commercially as plugs. Sod also can be made into plugs by cutting it into small squares. Spacing of plugs varies from 6 to 24 inches. The closer spacing provides full coverage in three to six months, and farther spacing covers in six to twelve months. Plugs are placed in holes of the same size or in open furrows and tamped into place. A thorough watering completes the installation. The turf should then be cared for like a sprigged lawn.

Fertilization

Proper fertilization of any lawngrass is an important component of the best management practices for your home lawn. Fertilization and other cultural practices influence the overall health of your lawn and can reduce or increase its vulnerability to numerous stresses, including weeds, insects, and disease.

It is advisable for homeowners to have soil tests done annually. Your local Extension Service office has instructions and supplies for taking soil samples and submitting them to the UF/IFAS Extension Soil Testing Laboratory for analysis. In particular, phosphorus levels should be determined by soil testing. Since many Florida soils are high in phosphorus, little or no phosphorus may be needed for satisfactory lawn growth.

Maintaining a good-quality lawn requires a properly planned fertility program. An acceptable-quality St. Augustinegrass lawn can be grown with a low to high level of fertility, depending on what the homeowner wants. First, decide how much time and effort can be spent on lawn maintenance. A lower-fertility lawn is best for those with little time to spend on lawn care. A high-fertility lawn may be better suited to those who desire a manicured appearance for their yard. This type of maintenance will require more time and money for lawn care.

In general, two weeks following spring regrowth, apply a complete fertilizer such as 15-0-15 at the rate of ½ (water-soluble) to 1 (slow-release) pound of nitrogen per 1000 square feet. The three numbers refer to the percentages of nitrogen, phosphorus, and potassium, respectively. For example, a 50-pound bag of 15-0-15 contains 15 percent nitrogen or 7.5 pounds total nitrogen. This bag will fertilize 7500 square feet at the rate of 1 pound of nitrogen per 1000 square feet. If applying water-soluble forms at the lower application rate, it will take more fertilizer applications to apply the total amount of fertilizer needed for the year than if applying a slow-release fertilizer form.

Table 1.8. St. Augustinegrass: recommended ranges of nitrogen rates

Location	Pounds N per 1000 sq ft
North Florida	2–4
Central Florida	2–5
South Florida	4–6

University of Florida guidelines for lawngrass fertility show a range of fertilizer rates over which a particular species may be successfully grown for various areas of the state. These ranges are included to account for individual homeowner preferences for low-, medium-, or high-input grass. Additionally, localized microclimate conditions can have a tremendous effect on turfgrass growth, and a range of rates allows for these environmental variations. An example of this would be a typical home lawn that is partially shaded and partially sunny. The grass growing in the shade should receive lower rates of fertilizer than that growing in full sun. The guidelines are also separated into three geographical locations statewide, as indicated in table 1.8 below. All rates are in pounds of nitrogen per 1000 square feet. For questions on how to apply these amounts, refer to chapter 2, "Fertilizing Your Florida Lawn."

Fertilizer should be applied to St. Augustinegrass in two to six applications from spring green-up through fall (table 1.9). Do not apply nitrogen too early in the growing season, particularly in north Florida, or subsequent frosts may damage the grass. Likewise, don't fertilize too late in the year, as this can slow regrowth the following spring. If applying water-soluble forms at the lower application rate, it will take more applications to apply the total amount of fertilizer needed for the year than if applying a slow-release fertilizer form.

On high-pH (greater than 7.0) soils or where high-pH water is applied, yellow appearance may be an indication of iron or manganese deficiency. For iron deficiency, spray ferrous sulfate (2 ounces in 3–5 gallons of water per 1000 square feet) or a chelated iron source (refer to the label for rates) to temporarily enhance color. Iron applications every six weeks will help maintain green color and, unlike nitrogen, will not promote excessive top growth. On soils with pH greater than 7.0 or where high-pH water is applied, manganese deficiency may also become evident. Lower the soil pH by applying 15 pounds of elemental sulfur per 1000 square feet prior to grass establishment. Once the grass is established, up to 5 pounds of elemental sulfur may be added per 1000 square feet, if it is immediately irrigated into the soil to prevent burn. Using ammonium nitrate or sulfate as a fertilizer source will also help to temporarily reduce soil pH. Apply manganese as a fertilizer with micronutrients or as straight manganese sulfate ($MnSO_4$) bimonthly at 0.41 pound per 1000 square feet (18 pounds per acre) to relieve deficiency symptoms, if present.

Mowing

Proper mowing practices are necessary to keep any lawn healthy and attractive. Most St. Augustinegrass cultivars should be maintained at a height of 3.5–4

Table 1.9. Calendar guide to annual St. Augustinegrass fertilization, by region[a,b]

Region[c] and Maintenance Level	J	F	M	A	M	J	J	A	S	O	N
North Florida											
Basic			C			Fe			C		
Moderate			C		SRN		Fe		C		
High			C		SRN	Fe	SRN		C		
Central Florida											
Basic			C				Fe		C		
Moderate			C		SRN		Fe	SRN	C	C	
High		C		N	SRN		Fe	SRN	C		
South Florida											
Basic			C		SRN		SRN			C	
Moderate		C		N		SRN		SRN			C
High		C		N	SRN		SRN		SRN		C

a. For initial spring application, particularly in North Florida, the recommended time to fertilize is after the last frost rather than on a specific calendar date.

b. C = complete fertilizer application (NPK), N = nitrogen application only, SRN = nitrogen only in a slow-release form, Fe = iron application only.

c. For purposes of this table, North Florida = north of Ocala, Central Florida = south of Ocala to a line extending from Vero Beach to Tampa, South Florida = the remaining southern portion of the state.

inches. Mowing at lower heights reduces drought tolerance and increases susceptibility to pest problems (plate 11). Repetitive low mowing reduces the density and vigor of St. Augustinegrass and can lead to weed problems. To obtain this height with most home rotary lawn mowers, the highest wheel height setting should be used. This height will help the grass develop a deep root system and give a better appearance to the turf. No more than one-third of the length of the leaf blades should be removed with any mowing. The mowing height should be increased to 4 inches during periods of moisture stress or if the grass is growing in shade. Newer semidwarf varieties have a lower growth habit, and should be mowed at 1½–2½ inches for optimum quality. Mowing too infrequently and watering improperly can cause a thatch buildup. See the section in chapter 4 titled "Thatch Control in Your Florida Lawn" for more information.

Either a rotary or reel mower can be used on St. Augustinegrass. It is important to keep the blades sharp and well-adjusted to get a clean cut. Dull blades will give the lawn a brownish cast, because a ragged cut shreds the leaf blades rather than cutting them. During the growing season, blades should be sharpened on a monthly basis.

Grass clippings can be left on a lawn that is mowed at the proper height and frequency. Under these conditions, clippings do not contribute to the thatch layer. Clippings should be left on lawns maintained with low to moderate fertility levels to help recycle nutrients. If clippings are excessive (e.g., clumping occurs), let them dry out and then disperse them.

Watering

The best way to irrigate an established lawn is on an as-needed basis. Grass blades will begin to wilt (e.g., fold, turn bluish green in color, and not recover from traffic or footprints) as the moisture begins to be depleted in the soil. If 30–50 percent of the lawn shows signs of slight wilting, it is time to irrigate with ½–¾ inch of water. The turf will fully recover within twenty-four hours. The turf should not be watered again until it shows signs of wilting. This irrigation schedule works for any soil type and any environmental condition. For further information on recommended watering practices, see "Watering Your Florida Lawn" in chapter 4.

Proper watering practices will help maintain a lawn that requires less mowing and has little thatch buildup. Proper watering will also help develop a deep root system and make the lawn less susceptible to damage by pests and environmental stresses. If brown patch or gray leaf spot diseases are a continuous problem, excessive watering and nitrogen fertilization may be responsible. Certain weeds (like pennywort and nutsedge) also thrive in soils that are continuously wet. Regulate these management practices closely to reduce disease and weed severity.

Irrigating as needed is an efficient way to water any grass, providing that the proper amount of water is applied when needed. Normally, fall through spring is the driest period of the year; therefore, irrigation is required during these seasons to replace water lost via evapotranspiration. Apply enough water to rewet the soil root zone and then wait until the turf shows signs of drought (e.g., wilting) again before the next irrigation (usually every seven to fourteen days in winter and every three to four days in April and May, depending on soil type and location in state). For most Florida soils, no more than ¾ inch of water is necessary to rewet the upper 8–12 inches of the soil profile, which is where the majority of the roots are. To determine rates from a sprinkler system, place several coffee cans throughout the irrigation zones to find out how long it takes to apply ½–¾ inch of water. The length of the irrigation period needed to apply this ¾ inch of water can stay constant year-round; only the *frequency* between irrigations should change. Therefore, irrigation programs set by automatic timers do not need to operate on a daily schedule. They need to operate only after the turf begins to show signs of drought and then to be programmed to apply an average of ¾ inch of water. Overwatering encourages nutrient leaching, increased pest problems, shallow rooting, and, of course, water waste. For further information refer to the section titled "How to Calibrate Your Sprinkler System" in chapter 4.

Pests

Several pest problems can affect St. Augustinegrass. Diagnosis and recommendations for treatment of pest problems are available from your county Extension Service.

Weeds

The best approach to weed control is a healthy, vigorous lawn. Weed problems in a lawn indicate that the turf has been weakened by improper management practices or damage from pests. Proper management practices can eliminate most weed problems. If weeds are a persistent problem, herbicides labeled specifically for St. Augustinegrass should be used. If an herbicide is needed, apply preemergence herbicides (i.e., pendimethalin, benefin, bensulide, atrazine, or others) to control crabgrass if it was present in previous years. Timing is critical for successful control. As a general rule, apply on Feb. 1 in south Florida, Feb. 15 in central Florida, and March 1 in north Florida. *Note: Preemergence herbicides will not control weeds that are actively growing.*

Apply postemergence herbicides (e.g., atrazine) in May as needed for control of summer annual and perennial broadleaf or grassy weeds. Do not apply these materials if the turf is under moisture stress or if air temperatures exceed 85°F. Check with your local county Extension Service office for positive weed identification and latest recommendations.

Many commercial "weed-n-feed" formulations will provide weed control, but they should not be used every time the lawn is fertilized. Read and follow any pesticide label before use. The section titled "Weed Management" in chapter 4 gives specific weed control recommendations.

Insects

The major pest of St. Augustinegrass is the chinch bug. These are foliar-feeding insects that suck plant juices through a needlelike beak, causing yellowish to brownish patches in turf. Injured areas are usually first noticed as the weather begins to warm, in areas along sidewalks, adjacent to buildings, and in other water-stressed areas where the grass is in full sun. Check for chinch bugs by removing the ends of a coffee can, inserting one end into the soil at the margin of suspected damaged areas, and filling with water. Chinch bugs will float to the water surface within five minutes. In areas where chinch bugs are a serious problem, a single, thorough insecticide treatment may offer only temporary control. Therefore, repeat applications may be required. Be sure to follow all label directions when applying any pesticide.

Other insect pests, including webworms, armyworms, grass loopers, and mole crickets, can damage St. Augustinegrass. Mole crickets damage turfgrass areas primarily by creating tunnels or soft mounds while searching for food. Additional damage may result from small animals digging through the soil profile in search of the mole crickets as food. Check for mole crickets by (1) examining an area for the tunnels, or (2) applying 2 gallons of water mixed with 1½ ounces of detergent or soap per 2 square feet in suspected damaged areas. Mole crickets will surface in several minutes.

High levels of nitrogen fertilizer encourage insect problems. Refer to the chapters on specific insect pests for descriptions and information about their control.

Diseases

Brown patch and gray leaf spot are two major disease problems of St. Augustinegrass. Brown patch occurs in warm, humid weather and is encouraged by excessive nitrogen. Brown patch is generally most noticeable during spring and fall months. Gray leaf spot occurs during the summer rainy season and is a problem primarily on new growth. Both diseases can be controlled with fungicides.

Other St. Augustinegrass disease problems originate in the root system. Take-all root rot (*Gaeumannomyces graminis* var. *graminis*) occurs under high moisture or stress conditions. When symptoms are noticeable aboveground, the disease is usually in an advanced state. Following proper cultural practices is the best defense against this disease. Refer to "Disease Management" in chapter 5 for additional information on diseases and their control.

Nematodes

Several types of nematodes infest St. Augustinegrass lawns. Population peaks of nematodes typically occur in late April to early May and again in late August to early September. Damage symptoms include thin stand density, less vigorous growth, a weakened root system, slow recovery following rain or irrigation application, and certain weed invasions (e.g., prostrate spurge and Florida pusley). Soil nematode levels can be positively identified only through laboratory procedures. Inquire with your local county Extension Service office on proper sample submission to the University of Florida Nematode Assay Laboratory. Encourage deep turfgrass rooting by raising the mowing height, irrigating less frequently but more deeply, and providing ample soil potassium and phosphorus. For more information, refer to "Nematode Management" in chapter 5.

Other Problems

Many other factors can decrease the quality of a lawn. To ensure a good St. Augustinegrass lawn, refer to other sections of this publication for recommended management practices, and follow label directions when applying fertilizers and pesticides.

Thatch Removal

Thatch is the layer of undecomposed leaf blades, stolons, roots, and crowns intermingled with soil. Contrary to popular belief, leaving mowing clippings on the lawn does not cause thatch. Excessive thatch develops when the grass is overfertilized, overwatered, and improperly mowed. If the thatch layer exceeds 1 inch, remove by vertical mowing in early spring (e.g., April) south of Orlando and late spring (e.g., May) north of Orlando. A 3-inch spacing between the dethatching blades is best. *Caution: Vertical mowing may result in damaged turf that will require a period of recuperation. Do not attempt vertical mowing unless the grass is actively growing (April–May). A professional landscaping maintenance service or the local county Extension Service office should be consulted before attempting lawn renovation.* Remove debris by raking, sweeping,

Table 1.10. Relative growth characteristics of St. Augustinegrass cultivars

Cultivars	Mowing Ht. (in.)	Cold Tolerance	Shade Tolerance	Chinch Bug Resistance	Green Color	Texture	Density
Normal Growth Habit							
Bitterblue	3–4	good	good	slight	dark	coarse	good
Common/Roselawn	3–4	poor	poor	poor	light	coarse	poor
Floralawn	3–4	poor	poor	slight	dark	very coarse	good
Floratam	3–4	poor	poor	slight	dark	coarse	good
Floratine	2–3	fair	good	slight	dark	medium coarse	good
FX-10	3–4	poor	poor	good	medium	coarse	good
Raleigh	3–4	very good	good	poor	medium	coarse	good
Semidwarf Growth Habit							
Delmar	2–2.5	very good	good	poor	dark	medium-fine	good
Jade	2–2.5	good	good	poor	dark	medium-fine	good
Palmetto	2–3	good	fair		dark	coarse	good
Seville	2–2.5	good	good	slight	dark	fine	good

or vacuuming, and follow with a conventional mowing to improve turf appearance. Immediately irrigate to prevent root zone dehydration. One week after vertical mowing, apply 1 pound soluble nitrogen per 1000 square feet (e.g., 3 pounds ammonium nitrate or 5 pounds ammonium sulfate per 1000 square feet) to encourage recovery. This material must be watered into the soil immediately following application to prevent plant burn. Periodic top dressing (adding a uniform layer of soil on top of the grass) with ¼ inch of soil similar to that underlying the turf is the best method to alleviate thatch accumulation; however, the physical labor required limits the practicality of this method for most homeowners. If top dressing, use soil that is free of weed seeds and nematodes. Do not exceed recommended top dressing rates, as this encourages brown patch disease.

Renovation

Replant large, bare areas by broadcasting sprigs (1 bushel per 1000 square feet), by planting 2-inch plugs every 12 inches, or by sodding. Keep these areas continuously moist with light, frequent irrigations several times daily until runners develop or sod is well-rooted. Over time, gradually reduce irrigation frequency but increase irrigation duration to apply ¾ inch of water, the amount needed to wet the top 8–12 inches of the root zone. Refer to "Establishing Your Florida Lawn" in chapter 2 for more information.

Zoysiagrass for Florida Lawns

Zoysiagrasses (*Zoysia* spp.) were introduced into the United States from Asia and provide attractive turf throughout much of the United States. Several species and varieties are used for residential and commercial landscapes, athletic fields, golf course tees, fairways, and roughs. An established, well-managed zoysiagrass provides a high-quality turf, but zoysiagrasses generally require a high level of maintenance. Improvements in zoysiagrass varieties, however, are a major objective of many turfgrass breeders. These improvements are aimed at maximizing the positive attributes of zoysiagrass, while minimizing the disadvantages.

Advantages

Zoysiagrasses are adapted to a variety of soils and have good tolerance to shade, salt, and traffic. They provide an extremely dense sod that resists weed invasion. Once established, the slow growth of some zoysiagrass varieties is an advantage because mowing frequency is reduced. When properly maintained, zoysiagrasses make excellent turf.

Disadvantages

The improved zoysiagrasses must be propagated vegetatively, and some varieties are extremely slow to establish. For some varieties, two growing seasons may be required for coverage when propagated by plugging or sprigging; others establish much more rapidly. All zoysiagrasses form a heavy thatch that will require periodic renovation. Other disadvantages of the older varieties include slow recovery from damage, poor growth on compacted soils, high fertility requirements, and poor drought tolerance. Some varieties are also prone to damage by nematodes, hunting billbugs, and several diseases. Zoysiagrass also tends to form shallow roots and is weakened when grown in soils low in potassium. Due to toughness of leaves and stems, a reel mower will provide the best cut.

Cultivars

Several species and cultivars of zoysiagrasses can be used in Florida. These vary widely in leaf color, texture, and establishment rate.

Zoysia japonica

This species was introduced into the United States in 1895 and is commonly called Japanese or Korean lawngrass. It is a very coarse-textured grass with hairy light green leaves. This species has a faster growth rate than most other zoysias. It also exhibits excellent cold tolerance. *Zoysia japonica* is the only zoysiagrass for which seed is commercially available; however, the seeded varieties generally do not produce as high a quality turf as do the vegetatively propagated varieties. They can be used for lawns or general turf areas where convenience of establishment by seed is more important than quality. Additionally, hunting billbugs and nematodes cause considerable damage to some varieties of this lawngrass.

Many cultivars of *Zoysia japonica* are available. They include:

'Belaire'

Belaire is an improved *Zoysia japonica* developed in Maryland by the USDA and released in 1985. It is noted for its excellent cold tolerance and medium green color. Compared to Meyer, Belaire has a more open growth habit, coarser leaf texture, and faster establishment rate. Brown patch disease may be a problem for this variety.

'Crowne'

Crowne is a coarse-textured, vegetatively propagated clone of *Zoysia japonica* released by Texas A&M University. Crowne is noted for its tolerance to low water use requirements, its cold hardiness, and its rapid recuperative ability. It was released for use on home lawns, industrial parks, highway rights-of-way, and golf course rough areas.

'El Toro'

El Toro is also an improved *Zoysia japonica* released in 1986 from California. It resembles Meyer but has a quicker establishment rate, improved cool-season color, better cold tolerance, and less thatch buildup. El Toro is also reported to have early spring green-up, increased shade tolerance, and improved resistance to rust disease.

'Empire'

Empire is a native proprietary selection of *Zoysia japonica*. It is said to be dark green in color with a wide leaf blade and open growth habit. It has performed well in sandy and clay soil types with aggressive growth from its stolons and rhizomes, but can be mowed with a standard rotary mower because of its broader leaf and open growth habit.

'Empress'

Empress is another native proprietary selection of *Zoysia japonica*; however, unlike Empire, this grass was selected for its fine-bladed texture, tight growth habit, and green color. Empress is best suited for applications where a fine, small-leaved, soft- textured turf is desired, such as home lawns, golf courses, parks, and sports fields.

'Meyer'

Meyer zoysiagrass, also called Z-52 or Amazoy, is an improved selection of *Zoysia japonica* released in 1951. Meyer is the zoysiagrass often advertised as the "miracle" grass in newspapers and magazines and has long been the standard zoysiagrass in use. It has a deep green color, medium leaf texture, and spreads much faster than other varieties, although it produces few rhizomes. Meyer makes an excellent turf once established. It is less shade tolerant than

Emerald, but is one of the most cold-tolerant zoysiagrasses. Hunting billbugs and nematodes pose serious problems with Meyer, limiting its use in Florida.

Palisades

Palisades is an improved *Zoysia japonica* that forms a medium- to coarse-textured turf. Released by Texas A&M University, Palisades produces a vigorous regrowth from stolons and rhizomes and is noted for its good winter hardiness, tolerance to low mowing, and good to excellent shade tolerance. It is said to be a low water user and has good salt tolerance. Palisades is being marketed for home lawns and golf courses. One concern with Palisades is the lack of research information on nematode susceptibility.

Zoysia matrella

Also called Manilagrass, this species was introduced into the United States in 1912 from Manila. It produces a finer and denser turf than *Zoysia japonica,* but is less winter-hardy and slower growing. Manilagrass resembles bermudagrass in texture, color, and quality and is recommended for a high-quality, high-maintenance turf where a slow rate of establishment is not a disadvantage. Some varieties of *Zoysia matrella* are highly susceptible to damage by nematodes.

'Cashmere'

Cashmere is a 1988 release from Pursley Turf Farms, located in Palmetto, Florida. It is dark green, has a fine leaf texture, and forms a dense turf. Its shade tolerance is not fully known, but it does lack cold hardiness, and is thus best adapted to the lower southern region.

'Cavalier'

Cavalier is another fine-textured *Zoysia matrella* cultivar and is appropriate for home lawns, sports fields, and golf course fairways and tees. A long-leaved variety, it is said to make a very attractive turf, especially during summer. It is rated as having good shade tolerance, good salt tolerance, and excellent fall color retention. In trials conducted at Texas A&M at Dallas, Cavalier showed good resistance to fall armyworms and moderate resistance to tropical sod webworms. Cavalier has done well in trials in Texas, the Midwest, and mid-Atlantic regions; however, limited research has been conducted in Florida on this grass.

'Diamond'

Diamond is an improved *Zoysia matrella* that is vegetatively propagated. It was released from Texas A&M University in 1996. Diamond is distinguished from other zoysiagrasses by its fine texture, excellent salt and shade tolerance, and faster growth. It performs best when mowed at a height of ½ inch or less. In fact, Diamond has been planted on several experimental golf greens mowed at ¼ inch or lower. Like other zoysiagrasses, it has poor cold tolerance, which may limit its use in northern parts of the state. It is also highly susceptible to tropical sod webworms.

Zoysia tenuifolia

Also called Mascarenegrass or Korean velvetgrass, this species is the finest textured and most dense zoysiagrass available. It has good wear tolerance but poor cold tolerance, and is adapted only to the central and southern areas of the state. It also produces an excessive thatch, giving it a puffy appearance.

Zoysiagrass hybrids

Emerald zoysiagrass is a selected hybrid between *Zoysia japonica* and *Zoysia tenuifolia* developed in Tifton, Georgia, and released in 1955. This hybrid combines the winter hardiness, color, and faster growth rate of one parent with the fine texture and density of the other parent. Emerald resembles Manilagrass in color, texture, and density, but is faster spreading and has a wider adaptation. Emerald zoysiagrass is highly recommended for top-quality lawns where time and money allow for adequate maintenance. Emerald produces an excessive thatch layer and is susceptible to dollar and leaf spot. Brown patch disease also can occur.

Zoysia sinica: a new species for turf?

Seashore zoysiagrass (not to be confused with seashore paspalum) is an obscure species that was previously not considered suitable for turf. However, breeding efforts have produced an improved cultivar, J-14. It most closely resembles *Zoysia japonica* as far as leaf texture, color, density, and general appearance are concerned. One major difference is that the seed for seashore zoysiagrass is much easier to handle and appears to propagate better.

Maintenance of Zoysiagrass

Establishment

With one exception, zoysiagrasses must be planted vegetatively by sod, plugs, or sprigs. *Zoysia japonica* is the only species for which seed is commercially available. Success with any propagation method is highly dependent on proper soil preparation.

Seeding

The practice of establishing zoysiagrass from seed is increasing in popularity. The seed, however, is extremely sensitive to light and cannot be covered with soil. Consequently, areas to be established by seed need to be covered with some type of erosion cloth to reduce any surface disruption caused by rain or irrigation. After seeding, frequent, light irrigations are necessary to keep the soil moist and encourage germination. Maintain this moisture regime until the planted area is completely covered.

Sodding

Sodding will produce an instant turf, as the entire area to be planted is covered with grass growing in squares of sod. Sod should be laid over only bare moist soil, with pieces laid in a staggered bricklike pattern and the edges fitted tightly together to avoid any open cracks. Rolling and watering thoroughly will ensure good contact with the soil for fast rooting. Sodded areas should be watered at least twice per day with ¼–½ inch of water until the sod is held fast (usually ten to fourteen days) to the soil by new roots; then watering should be reduced to an as-needed basis.

Plugging

Because of the relatively slow establishment rate of zoysiagrass, plugs are usually planted on 6–8-inch centers. This means that plugs are planted every 6–8 inches in a row and rows are spaced 6–8 inches apart. Even with 6-inch spacing, at least one full season (and longer for some varieties) will be required for complete coverage. Plugs should be tamped firmly into the soil and watered in. During grow-in, the soil should be kept moist until the grass is well rooted. Extra attention to weed control is necessary during this type of establishment.

Sprigging

Planting zoysiagrasses by sprigs is a laborious but effective method of establishment. Fresh sprigs with at least 2 or 4 nodes should be planted in rows that are 6 inches apart. Plant the sprigs end-to-end or no more than 6 inches apart in the row, and cover them with soil about 1–2 inches deep, leaving part of each sprig exposed to light. A roller can be used to press sprigs into the soil. Soil must be kept moist until plants initiate new growth and the area is completely covered.

Fertilization

Proper fertilization is an important component of the best management practices of your turf. Fertilization and other cultural practices influence the overall health of the turf and can reduce or increase its vulnerability to many stresses, including weeds, insects, and disease.

Having soil tests done annually to determine the exact fertility need is advisable. Your county Extension Service office has instructions and bags for taking soil samples and submitting them to the UF/IFAS Extension Soil Testing Laboratory for analysis. These tests form the basis for your turf fertility program, and recommendations from the soil tests should take precedence over recommendations given in publications or on fertilizer bags. In particular, phosphorus levels should be determined by soil testing. Since many Florida soils are high in phosphorus, little or no supplementary phosphorus may be needed for satisfactory turf growth. The exception to this may be during establishment.

In general, two weeks after complete spring green-up, apply a fertilizer at the rate of ½ (water-soluble) to 1 (slow-release) pound of nitrogen per 1000 square feet. The three numbers on a fertilizer bag refer to its percentages of nitrogen, phosphorus, and potassium, respectively. For example, a 50-pound bag of 15-2-

Table 1.11. Zoysiagrass: recommended ranges of nitrogen rates

Location	Pounds N per 1000 sq ft
North Florida	3–5
Central Florida	3–6
South Florida	4–6

Table 1.12. Calendar guide to annual zoysiagrass fertilization, by region[a,b]

Region[c] and Maintenance Level	J	F	M	A	M	J	J	A	S	O	N
North Florida											
Basic			C		SRN				C		
Moderate			C		SRN		SRN		C		
High			C	N	SRN		SRN		C		
Central Florida											
Basic			C		SRN				C		
Moderate			C		SRN			SRN		C	
High		C		N	SRN		SRN		N		C
South Florida											
Basic			C		SRN		SRN			C	
Moderate		C		N		SRN		SRN			C
High		C		N	SRN		SRN		SRN		C

a. For initial spring application, particularly in North Florida, the recommended time to fertilize is after the last frost rather than on a specific calendar date.

b. C = complete fertilizer application (NPK), N = nitrogen application only, SRN = nitrogen only in a slow-release form, Fe = iron application only.

c. For purposes of this table, North Florida = north of Ocala, Central Florida = south of Ocala to a line extending from Vero Beach to Tampa, South Florida = the remaining southern portion of the state.

15 contains 15 percent nitrogen or 7.5 pounds total nitrogen. This bag will fertilize 7500 square feet at the rate of 1 pound of nitrogen per 1000 square feet. To look their best, zoysiagrasses require frequent fertilization. They should receive 3–6 pounds of nitrogen during the growing season in most parts of the state.

University of Florida guidelines for lawngrass fertility show a range of fertilizer rates over which a particular species may be successfully grown for various areas of the state. These ranges are included to account for individual homeowner preferences for low-, medium-, or high-input grass. Additionally, localized microclimate conditions can have a tremendous effect on turfgrass growth, and a range of rates allows for these environmental variations. An example of this would be a typical home lawn that is partially shaded and partially sunny. The grass growing in the shade should receive lower rates of fertilizer than that growing in full sun. The guidelines are also separated into three geographical locations statewide, as indicated in table 1.11 below. All rates are in pounds of nitrogen per 1000 square feet. For questions on how and when to apply these amounts, refer to "General Recommendations for Fertilization of Turfgrasses in Florida Soils" in chapter 3.

Fertilizer should be applied to zoysiagrass in three to six applications from spring green-up through fall. Do not apply nitrogen too early in the growing season, particularly in north Florida, or subsequent frosts may damage the grass. Likewise, don't fertilize too late in the year, as this can slow regrowth the following spring. If utilizing water-soluble forms at the lower application rate, it will take more applications to apply the total amount of fertilizer needed for the year than if using a slow-release fertilizer form.

Mowing

If fertilized as recommended, zoysiagrasses will require frequent mowing (e.g., weekly) during the summer to look their best. *Zoysia japonica* should be mowed every seven to ten days, or when it reaches a height of 3–4 inches. It should be mowed at a height of 2–3 inches with a rotary mower. Meyer zoysiagrass looks best when cut at 1–2 inches every ten to fourteen days, or when it reaches a height of 2–2½ inches, using a reel mower. Emerald and Manilagrass should be cut with a reel mower at ½–1 inch every ten to fourteen days, or when they reach a height of ¾–1½ inches. Because zoysiagrass leaves are very coarse, they can be quite difficult to mow. A sharp, well-adjusted rotary or reel mower should be used.

Watering

Zoysiagrasses require watering especially if parasitized by nematodes, which greatly restrict the root system. During prolonged droughts, watering zoysia-grass every other day may be necessary. Irrigating as needed is an excellent way to water any grass, provided the proper amount of water is applied when needed, not at a later or more convenient time. When using this approach, water at the first sign of wilt and apply ½–¾ inch of water per application.

Thatch Control

Zoysiagrasses typically develop a thick thatch layer in the years after establishment. This thatch must be controlled or removed mechanically to maintain a uniform grass appearance. This is most often done using a vertical mower or core aerator. Research on some of the newer, fine-textured zoysiagrasses have shown good results with alternating conventional mowing and vertical mowing.

Pests

Zoysiagrasses are troubled by several insects, diseases, and nematodes. Periodic control of one or more of these problems will be necessary to grow a high-quality turf.

Insects

The most serious insect pest of zoysiagrass is the hunting billbug. Billbugs destroy and feed on roots, causing grass to die in irregularly shaped patches. Billbugs may require periodic chemical control. Lawn caterpillars may also damage zoysiagrasses.

Nematodes

Probably the most serious pests on zoysiagrasses are nematodes. These soilborne, microscopic worms attack the grass roots, and if not controlled, can ultimately kill the entire turf.

Diseases

Disease problems of zoysiagrass include dollar spot, brown patch, and rust. These are generally suppressed in properly fertilized and watered turf.

2

Preparation and Establishment

Preparing to Plant a Florida Lawn

Proper soil preparation prior to grass planting is critical to ensure the establishment of a quality turf. Preparation will determine how quickly the lawn becomes established and its long-term maintenance requirements. Soil should be prepared whether you are planting a new lawn or replanting an old one and whether you are seeding or propagating vegetatively. The following steps provide a general guideline for preparing to plant a lawn.

Clean and Rough Grade

Remove all construction debris, brush, large roots, rocks, weeds, and old tree stumps. If extensive grading is needed, remove the topsoil and stockpile it for replacement after the rough grade is established. The site should be sloped at 1–2 percent (e.g., ½–1 foot drop per 50 feet) away from the house (pl. A). The rough grade should conform to the final grade after the topsoil is replaced. Swales or mounds with steep slopes of more than 10 percent should be sodded and not seeded because of erosion problems. The steep slopes and mounds currently used as catch basins around many condominium and commercial buildings should be avoided; establishing grass and maintaining proper moisture levels there is difficult, and mowing there is dangerous. If an area cannot be leveled, use ground cover plants other than turfgrass. Control of perennial weeds such as bermudagrass and torpedograss should be performed during site preparation. Several applications of a nonselective herbicide such as glyphosate (Roundup) or commercial fumigation may be necessary for complete weed control.

Soil Analysis

You should always obtain a soil analysis before planting. A representative soil sample can be obtained by collecting small plugs or garden trowels of soil at 15–20 locations around the yard from the top 6 inches of soil. Samples should be combined in a pan or bucket and thoroughly mixed. A portion of this can then be submitted to the UF/IFAS Extension Soil Testing Laboratory. Local county extension offices can supply additional information on soil testing. A soil test will determine the pH value and the report will indicate whether pH adjustment is necessary. If the soil is too acidic (pH too low), dolomitic limestone (dolomite) is recommended for increasing soil pH. Application should be based on a lime requirement that considers both soil buffering capacity and soil pH value. If the soil is analyzed by the UF/IFAS Extension Soil Testing Laboratory in Gainesville, a lime requirement determination will be provided. If the county Extension Service or commercial laboratory makes the analysis, this may not be included unless requested.

In lieu of a lime requirement analysis, the application of 1 ton of dolomite per acre or 50 pounds per 1000 square feet is sufficient to increase the pH of most Florida soils one pH unit; for example, from pH 5.0 to 6.0. A desirable pH range for most turfgrasses is 5.5–7.0. Certain soils in Florida are basic, meaning that their pH levels are greater than 7.0. Turfgrass grown on soils with pH levels greater than 7.0 often displays deficiencies in minor nutrients such as iron and manganese. Further details on soil pH adjustment can be obtained from your county extension office. The soil test analysis will provide the basis for your lawn fertility program. Phosphorus is generally found in sufficient quantity in Florida soils and is not often required when fertilizing your lawn. Fertilization ratios and analysis used will depend primarily on soil test results and local product availability. A general recommendation is to use a turf-type fertilizer in 4-1-2 or 1-0-1 ratios with micronutrients. Apply at a rate of ½–1 pound of soluble nitrogen per 1000 square feet. See "Fertilizer Recommendations for Your Florida Lawn" in chapter 3 for further information.

Installation of Irrigation Equipment

If an irrigation system is desired, it should be designed by an irrigation specialist and installed according to design specifications. An irrigation system's capacity to perform properly is limited by its design, construction, and operation. A poorly designed or improperly installed system will never operate satisfactorily. For proper irrigation of lawn areas, it is important to have an irrigation system that delivers water uniformly and in the amount needed by the grass. It is advisable to turn off the automatic setting on the system and irrigate on an as-needed basis. For more information on this, see "Watering Your Florida Lawn" in chapter 4. It is also important that systems are designed to irrigate shrubbery and other plantings separately from turfgrass.

Soil Amendments

The majority of Florida's soils are sand based, with little organic matter and low water- and fertilizer-holding capacities. Addition of proper amendments to these soils can improve their physical and chemical properties. Amendments may be organic or inorganic; however, organic amendments like peat and compost are rapidly decomposed by soil microorganisms. Inert amendments such as colloi-

Table 2.1. Comparison of selective soil amendments

Soil Amendment	pH	Water Holding Capacity	Cation Exchange Capacity	Compaction Resistance	Durability
Peat Humus	Acid	Good	Good	Fair	5 yr.
Reed-Sedge Peat	Acid	Good	Good	Fair	4–5 yr.
Sphagnum Peat Moss	Acid	Excellent	Good	Fair	1–3 yr.
Sawdust	Acid	Fair	Fair	Fair	1 yr.
Sludge	Acid	Fair	Good	Fair	1–2 yr.
Calcined Clay	Neutral	Good	Poor	Good	>10 yr.
Colloidal Phosphate	Neutral	Good	Good	Good	>10 yr.
Perlite	Neutral	Fair	Poor	Good	>10 yr.
Sand	Neutral	Poor	None	Good	Infinite
Manure	Neutral	Good	Fair	Fair	6 mo.–1 yr.

dal phosphate are permanent. All organic materials should be sterilized to prevent the incorporation of weed seed. A general guideline is to add 1–2 cubic yards of colloidal phosphate or organic material (5 percent by volume), such as peat moss, shredded pine bark, or rotted sawdust, per 1000 square feet of area. Two pounds of actual nitrogen for each cubic yard of sawdust should be added to the soil to aid decomposition and to ensure an adequate supply of nitrogen for the grass. Table 2.1 lists selective soil amendments.

Deep Tillage

Rototilling loosens compacted soil and improves the speed and depth of rooting. If soil amendments, lime, or fertilizer have been added in the preceding steps, the soil should be tilled as deeply as possible, preferably 6–8 inches. A tractor-mounted or self-propelled rotary tiller will do an adequate job of tilling the soil.

Final Grading

Final grading completed just prior to planting provides a smooth planting bed. The site can be hand-raked and dragged with a hand-pulled drag, such as a metal doormat. Large areas can be smoothed by tractor-drawn equipment with a tiller rake or grading box and then hand-finished. Soil particles should be no larger than golf ball size, with even smaller sizes preferable. To achieve a uniformly firm planting bed and to reduce erosion, loose soil can be compressed with a water ballast roller. Care should be taken not to add too much weight and cause soil compaction. Driveways and walks should be level with, or slightly above, the final grade. A good job of grading will result in a more level site and a more attractive lawn that is easy to mow. Irrigation can be used to settle the soil before planting. Hand raking to break up a crusty surface is necessary prior to seeding.

Plate A. Rough grading needs to be done following construction. The effort spent to ensure a smooth surface will result in easier establishment and maintenance.

Plate B. Sod pieces should be fitted together as tightly as possible.

Plate C. Plugs, or small cut pieces of sod with roots and shoots, planted on 6–12-inch centers.

Plate D. Drop (gravity) spreader. Fertilizer is dropped through openings in bottom of spreader.

Plate E. Rotary (centrifugal) spreader. Blades propel fertilizer farther than a drop spreader.

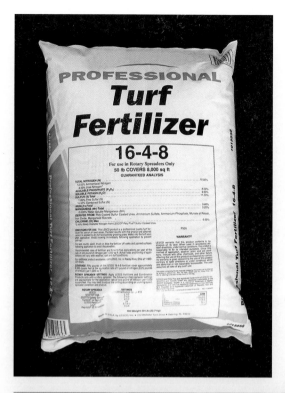

Plate F. Example of a fertilizer label.

Plate G. Skip in fertilizer application.

Plate H. The lawn on the right has been mowed too low. This leaves the grass in a weakened condition and susceptible to other stresses.

Plate I. Rotary mower.

Plate J. Reel mower.

Plate K. Mulching mower.

Plate L. St. Augustinegrass mowed with dull mower blade.

Plate M. St. Augustinegrass mowed with sharp mower blade.

Plate N. Irrigation is one of the most important cultural practices for your lawn. Improper irrigation is often the cause of lawn injury or death.

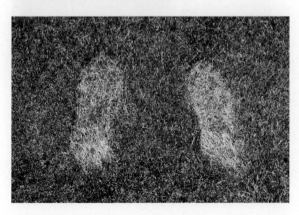

Plate O. Footprints that remain visible or folded leaf blades indicate that the lawn needs to be watered. Irrigate when 40–50 percent of the lawn shows these symptoms.

Plate P. It is important to calibrate your sprinkler system periodically so that water is not wasted.

Plate Q. Calibrating your sprinkler system ensures uniform and adequate water distribution.

Plate R. Overseeding with a cool season grass will give your lawn year-round green color. It is important to realize that this practice will also increase mowing, irrigation, and fertilization needs.

Plate S. Overseeding is a common practice on many Florida golf courses to provide year-round color.

Plate T. Excess thatch can accumulate in a lawn over time. This can reduce irrigation efficiency and increase insect pressure.

Plate U. Example of a thatchy lawn.

Plate V. Verticutting is one recommended procedure for thatch removal. The blades of the vertical mower tear out the thatch and reduce shoot material.

Plate W. Core aeration or cultivation removes soil cores from below the soil, opening up the soil and increasing microbial activity to enhance tissue decomposition.

Plate X. Topdressing often follows verticutting or aeration and is the application of a thin layer of soil or sand to the top of the lawn.

Plate 1. Bahiagrass lawn in a low maintenance scenario.

Plate 2. Choose grass carefully for shaded areas, or omit it completely from these areas.

Plate 3. St. Augustinegrass produces a nice manicured look for southern landscapes.

Plate 4. Bahiagrass lawn showing fertilizer deficiency. While bahiagrass prefers low fertility, it is important to apply some fertilizer to keep the turf growing.

Plate 5. Bahiagrass does not have good wear tolerance, as seen here.

Plate 6. Bermuda-grass provides a lush lawn with higher mainte-nance require-ments than many other lawn grasses.

Plate 7. Seashore paspalum forms a tight, dense turf with the ability to outcompete many weeds and forms an attractive lawn when properly maintained.

Plate 8. Seashore paspalum plugs will grow in rapidly during summer months. Two applications of ¼–½ pound of soluble nitrogen per 1000 square feet in the first month after planting will hasten cover, producing a lawn more quickly.

Plate 9. St. Augustinegrass is the most common home lawn grass in Florida.

Plate 10. St. Augustinegrass has relatively good shade tolerance, but requires some sunlight to grow. In this heavy shade, where humidity is higher and there is less air movement, conditions are perfect for disease problems to occur, as seen here.

Plate 11. St. Augustinegrass should not be mowed lower than 3–4 inches in height. If scalped, it is more susceptible to other stresses such as insect, disease, or weed pressure.

Plate 12. A healthy dense lawn that receives the proper care and fertilizer rates will be less prone to problems with weeds, insects, or disease.

Plate 13. Hairy Beggarticks (*Bidens alba*)

Plate 14. Red Spiderling (*Boerhavia diffusa*)

Plate 15. Shepherds Purse (*Capsella bursa pastoris*)

Plate 16. Spotted Spurge (*Chamaesyce maculata*)

Plate 17. Pinnate Tansymustard (*Descurainia pinnata*)

Plate 18. Dichondra (*Dichondra repens*)

Plate 19. Virginia Buttonweed (*Diodia virginiana*)

Plate 20. Rough Fleabane (*Erigeron strigosus*)

Plate 21. Dogfennel (*Eupatorium capillifolium*)

Plate 22. Catchweed Bedstraw (*Galium aparine*)

Plate 23. Carolina Geranium (*Geranium carolinianum*)

Plate 24. Wandering Cudweed (*Gnaphalium pensylvanicum*)

Plate 25. Oldworld Diamondflower (*Hedyotis corymbosa*)

Plate 26. Pennywort (Dollarweed) (*Hydrocotyle* spp.)

Plate 27. Henbit (*Lamium amplexicaule*)

Plate 28. Virginia Pepperweed (*Lepidium virginicum*)

Plate 29. Black Medic (*Medicago lupulina*)

Plate 30. Cuban Purple Woodsorrel (*Oxalis intermedia*)

Plate 31. Yellow Woodsorrel (*Oxalis stricta*)

Plate 32. Longstalked Phyllanthus (*Phyllanthus tenellus*)

Plate 33. Chamberbitter (*Phyllanthus urinaria*)

Plate 34. Buckhorn Plantain (*Plantago lanceolata*)

Plate 35. Broadleaf Plantain (*Plantago major*)

Plate 36. Florida Pusley (*Richardia scabra*)

Plate 37. Eastern Blue-eyed Grass (*Sisyrinchium angustifolium*)

Plate 38. Greenbriar (*Smilax* spp.)

Plate 39. Spiny sowthistle (*Sonchus asper*)

Plate 40. Common Sowthistle (*Sonchus oleraceus*)

Plate 41. Florida Betony (*Stachys floridana*)

Plate 42. Common Chickweed (*Stellaria media*)

Plate 43. Large Hop Clover (*Trifolium campestre*)

Plate 44. White Clover (*Trifolium repens*)

Plate 45. Narrowleaf Vetch (*Vicia sativa* subsp. *nigra*)

Plate 46. Asiatic Hawksbeard (*Youngia japonica*)

Plate 47. Blanket Crabgrass (seedling) (*Digitaria serotina*)

Plate 48. Blanket Crabgrass (mature) (*Digitaria serotina*)

Plate 49. Goosegrass (*Eleusine indica*)

Plate 50. Annual Bluegrass (*Poa annua*)

Plate 51. Kyllinga rhizomes (*Cyperus brevifolia*)

Plate 52. Purple nutsedge (*Cyperus rotundus*)

Plate 53. Globe Sedge (*Cyperus globulosus*)

Plate 54. A well-maintained, properly fertilized lawn is your best defense against weeds.

Plate 55. Thinning or injured turf is prone to weed pressure.

Plate 56. Fall armyworm caterpillar. Photo by J. Castner.

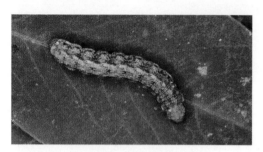

Plate 57. Granulate cutworm. Photo by J. Castner.

Plate 58. Hunting billbug adult (*left*) and larva (*right*). Photo by J. Castner.

Plate 59. Chinch bug adult (*bottom*) and older nymph (*top*). Photo by J. Castner.

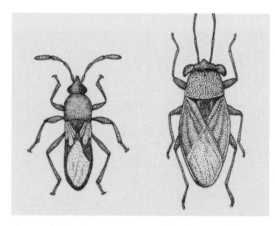

Plate 60. Southern chinch bug (*left*) and big-eyed bug (*right*) adults.

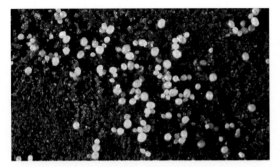

Plate 61. Ground pearls. Photo by J. Castner.

Plate 62. Tawny mole cricket adult. Photo by J. Castner.

	Pronotum	Dactyls	Identification
Tawny mole cricket			**Pronotum with central band; dactyls nearly touch at base ("V")**
Southern mole cricket			**Mottled or 4-dot pronotum; dactyls separate at base ("U")**
Shortwinged mole cricket			**Mottled and spotted pronotum; dactyls form a "U"; adult has short wings**

Plate 63. Important characters used to identify exotic mole crickets. Photos by L. Buss.

Plate 64. Twolined spittlebug adult. Photo by L. Buss.

Plate 65. Tropical sod webworm. Photo by D. Caldwell.

Plate 66. White grub. Photo by E. A. Buss.

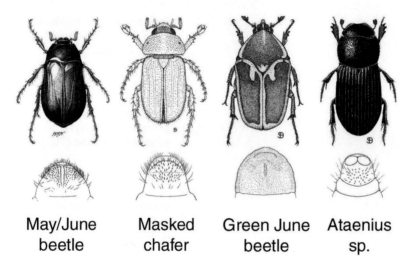

| May/June beetle | Masked chafer | Green June beetle | Ataenius sp. |

Plate 67. Adults and raster patterns of some white grubs found in Florida. Drawings do not indicate true size. Adapted by Ohio State University Cooperative Extension Service.

Plate 68. Damage from an excessive rate of herbicide—no disease.

Plate 69. St. Augustinegrass mowed too short, resulting in scalped turfgrass—no disease.

Plate 70. Dry patches in St. Augustinegrass—no disease.

Plate 71. Anthracnose symptoms on centipedegrass.

Plate 72. Base of leaf is rotted as a result of brown patch disease.

Plate 73. Brown patch symptoms on St. Augustinegrass.

Plate 74. Brown patch symptoms on zoysiagrass. Note the darker color of the outer edge, indicating the fungus is active at this point.

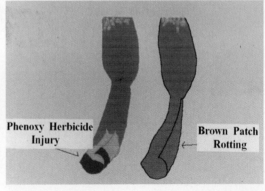

Plate 75. Comparison of phenoxy herbicide damage (*left*) and basal leaf rot due to brown patch (*right*).

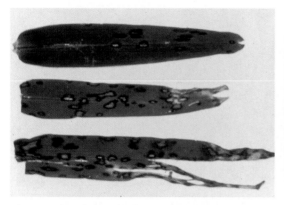

Plate 76. *Cercospora* leaf spot symptoms on St. Augustinegrass.

Plate 77. Dollar spot symptoms on St. Augustine-grass. Note that the patch is very small (about 3 inches in diameter) compared to brown patch symptoms in plates 72 and 73.

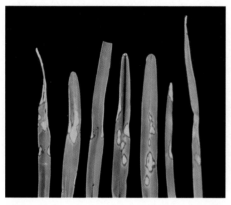

Plate 78. Leaf lesions due to dollar spot disease on St. Augustinegrass.

Plate 79. Dollar spot disease control with application of either a fungicide (*left*) or a quick-release nitrogen fertilizer (*right*).

Plate 80. Type II fairy ring with dark ring of turfgrass and mushrooms.

Plate 81. Type III fairy ring with only mushrooms present.

Plate 82. The mushroom of the poisonous fairy ring fungus *Chlorophyllum*.

Plate 83. Gray Leaf Spot on St. Augustinegrass.

Plate 84. Severe Gray Leaf Spot symptoms. Note leaf tip dieback.

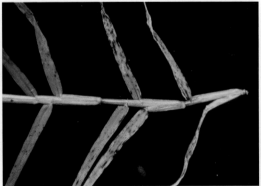

Plate 85. *Helminthosporium* leaf spot symptoms on bermudagrass.

Plate 86. Rust symptoms on zoysiagrass.

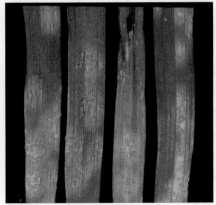

Plate 87. Rust symptoms on ryegrass. Orange spores will rub off.

Plate 88. St. Augustinegrass roots rotted as a result of take-all root rot.

Plate 89. Early aboveground symptoms of take-all Root Rot.

Plate 90. Severe symptoms (death) of take-all Root Rot.

Plate 91. Healthy bermudagrass (*green strip at top*) cut at the correct height, compared to severely diseased bermudagrass (*bottom*) cut too low.

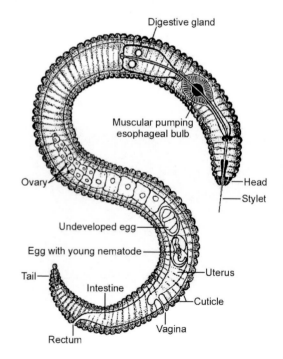

Plate 92. Diagram of a typical plant-parasitic nematode.

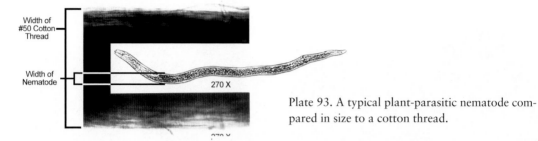

Width of #50 Cotton Thread

Width of Nematode

270 X

Plate 93. A typical plant-parasitic nematode compared in size to a cotton thread.

Plate 94. A typical plant-parasitic nematode stylet resembles a hypodermic needle.

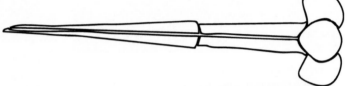

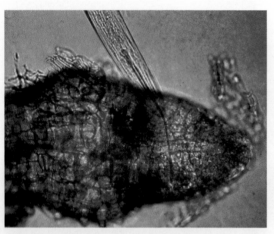

Plate 95. An ectoparasitic nematode feeding by inserting its stylet into a root tip.

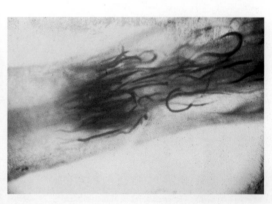

Plate 96. Endoparasitic nematodes burrowing within a root.

Plate 97. Healthy grass roots (*left*) and dark, rotting grass roots damaged by nematodes.

Plate 98. Typical nematode symptoms on a lawn; irregular patches of yellowing, wilting, and browning grass.

Plate 99. Spurge, a weed often associated with turf declining from nematode injury.

Plate 100. Sedge, a weed often associated with turf declining from nematode injury.

Plate 101. Florida pusley, a weed often associated with turf declining from nematode injury.

Plate 102. A T-type soil sample tube is ideal for collecting nematode samples from turf.

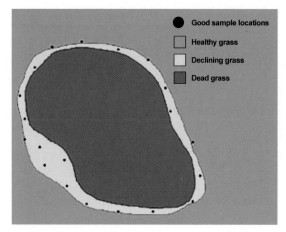

Plate 103. Collect cores for a nematode sample from the edges of declining areas.

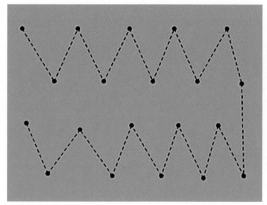

Plate 104. When sampling turf that appears healthy, collect cores in a zig-zag pattern across the area.

Plate 105. Insufficient nitrogen hinders healthy growth, leaving a weakened turf system that is outcompeted by weeds.

Plate 106. Scalping a lawn forces it to regrow after the injury, depleting its stored carbohydrates.

Plate 107. A lawn growing in a stressed situation should not be forced to grow by application of excess nitrogen.

Plate 108. Under mandatory watering restrictions, it may be difficult to supply your lawn with as much water as it needs. By preconditioning your lawn, you can make it more resistant to the effects of drought.

Plate 109. A healthy lawn, showing proper irrigation and fertilization practices.

Plate 110. Turfgrass species vary in their tolerance to drought. Bahiagrass is drought tolerant because it goes dormant (brown) when water is limited and then becomes green once water is applied in ample quantities.

Plate 111. In many parts of Florida, warm-season grasses go into winter dormancy. This is a normal condition and growth resumes when temperatures increase.

Plate 112. Turfgrass needs a certain amount of light to produce acceptable growth. In environments with excess shade, grass will continually decline over time.

Plate 113. Turfgrass will grow more slowly and less densely in the shade. It requires less fertilizer and water than grass growing in full sun.

Plate 114. Seashore paspalum has far better wear tolerance than St. Augustinegrass or bahiagrass.

Plate 115. Bahiagrass showing effects of vehicular traffic.

Soil Fumigation

Soil fumigation is necessary on sod farms, golf courses, and athletic fields, but it is not recommended or available for home lawns. Sterilization utilizes lethal gases to kill weed seeds, insects, disease organisms, and nematodes in the soil. Because the materials used for sterilization are toxic and require special handling, this work must be done by professionals.

Establishing Your Florida Lawn

The two primary methods of establishing turfgrass are seed and vegetative propagation. Vegetative propagation includes sodding, sprigging, and plugging. Although propagating vegetatively is labor intensive, all warm-season grasses can be planted by this method. Seeding is usually the easiest and most economical method of planting grasses, but not all warm-season grasses can establish from seed. It also requires a longer period of time to achieve complete grass cover. Tables 2.2 and 2.3 show recommended planting rates for each turfgrass species.

Regardless of the method of planting, it is essential that a proper seedbed be prepared before planting. A healthy, attractive, long-lived lawn can be established only if you select high-quality seed or planting material and select turfgrasses that are well adapted to the soil and climate. Refer to "Preparing to Plant a Florida Lawn" in this chapter for instructions on site preparation and grass planting.

Seeding

Seeding is the easiest and most economical way to establish a lawn. Success depends on seed quality, proper seeding time, seeding rate, and method of seeding. Warm-season turfgrasses that can be grown from seed include bahiagrass, some bermudagrasses, carpetgrass, centipedegrass, and some zoysiagrasses.

Seed Quality

In order to successfully establish a lawn from seed, top-quality seed must be used. Federal and state laws require that each container of seed bear a tag listing turfgrass species and cultivar, purity, percentage of germination, and weed content. Purity describes the amount (as a percentage) of the desired seed and any other seed and inert matter. Percentage of germination describes the amount of seed expected to germinate under optimum conditions. The quantity of weed seeds is also listed. Read the tag thoroughly to be sure you are purchasing good-quality seed. Try to purchase seed that has a purity of 90 percent or higher and a germination of 85 percent or higher. Always select the best-quality seed of the cultivar you wish to plant. Many times, contractors buy seed with poor germination (less than 50 percent) and poor purity (less than 80 percent) in order to save money. Usually this results in weed invasion and/or poor stand establishment. Text box 1 is an example of a seed label.

Seeding Time and Rate

The best time to seed warm-season grass is during the spring and summer months, from April through July, since this permits a full growing season before cold weather. Seed may be planted as late as September or early October, but establishment will be much slower because of the cooler weather. In south Florida, seed may be planted year-round. In north Florida, young seedling grasses may be winter-killed if planted too late in the fall. Seeding rates are shown in table 2.2. Rates vary with species and cultivars of grasses. Economics must be considered; certain turfgrass seeds are quite expensive and therefore optimum seeding rates are not always practical. The seeding rates suggested will give adequate coverage and produce a mature lawn if given good post-planting care. Rates vary from 4 ounces per 1000 square feet for centipedegrass, which has a very small seed, to 10 pounds per 1000 square feet for bahiagrass, which has a large seed. Seeding rates can be reduced, but the trade-off is a more open turf area subject to weed invasion and erosion.

A hard, impermeable seed coat that restricts the entrance of water or gases into the seed can prevent or seriously delay germination even under favorable conditions. Seed germination is enhanced by scarification processes that disrupt the impermeable coat and permit the entrance of moisture and gases. Bahiagrass seed is often scarified either by soaking in a mild acid solution for a period of time or by physical abrasion to help remove its impermeable seed coat. Bahiagrass seed that has been scarified has an increased germination percentage.

Many seeding methods are used, ranging from planting by hand to the use of mechanical equipment for large turf areas. Evenness of seed distribution is important from the standpoint of overall uniformity of the resulting turfgrass stand. The seedbed should be moist, well prepared, and leveled. Rake the entire area with a heavy garden rake to produce furrows into which seeds are planted. Seed should be applied mechanically, with either a drop-type or rotary spreader. Mechanical seeders provide a more uniform distribution of seed than hand seeding. For best distribution of seed, apply half the required amount in one direction and apply the remainder at right angles to the first seeding. For easier and more uniform application when sowing very small seed like centipedegrass or bermudagrass, mix seed with sand, topsoil, or another convenient carrier that adds bulk to the spreader.

After sowing, seeds should be lightly covered by working them into the soil with a rake. Ideally, seed should be topdressed with ¼–½ inch of soil, but this may not be practical for most home lawns. In the absence of topdressing, seeds can be covered reasonably well by raking. If the seedbed was furrowed before seeding, then raking or dragging with a board will work the seed into the furrows and adequately cover it. Roll the seeded area with a lightweight roller to

Table 2.2. Seeding rates for Florida turfgrasses

Turfgrass	Pounds seed per 1000 sq ft
Bahiagrasses	7–10 (scarified)
Bermudagrass (common)	2 (hulled)
	4 (unhulled)
Carpetgrass	2
Centipedegrass	0.25

firm up the soil and to ensure good contact between seed and soil. The area should then be mulched with weed-free grass, hay, or straw, so that 50–75 percent of the bare ground is protected. Mulching helps conserve soil moisture, moderates soil temperature, and prevents erosion of topsoil and washing of seed. As a general rule, one bale of hay will cover approximately 1000 square feet. Proper watering is the most critical step in establishing turfgrasses from seed. The soil must be kept continuously moist but not excessively wet until seeds have germinated. Supplying water two or three times a day in small quantities for approximately two weeks will ensure adequate moisture for germination. If the surface of the soil is allowed to dry out at any time after the seeds have begun to swell and before roots have developed, many of the seedlings will die. *Improper watering is the most common cause of seeding failure.* Initial watering should be from a fine spray, if possible, or from sprinklers with a low precipitation rate. Coarse spray and high water pressure or high precipitation rates will wash the soil and uncover buried seeds. Avoid overwatering and saturating the soil. This can cause the seeds to float and increases the incidence of disease that can kill the seedling plants. As the seedlings mature and root systems develop, the number of waterings can decrease, but the volume should increase so that the entire root zone is wetted, not just the soil surface. If water is not available, avoid planting in April, May, and October, since these are traditionally Florida's driest months.

Vegetative Planting

Vegetative planting is simply transplanting large or small pieces of grass. Solid sodding covers the entire seedbed with vegetation. Plugging or sprigging refers to planting pieces of sod or individual stems or runners called stolons or rhizomes.

Sod

Sodding is more expensive than sprigging or plugging, but it produces a so-called "instant lawn." Without proper site preparation and post-installation care, however, the sod can die almost as easily as any other newly planted area. Before buying sod, inspect it carefully to guarantee the absence of weeds, insects, and disease. Store the sod in a cool, shady place until ready to plant. Sod life on pallets during summer months is less than forty-eight hours. The area to be planted should be properly prepared (i.e., tilled and raked smooth) and moistened at the time of laying sod. Sod pieces should be fitted together as tightly as possible, but the sod should not be stretched to fit an area (pl. B). If cracks are evident between pieces, they should be filled with topsoil. Tamp or roll the sod to remove air pockets and ensure good soil contact. If the root is not in contact with the underlying soil, it will dry out and die. Do not let the soil dry out until there is a good union between the sod and the soil surface. Light, frequent applications of soil topdressing will help to smooth out the lawn surface. Sodding is expensive, but is recommended where immediate cover is desired for aesthetics or prevention of soil erosion.

Sprigs

Sprigging is the cheapest vegetative planting method. A sprig is an individual stem or piece of stem of grass with at least one node (joint) that has the potential to develop into a grass plant. There is no adhering soil on a sprig. Sprigs may also be called runners, rhizomes, or stolons. Sprigging is simply the planting of individual grass stems at spaced intervals. A suitable sprig should have 2–4 nodes from which roots can develop. Sprigs can be bought by the bushel, but more commonly sod is used and cut or pulled apart into sprigs.

There are several methods of planting sprigs. One method is to cut shallow furrows in the prepared planting area by using a push-plow or the edge of a hoe. Place the sprigs end-to-end or every 6–12 inches along the row, cover a part of each sprig with soil, and firm it by rolling or stepping on the furrow. The closer together sprigs are planted, the faster the grass will cover the soil. Rows should be placed no more than 6–8 inches apart. A second method is to place sprigs on the soil surface at the desired interval end-to-end, about 6 inches apart, and then press one end of the sprig into the soil with a notched stick or blunt piece of metal like a dull shovel. A portion of the sprig should be left aboveground, exposed to light. Each sprig should have some leaves, but a node will do if the stolon has no leaves. Regardless of the planting method, each sprig should be tamped or rolled firmly into the soil. This will help keep the sprigs from drying out and dying. As with seeding, soil must be kept continually moist—not wet—until adequate rooting has occurred. Water lightly once or twice daily after planting until roots develop. After the first few weeks, gradually back off the multiple irrigations until you reach a point where you are irrigating every other day. Reduce that frequency over the course of ten to fourteen days, gradually getting to irrigation intervals of twice a week or less. Mulching can also be used in vegetative planting for moisture conservation and erosion control.

Another method of sprigging, which is used where rapid cover is needed, is "stolonizing" or "broadcast sprigging." The sprigs are prepared either by mechanical shredding or by hand-tearing of sod into individual sprigs, or they may be purchased by the bushel (most common with bermudagrasses). The material is broadcast, like a mulch, over the area by hand. Sprigs are then cut into the soil with a light disc or covered with ½ inch of soil topdressing, rolled, and watered. This method provides very fast coverage. Since the sprigs are planted at a shal-

Table 2.3. Spacing and planting material from sod for vegetative hand planting (nonbroadcast)[a]

Turfgrass	Spacing (inches)	Sq ft of sod per 1000 sq ft of lawn[b]
St. Augustinegrass		
2-inch plugs	6–12	30–50
Sprigs	6–12	10–15
Centipedegrass		
2-inch plugs	6	100–150
Sprigs	6	30–50
Zoysiagrass		
2-inch plugs	6	100–150
Sprigs	6	8–15
Bermudagrass		
2-inch plugs	12	30–50
Sprigs	12	2–5

a. Broadcast sprigging or stolonizing is used for planting large areas such as golf courses, football fields, etc. Usually 5–10 bushels of sprigs are required per 1000 square feet (approximately 200–400 bushels/acre) for best results.
b. Based on estimates of 1 sq ft of sod = 80 linear ft of sprigs; 1 sq yd of sod = 1 bushel of sprigs; and 1 sq yd of sod = 324 2-inch plugs. The numbers in the column refer to the square feet of solid sod from which either 2-inch plugs or sprigs can be obtained.

low depth, they are very susceptible to drying out. Light, frequent waterings are necessary until roots become well established. This is the method often used to plant bermudagrass golf greens and fairways.

Plugs

Plugging is the planting of 2–4-inch circular or block-shaped pieces of sod at regular intervals (pl. C). Three to ten times as much planting material is necessary for plugging as sprigging (table 2.3). Several turfgrasses are currently available commercially as plugs in trays. These commercial plugs usually have well-developed root systems and are treated as other plugs described in table 2.3.

Square plugs can be cut from sod with a shovel, axe, or machete, while round plugs are cut with special steel pluggers similar to a bulb planter. The plugs are then placed in correspondingly sized holes made in the soil. These should be planted on 6–12-inch centers. Wider spacing prolongs the establishment phase. Plugs will grow in more slowly than sprigs, but they are less susceptible to desiccation. Mulching will help improve moisture retention and prevent erosion of the soil between the plugs.

Post-Planting Care

As previously mentioned, proper water management after planting is crucial. For seeded areas, keep the seedbed continuously moist with light, frequent sprinklings several times daily. Do not flood the seedbed or apply water in a hard stream, as this can cause seed movement and soil erosion. As seedlings or planted material take root and grow, decrease watering frequency and increase the amount of water applied each time. Fertilize new seedlings one week after emergence. Apply a complete (N-P-K) turf-type, slow-release nitrogen fertilizer (e.g., 16-4-8) to provide 1 pound of actual nitrogen per 1000 square feet. Fertilize vegetatively established grasses with ½–1 pound of nitrogen per 1000 square feet every two to three weeks once stolons begin to spread. Continue this until a solid stand of grass is achieved. Once a solid stand results, follow the fertilizer programs listed in other chapters for established turf. Look for the words "slow release" or "insoluble" on the fertilizer labels. Nitrogen in this type of fertilizer will not burn or wash away as readily as quick-release nitrogen sources. Don't be fooled by the word "organic." Some organic fertilizers are water soluble and can leach as quickly as inorganic fertilizers.

Begin mowing as soon as the grass reaches 30 percent greater than the desired height. For example, mow bahiagrass back to 3 inches when it reaches 4–4½ inches. Use a mower with a sharp blade. If a sharp blade is not used, seedlings may be torn from the ground or the grass will have a ragged appearance. Do not mow when the grass is wet. If clippings are heavy enough to shade the grass, catch them or rake and remove them. Otherwise, clippings should be left on the ground, as they result in a 20–30 percent reduction of fertilizer usage.

Newly planted areas often become infested with weeds. Proper mowing height and frequency are the best method of controlling many weeds in newly established lawns. Remaining weeds may be controlled with herbicides or by hand removal. *Do not apply herbicides until the lawn has been mowed at least three times.* Refer to "Weed Management" in chapter 5 for the latest herbicide recommendations.

Tips For Turfgrass

Follow these tips to reduce runoff, save fertilizer, and prevent pollution of ground or surface water. Remember, your objective is to get water and fertilizer to the root zone, where it will be taken up by the grass.

- Apply ½–¾ inch of water per irrigation. If you have just fertilized your lawn, apply only ¼ inch of water.
- Make sure your sprinkler system applies water uniformly. Do not mix sprinkler head types or let the reach of two sprinklers overlap excessively.
- Know how much water your system applies over a time period. Simply place coffee cans in a straight line from your sprinkler to the edge of the watering pattern. Turn the water on for fifteen minutes and measure the average depth of water in each can with a ruler. Then multiply this number by 4 to determine the irrigation rate in inches per hour.
- Adjust irrigation to the season and rainfall pattern. Warm-season grasses require more water in the summer when they are actively grow-

ing. Rainfall may or may not provide adequate irrigation. In winter, you will normally be able to reduce irrigation substantially. Watch the grass for a bluish gray color, slow recovery from foot or tire traffic, or the folding of grass blades. These symptoms indicate the grass is wilting and needs to be watered.

- Do not water when rain is forecast for your particular area.
- Increase mowing height of lawns; this allows the plant to develop a more extensive root system.

Renovation

Prior to renovating an established lawn, ask these questions:

- Were improper management practices the cause of the need for renovation? If so, these practices should be reviewed and adjusted as recommended by the University of Florida.
- Will another turf species replace the current grass?
- Is more than 50 percent of the present lawn in need of renovation?
- Are there adequate time and resources available for renovation and subsequent maintenance?

If an area is to be completely replanted and if more than 50 percent of plants currently present are weeds, or if the turf species is to be changed, the areas should be treated with a nonselective herbicide, such as glyphosate (Roundup). It will typically require more than one application of Roundup to completely remove existing vegetation. A second application should be made approximately fourteen days after the first. If removing bermudagrass, a third application may be advisable. This area should then be de-thatched using a verticutter, power rake, or slicer/groover. A soil test should be done at this time to determine fertilization requirements or necessary pH adjustments. Depending on soil test results, starter fertilizer or lime may be added. Any required irrigation should also be installed prior to planting.

If establishing by seed, lightly rake sown seeds to encourage contact with soil. If the area is replanted by vegetative means, such as sprigs or sod, the glyphosate-treated turf should be removed with a sod cutter, the surface regraded, soil amendments and starter fertilizer added; then the grass may be planted. If the existing area does not need treatment with a nonselective herbicide, sprigs may be planted directly into the current turf.

Text Box 1. **Example of a seed label.**

Brand name: Centipedegrass Seed
   98.75% Pure Seed
Other Ingredients
   0.00% Other Crop Seed
   1.00% Inert Matter
   0.25% Weed Seeds
   85.00% Germination
Tested 12/94
LOT 0001-A

3

Fertilizing Your Florida Lawn

Fertilizer Recommendations for Your Florida Lawn

Many people think a beautiful lawn is unattainable, but that is not necessarily true. A few basics concerning fertilization, watering, pest control, and mowing are necessary, and here we present some of the basic facts relating to fertilization. By far the best approach to a proper fertilization program is to test the soil, but if a soil test is not available, these guidelines can be used for a general turfgrass fertilization program.

Essential Elements

All plants require certain chemical elements for proper growth and appearance. Of these nutrients, at least sixteen are known to be essential elements; these are listed in table 3.1 along with their sources. All essential elements except carbon, hydrogen, and oxygen are obtained from the soil and absorbed by plant roots. If nutrient availability is inadequate in the soil, turfgrass growth and quality may be limited and application of fertilizer will be necessary to promote proper turfgrass growth.

Turfgrasses require the macronutrients nitrogen (N), phosphorus (P), and potassium (K) in greatest quantities. Calcium (Ca), magnesium (Mg), and sulfur (S) are required in smaller quantities. The micronutrients iron (Fe), manganese (Mn), zinc (Zn), copper (Cu), chlorine (Cl), molybdenum (Mo), and boron (B) are required in very minute quantities, and less often than the macronutrients. Micronutrients are as essential as the macronutrients, but are required in much smaller amounts.

Types of Fertilizers

Fertilizers are identified by analysis and/or brand name. Many common commercial fertilizers are known by their grade, such as 16-4-8 or 15-2-15. A complete fertilizer contains N, P, and K, in that order, in percentages indicated by the numbers. A 16-4-8 fertilizer, for example, contains 16 percent total nitrogen, 4 percent available phosphorus expressed as P_2O_5, and 8 percent soluble potash

Table 3.1. Essential elements required by turfgrasses

Macronutrients		Micronutrients
From Air/Water	From Soil	From Soil
Carbon	Nitrogen	Iron
Hydrogen	Calcium	Copper
Oxygen	Phosphorus	Manganese
	Potassium	Molybdenum
	Magnesium	Zinc
	Sulfur	Boron
		Chlorine

expressed as K_2O. Thus a 100-pound bag of 16-4-8 contains 16 pounds of total nitrogen, 4 pounds of available phosphate, and 8 pounds of potash. These three constituents, N, P, and K, are called the primary plant foods; if all three are present, the fertilizer is a "complete" fertilizer. Complete fertilizers like 16-4-8, 12-4-8, and 15-2-15 are commonly used in turfgrass fertilization. Besides the primary elements (N, P, and K), the fertilizer may contain secondary plant foods, including Ca, Mg, S, Mn, Zn, Cu, Fe, and Mo.

Both primary and secondary elements, if present, are listed on the fertilizer label. The label also describes the materials from which the fertilizer has been made. This information appears beside the "derived from" statement. An example of a mixed fertilizer containing several different sources of N is shown in plate F.

In addition to complete fertilizers, some materials are used almost exclusively to supply N to turfgrasses for rapid growth and dark green color. These materials include soluble forms of N, such as ammonium nitrate (33% N), ammonium sulfate (21% N), urea (46% N), calcium nitrate (15.5% N), potassium nitrate (13% N and 44% K_2O), as well as slow-release N sources such as ureaformaldehyde (38% N), isobutylidene diurea (31% N), sulfur-coated urea (36% N), Nutralene (40% N), and Polyon (42% N). Turfgrasses commonly require higher rates and more frequent applications of N source fertilizers than other nutrient sources. In most cases, slow-release N sources can be used to reduce the potential for leaching losses of applied N. In order to obtain the desired growth and color response, a mixture of soluble and slow-release N sources is generally recommended for use on turfgrasses. Many fertilizers available for homeowner use have varying ratios of soluble to slow-release N. Look for a product with a relatively high slow-release content, such as 30–50 percent.

Although slow-release fertilizers provide benefits in terms of less opportunity for leaching and longer-term response from the fertilizer application, it is important to realize that turfgrasses are very efficient N-absorbing ground covers. University of Florida research has shown that N does not leach from a turfgrass system that has been fertilized at the recommended rate and frequency. Poor-quality, slow-growing, and improperly fertilized turfgrasses actually leach much more N than do turfgrasses growing at optimum levels.

For Florida turfgrasses, the best yearly fertilization program usually includes a combination of one or two applications of multiple nutrient fertilizations and several supplemental applications of an N fertilizer. Nitrogen fertilization is often based on the desired growth rate and type of turfgrass being grown. As a result of past fertilizer applications and the inherent nature of some Florida soils, phosphorus fertilization is not always required. One should depend on a recent soil test to determine if P is required for optimum turfgrass growth. If your soil test indicates an adequate level of extractable soil P, choose a fertilizer blend that does not contain P as one of the supplied nutrients. That blend would be represented as X-0-X, such as 15-0-15. Excess P application can result in enrichment of the P status of run-off or leachate waters, leading to enhanced growth of submerged plants and resulting loss of dissolved oxygen in adjacent bodies of water, a process known as eutrophication.

Second only to N in total fertilization requirement is potassium, otherwise known as K. Potassium influences root growth and water- and stress-tolerance relationships in turfgrasses and should be maintained at adequate levels for optimum growth. Potassium should generally be applied at equal or one-half the amount of N, such as in a 15-2-15 or 16-4-8 blend.

Fertilizer Application

Most fertilizers are applied at a rate determined by the type and amount of nitrogen present in the material. Nitrogen is the nutrient most used by a turfgrass but at the same time the material that burns the turfgrass if applied at excessive rates.

In the past, it was customary to recommend the application of 1 pound of actual nitrogen per 1000 square feet of turfgrass. In light of potential environmental concerns, it is now recommended that no more than ½ pound of the nitrogen in the application be in soluble form. Therefore, in order to make an application of 1 pound of actual nitrogen per 1000 square feet of turfgrass, you need to use a blended fertilizer product containing no more than 50% of the total N in soluble form with the rest of the nitrogen originating from a slow-release N source. The pounds of actual N in every fertilizer can be determined by dividing the percent N listed on the label into 100. For example, if applying soluble N from ammonium sulfate, divide 21% (the N content of ammonium sulfate) into 100 to find the number of pounds of ammonium sulfate that will supply 1 pound of N. Since 100 divided by 21 equals about 5, 5 pounds of ammonium sulfate supplies 1 pound of N. Therefore, to apply the equivalent of ½ pound of soluble N per 1000 square feet of turfgrass surface, one would need to apply 2½ pounds of ammonium sulfate. If applying N as a 16-4-8 fertilizer containing a 50/50 mixture of soluble and slow-release N, one could apply 1 pound of total N per 1000 square feet. In order to calculate the quantity of 16-4-8 to apply, divide 100 by 16 (16 is the percentage of N in the fertilizer), which equals approximately 6. Thus, apply 6 pounds of the 16-4-8 fertilizer per 1000 square feet to supply 1 pound of N (50% soluble and 50% slow-release N).

Table 3.2. A guide to fertilizer rates on Florida turfgrasses

Nitrogen Fertilizers	Composition	Pounds needed to apply 0.5 pounds of actual N per 1000 sq ft
Soluble N Sources (Inorganic)		
Ammonium Nitrate	33.5% N	1.5
Ammonium Sulfate	21% N	2.5
Calcium Nitrate	15.5% N	3.2
Potassium Nitrate	13-0-44	3.8 also 1.7 lbs K_2O
Sodium Nitrate	16% N	3.1
Nitrate of Soda Potash	15-0-16	3.3 also 0.5 lbs K_2O
Monoammonium Phosphate	11-48-0	4.5 also 2.2 lbs P_2O_5
Diammonium Phosphate	18-46-0	2.8 also 0.4 lbs P_2O_5
Soluble N Sources (Organic)		
Urea	46% N	1.1
Calcium Cyanamide	21% N	2.4
Slow-Release N Sources (Synthetic)		
Ureaform/Nitroform	38% N	1.3
Nutralene	40% N	1.25
Isobutylidene diurea (IBDU)	31% N	1.6
Sulfur-coated Urea	38% N	1.3
Polyon	42% N	1.2
Slow-Release N Sources (Natural Organics)		
Sewage Sludge	6-2-0	8.3 also 0.2 lbs P_2O_5
Cow Manure	2-0-0	25
Poultry Manure	4-0-0	12.5
Cottonseed Meal	7% N	7.1
Alfalfa Meal	6% N	8.3
Blood Meal	3-22-0	16 also 3.7 lbs P_2O_5
Processed Tankages	5–10% N	10 to 5
Garbage Tankages	2–3% N	20 to 15

Potassium and Phosphorus Fertilizers	Composition	Pounds needed to supply 0.5 lbs of actual Potash or Phosphate per 1000 sq ft
Potassium Chloride (Muriate of Potash)	60% K_2O	0.83
Potassium Sulfate	50% K_2O	1
Potassium Nitrate	13-0-44	1.1 also 0.1 lbs N
Sulfate of Potash Magnesia	22% K_2O, 11% Mg, 8% S	2.2 also 0.2 lbs Mg & S
Concentrated Superphosphate	46% P_2O_5	1

Several fertilizer materials are listed in table 3.2, and the rate of application for ½ pound of N is already calculated. For example, if using ammonium nitrate on a turfgrass, note that the table lists the rate of application at 1½ pounds of material per 1000 square feet to apply the equivalent of ½ pound of N. Therefore, if you have a 5000-square-foot lawn, use 7½ pounds of ammonium nitrate.

When a soil test of a turfgrass area is not available, table 3.3 can be used as a guide for turfgrass fertilization programs at three levels of maintenance for

Table 3.3. Fertilization guide for turfgrasses maintained without the benefit of a soil test[a]

Region[b] and Turfgrass	Maintenance Level	J	F	M	A	M	J	J	A	S	O	N	D
North Florida													
Bahiagrass	Basic			C						C			
	Moderate			C		N		Fe		C			
	High		C		N	SRN		Fe		C			
Bermudagrass	Basic			C		N				C			
	Moderate			C		SRN			SRN			C	
	High		C	N	SRN	C		Fe	SRN			C	
Centipedegrass	Basic			C						C			
	Moderate			C	Fe			Fe		C			
	High			C	Fe	SRN		Fe		C			
St. Augustinegrass	Basic			C			Fe			C			
	Moderate			C		SRN		Fe		C			
	High		C	SRN	Fe			SRN		Fe	C		
Zoysiagrass	Basic			C						C			
	Moderate			C		SRN			SRN			C	
	High		C		N	SRN			SRN			C	
Central Florida													
Bahiagrass	Basic			C		N				C			
	Moderate			C		N			Fe		C		
	High		C		N		SRN		Fe		C		
Bermudagrass	Basic			C		N		Fe		C			
	Moderate		C		N		SRN		Fe			C	
	High		C	N	SRN	C		Fe		SRN		C	
Centipedegrass	Basic			C			Fe			C			
	Moderate			C	N			Fe		C			
	High			C		N		Fe		SRN		C	
St. Augustinegrass	Basic			C		N		Fe		C			
	Moderate			C			SRN	Fe		SRN		C	
	High		C		N		SRN	Fe		SRN		C	
Zoysiagrass	Basic			C			SRN			C			
Zoysiagrass	Moderate			C			SRN		SRN			C	
	High		C		N	SRN		SRN		N		C	
South Florida													
Bahiagrass	Basic	C						Fe		C			
	Moderate	C			N			Fe		C			
	High	C			N	SRN		Fe		N		C	
Bermudagrass	Basic	C			N		SRN			C			
	Moderate	C			N		C		Fe	C			
	High	C			N	SRN	C	Fe		SRN		C	
Centipedegrass	Basic			C				Fe		C			
	Moderate	C			N			Fe		C			
	High	C			N		SRN		Fe			C	
St. Augustinegrass	Basic			C		N			Fe	C			
	Moderate	C		SRN			Fe		SRN	C			
	High	C			N		SRN		Fe		SRN		C
Zoysiagrass	Basic			C		SRN				C			
Zoysiagrass	Moderate	C		SRN					SRN		C		
	High	C			N		SRN			N			C

This guide is for turfgrass fertilization under circumstances where a soil test does not exist. In order to determine the correct rates of P and K, a soil test is required and is always recommended.

a. Complete fertilizer applied at 1 pound N per 1000 sq ft containing a 50% soluble and 50% slow-release N. N = soluble N applied at 0.5 pounds N per 1000 sq ft. SRN = slow-release N applied at 1 pound N per 1000 sq ft. Fe = apply iron to provide dark green color without stimulating excessive growth. For foliar application use ferrous sulfate (2 oz/3–5 gal water/1000 sq ft). If the Fe is applied to an acidic soil, use 1 pound of iron sulfate per 1000 square feet. If the soil is calcareous, use the container label recommended rate of an iron chelate.

b. For purposes of this table, North Florida = north of Ocala, Central Florida = south of Ocala to a line extending from Vero Beach to Tampa, South Florida = the remaining southern portion of the state.

Table 3.4. Inorganic and organic nitrogen fertilizer sources compared

Advantages	Disadvantages
Inorganic Nitrogen Sources	
Readily available N	Leach rapidly
Low cost per pound of N	Danger of fertilizer burn
Easily controlled N levels	High salinity potential
Little problem of residual N	Must be applied frequently at low rates
May have greater efficiency	Usually acid forming
Organic Nitrogen Sources	
Slow release of N	May be very expensive per pound of N
Less subject to leaching loss	Not released at adequate rate during cool season
Small danger of turfgrass burn	Application response may be slow
May be applied infrequently at high rates	May contain weed seeds that contaminate turfgrass

each type of turfgrass for three regions of the state. Note that most programs use a combination of complete fertilizers and nitrogen fertilizers applied during different times of the year. Recall that the complete fertilizer should be used only when the soil test calls for both P and K. When P is not required, apply only those nutrients that are recommended by the soil test report.

The range of recommended fertilization rates vary to account for different needs. There is a minimum- or low-maintenance recommendation that will produce only a moderate-quality turfgrass. The maximum- or high-maintenance program should produce a high-quality turfgrass. A program can also be chosen between the two extremes. The correct schedule is the one that produces the quality of turfgrass that you desire.

To use table 3.3, find the particular turfgrass and part of the state that applies to you, then apply the fertilizer indicated during the month(s) recommended. For rates of various materials, refer to table 3.2. For example, to obtain a desirable centipedegrass lawn in Gainesville (north Florida), apply a complete fertilizer (designated as "C" in the table) in March and September, then apply a soluble N material like ammonium sulfate in June. Rates for individual N fertilizer materials are given in table 3.2, and the rate for a complete fertilizer is shown at the bottom of the fertilization chart (table 3.3).

Organic vs. Inorganic Fertilizers

There is much confusion over whether to use organic or inorganic fertilizers on turfgrasses. Both types have advantages and disadvantages; however, the type of fertilizer makes no difference to the turfgrass. Grasses absorb N as nitrate or ammoniacal N. Organic N is not used directly by the plant but must first be converted to one of the above chemical forms by soil microorganisms before being taken up by the plant.

The advantages and disadvantages of organic vs chemical fertilizers relate to the consumer, not to the turfgrass. Both organic and inorganic N fertilizers have advantages and disadvantages; these are compared in table 3.4. Select an N source after considering the pros and cons of the various forms. A mixture of the two will most likely result in the best response.

Supplemental Iron Application

Many times turfgrasses such as centipedegrass, bahiagrass, and St. Augustine-grass turn yellow during the summer because of lack of N fertilizer. However, fertilization with N in summer is not always desirable since this often encourages disease and insect problems. Many times the addition of iron (Fe) to these grasses provides the desirable dark green color, but does not stimulate excessive grass growth, as N fertilization does. Usually, iron sulfate (2 ounces per 3–5 gallons of water per 1000 square feet) or a chelated iron source is used to provide this greening effect. The effect from supplemental iron application is only temporary (approximately two to four weeks); therefore, repeat applications are necessary for summer-long color.

Precautions

All soluble fertilizers may burn turfgrass if improperly applied. To avoid burn, never apply fertilizer at greater than the recommended rate of ½ pound of soluble N per 1000 square feet per application or 1 pound of N when a 50/50 combination of soluble and slow-release N is applied. Apply P and K only when required based on a recent soil test, and do not exceed the recommended rate of application, especially for P. Always apply fertilizers when the turfgrass leaves are *dry* and water thoroughly after application. Apply enough water to solubilize the fertilizer and move it below the surface. This can generally be accomplished by applying ¼ inch of water through the irrigation system, which can usually be accomplished by running a typical turfgrass irrigation system for fifteen to twenty minutes. Excess irrigation may leach the soluble N source below the root zone, so great care should be taken not to water too much.

The Florida Fertilizer Label

Fertilizers are manufactured from a wide variety of materials to supply required plant nutrients. Once these materials are mixed, it becomes difficult to distinguish the materials present. In the past, a few unscrupulous manufacturers have taken advantage of this to increase their profits. To protect consumers and legitimate manufacturers from such practices, the Florida legislature enacted the first fertilizer law in 1889 and has amended it many times since its enactment. These laws regulate the manufacture and sale of fertilizers in the state.

The law requires that the manufacturer purchase and affix a label to each bag, package, container, or lot of fertilizer offered for sale in the state. The law requires that each label show specific information about the analysis and composition of the mixture or material.

Information on the Fertilizer Label

Fertilizer labels (pl. F) contain the following information:

1. The Fertilizer License Number is identified on all fertilizer labels with a capital "F" preceding the license number. The number must be clear, legible, and appear prominently and conspicuously on the label in proximity to the brand name or guaranteed analysis.
2. A brand name is the name used by the licensee to identify his product. Brand means a term, design, or trademark used in connection with one or several grades of fertilizer. The label shall also include a grade in close proximity to the brand. The "grade" means the percentages of total nitrogen expressed as N, available phosphate expressed as P_2O_5, and soluble potassium expressed as K_2O, stated in whole numbers, in that order.
3. The net weight is the actual weight present in the package or container. If sold in bulk, five labels containing all the required information must accompany a delivery ticket that shows the certified net weight of the bulk material.
4. The name and street address of the manufacturer or registrant of the fertilizer must be included.
5. When the term "organic" is used on the label, the specific organic nutrient must be identified and qualified as synthetic and/or natural, with the respective percentage of each specified, as in the following examples:
a. Nitrogen—50% organic (30% synthetic, 20% natural)
b. 50% of Nitrogen is organic (30% synthetic, 20% natural)
6. The "guaranteed analysis" section of the label gives the percentage of total nitrogen (the sum of all forms of nitrogen present in the mixture), the available phosphate, the soluble potassium, and a statement of each secondary plant nutrient present in the mixture. The chlorine content is guaranteed as the maximum percentage present, when applicable, in agricultural fertilizer. Specialty fertilizer—49 pounds and less, designed for home and garden use—is exempt from the chlorine requirement.
7. A "derived from" section is a listing of the actual source materials that constitute the primary and secondary plant nutrients guaranteed to be contained.

Total Nitrogen

Nitrogen may be included in the form of: (1) nitrate nitrogen, (2) ammoniacal nitrogen, (3) water-soluble organic nitrogen and/or urea nitrogen, and (4) water-insoluble nitrogen. A statement of the percentage of each form present in the fertilizer must be given. Nitrate nitrogen includes all of the nitrate (NO_3^-) forms in the fertilizer mixture. Ammoniacal nitrogen includes all the ammonium forms of nitrogen in the fertilizer. The statement of "and/or urea nitrogen" is optional for the manufacturer. The guarantee may be shown as the water-soluble organic nitrogen only. If only urea nitrogen is present, the guarantee may be shown as urea nitrogen or water-soluble organic nitrogen. If both urea and other forms of water-soluble organic nitrogen are present, the guarantee may be shown as all water-soluble organic nitrogen or as urea nitrogen and water-soluble organic nitrogen.

Water-insoluble nitrogen originally meant such natural organic materials as dried blood and tankage. Recently, however, many forms of water-insoluble nitrogen have been developed, so now any water-insoluble source is included in this figure. Insoluble sources may be materials such as urea-formaldehyde, isobutylidene diurea, magnesium ammonium phosphate, or other similar materials. A product made by coating urea with sulfur is also sparingly soluble for a period of time in the soil, but the method of analysis used in the fertilizer laboratory currently prohibits the characterization of the material as a water-insoluble nitrogen source. The natural organic sources become available by microbial action that converts the nitrogen first to ammonium and then to the nitrate form. Some water-insoluble nitrogen forms are rendered insoluble by coating with sulfur or plastic-based materials, by chemical combination with other elements, or by inhibiting the activity of microorganisms that release the nitrogen from insoluble forms. Many of these sources are treated in such a way as to provide for a long, continued release of nitrogen. Listing of source materials in which availability of nitrogen is controlled through slow hydrolysis of water-soluble organic compounds constitutes a claim of slow or controlled release of a nutrient, and a guarantee for such nutrient sources is required.

Available Phosphoric Acid

This is the water-soluble plus the citrate-soluble phosphorus (soluble in weak acids). The soil solution is a weak acid in which the citrate-soluble materials are readily made available for plant use. The guaranteed available phosphoric acid is the oxide equivalent of the actual phosphorus in the mixture. Elemental phosphorus makes up 44% of the amount of available phosphoric acid guaranteed in the mixture. The actual form of phosphorus is the mono-basic phosphate ion $(H_2PO_4^-)$, which is water soluble, or the dibasic phosphate ion (HPO_4^{2-}), which is citrate soluble.

Soluble Potash

This is the oxide equivalent of the potassium present in the mixture. Elemental potassium makes up 83% of the guaranteed soluble potash in the mixture. The actual form of potassium in the fertilizer is the potassium ion, K^+. Soluble potash is that portion of the potash contained in fertilizer or fertilizer materials that is soluble in aqueous ammonium oxalate, aqueous ammonium citrate, or water, according to the applicable AOAC International Method. All of the potassium guaranteed on a fertilizer label is soluble K, which implies that it goes into solution readily when applied to the soil and is immediately available for plant uptake.

Total Available Primary Plant Nutrient

This is the sum of the total nitrogen, available phosphoric acid, and soluble potash. The fertilizer law defines these as the primary plant nutrients. The three figures, e.g., 10-30-10, are known as the guaranteed analysis of the material. The sum of these, the total available primary plant nutrient, makes up the grade of the mixture. A statement of "Total Available Primary Plant Nutrient" is no longer required on the label and does not appear in the sample label shown here. However, the law states that a mixture of less than 16% total available primary plant nutrient cannot be sold unless a special permit is received from the agriculture commissioner and the label states "Low Analysis Fertilizer" in as conspicuous a manner as the brand name. The guaranteed analysis must be in whole numbers except for specialty fertilizers.

Specialty fertilizers are fertilizers packaged, marketed, and distributed for home and garden use and packaged in containers or bags with net weight of 49 pounds or less. Specialty fertilizers require registration, label approval, and registration fee(s).

Chlorine, Not More Than

The quantity of chlorine must be stated as "not more than" because this element may be toxic to many plants and/or reduce quality and yields. Tobacco is especially sensitive to chlorine, as it reduces the burning quality of the leaf. In addition, some vegetable crops and greenhouse flowers show toxicity symptoms and reduced quality and yields from excessive chlorine. It is required that the statement "Chlorine, Not More Than" be placed on the label so that the purchaser is aware of the content of this material in the mix.

Derived From

This is a statement of the actual source materials for the primary or secondary plant nutrients guaranteed.

Secondary Plant Nutrients

The Guaranteed Analysis specifies secondary plant nutrients in elemental form. Magnesium, iron, zinc, copper, and manganese must be expressed as total and/or water-soluble/soluble depending upon the source materials formulated in the product. Chelated elements are guaranteed separately when a chelating agent is denoted in the derivation statement below the guaranteed analysis. Sulfur must be guaranteed as sulfur (combined) and/or sulfur (free) in the elemental form, depending upon the source material in the formulation.

A derived from statement is also required to give the sources of secondary elements contained in the mixture, such as magnesium sulfate and manganese sulfate. When a chelated form of a plant nutrient is claimed in addition to another form of the same element, the chelated portion is guaranteed separately.

Some fertilizer mixtures contain pesticides. These mixtures must have a yellow label with lettering in a contrasting color to be conspicuous. Only the pesticides allowed (by law) may be included in the mixtures and in amounts not to exceed the maximum allowed. The label must include the crops for which the pesticide(s) are recommended and directions for use. It must also include the required precautionary statements, the percent active ingredient by weight, and the actual number of pounds per ton in the mixture.

Labels are required for all materials used as fertilizers in the state when sold as separate materials. The guarantees are similar to those on the fertilizer label for mixed fertilizers.

All manipulated manures, composts, soil conditioners, soil amendments, and soil additives are defined as fertilizers by law and as such must be labeled according to the law. The label includes the brand name, the common name of the product, and the grade numerals in terms of primary plant nutrients (table 3.5).

Soil Additives, Soil Amendments, and Soil Conditioners

Proof of beneficial claims may be required before registering any potting soil, mulch, compost, soil additive, soil conditioner, and soil amendment. If no claims are made, scientific evidence of the usefulness and agronomic value of the soil amendment may be required. To label the product, the following is required:

Soil Amending Ingredients

1. Name of ingredient _____% (identify and list all soil amending ingredients)

   Total of other ingredients _____%

2. Purpose of product

3. Directions for application

4. Net volume, in lieu of net weight, may be used for labeling mulch products or materials sold for use as aboveground dressings

Slow- and Controlled-Release Nutrients

When one or more slow- or controlled-release nutrients are claimed or advertised, the guarantees for such nutrients is shown as a footnote following the listing of source materials and expressed as percent of the actual nutrient.

Listing of source materials providing slow- or controlled-release characteris-

Table 3.5. The Florida fertilizer label

Florida License Number

Brand Name

Name and Address of Registrant
Net Weight
Nitrogen—50% Organic (30% synthetic, 20% natural)

Guaranteed Analysis

Total Nitrogen	%
Nitrate Nitrogen	%
Ammoniacal Nitrogen	%
Water Soluble Organic Nitrogen	%
And/or Urea Nitrogen	%
Water Insoluble Nitrogen	%
Available Phosphoric Acid	%
Soluble Potash	%
Chlorine, Not More Than	%

Derived from: (Actual source materials for primary plant nutrients; e.g., urea, concentrated superphosphate, potassium chloride, Milorganite, etc.)

Statement of Secondary Plant Nutrients

Total Magnesium as Mg	%
Water Soluble Magnesium as Mg	%
Total Manganese as Mn	%
Soluble Manganese as Mn	%
Total Copper as Cu	%
Soluble Copper as Cu	%
Sulfur (combined) as S	%
Sulfur (free) as S	%

Derived from: (Actual materials and in forms used in the fertilizer mixture; e.g., manganese oxide or manganese sulfate, etc.)

tics by controlling the water solubility of a naturally soluble material (as coating or occlusion) or through slow hydrolysis of water-soluble organic nitrogen compounds constitutes a claim of controlled-release nutrient, and a guarantee for such nutrient is required.

No guarantee, claim, or advertisement is made or required when a slow- or controlled-release nutrient is less than 15% of the total guarantee of that nutrient.

For further information contact:
Florida Department of Agriculture & Consumer Services
Bureau of Compliance Monitoring
3125 Conner Boulevard, Building ME-1
Tallahassee, Florida 32399-1650
Ph (850) 487-2085, Fax (850) 488-8498
For a copy of the Florida Commercial Fertilizer Law, Chapter 576 Florida Statutes and Chapter 5E-1 Florida Administrative Code, send an e-mail to Coxb@doacs.state.fl.us.

Spreader Calibration

Fertilizer application is effective only if you ensure uniform coverage. Dry fertilizers can be applied with either a drop (gravity) spreader or a rotary (centrifugal) spreader.

A drop spreader (pl. D) has the advantage of applying a fairly exact pattern because the area of application is limited to the distance between the wheels. This exact delineation allows a "tight" pattern (line) to be cut but requires that each pass meet precisely with the previous one, or skips will be noticeable. Drop spreaders wider than 6 feet can be cumbersome in the landscape by limiting access around trees, shrubs, and gates. The grinding action of the agitator in the bottom of a drop spreader may break the coating of some slow-release fertilizers, such as sulfur-coated urea. Friction generated by the agitator may cause a reduction in the desirable physical properties of some fertilizer mixtures, causing spreading and application problems.

The cyclone spreader (also known as rotary or centrifugal, pl. E) has a wider and less uniform distribution pattern than a drop spreader, and thus can cover a larger area. The uniformity of the application pattern of the cyclone spreader gradually diminishes as the distance from the spreader increases, reducing the probability of an application skip (pl. G). The uneven, wide pattern of the cyclone spreader is initially more difficult to calibrate, and heavier fertilizer particles tend to sling farther away from the machine. However, proper calibration and experience can minimize these influences.

A recent improvement in fertilizer spreader technology is the use of air to apply the material to the turf. This produces a fairly wide pattern (like the cyclone spreader) that is somewhat exact (like the drop spreader) without damaging the granules or slinging heavier particles farther. Wind and rain effects also are reduced with this technology, but initial equipment expense and requirement for application expertise are higher.

Spreader calibration involves measurement of the fertilizer output as the spreader is operated over a known area. One way to ensure uniform application of a material is to divide the material into equal portions. Use a spreader calibration that will deliver one-half of the desired amount of material. Make an application over the entire area, turn the spreader direction 90° from the initial application, and make a second application. This eliminates skips in coverage. Accordingly, calibration of the spreader should be based on one-half desired application rates. A flat surface, a method of collecting the material, and a scale for weighing the material is needed for calibration. The following sequence of steps will aid in calibrating a fertilizer spreader:

Calibrating a Drop-Type (Gravity) Spreader

1. Check the spreader to make certain all the parts are functioning properly.
2. Mark off a distance which when multiplied by the width of the spreader

will give 100 square feet of area. For example, the distance required for a 1.5-, 2-, and 3-foot spreader is about 67, 50, and 33 feet, respectively.

3. Fill the spreader with the material you wish to apply (fertilizer, seed, herbicide, lime, other).

4. Make several trial runs over the distance and practice opening the spreader as you cross the starting line and closing it as you cross the finish line. Opening the spreader before it is in motion will result in nonuniform distribution. Walk at the pace that will be used when applying the actual material. Open and close the spreader gradually, not with a fast, jerky motion.

5. The weight of the material applied by the spreader must be determined. It can be swept up from a hard surface or caught on a large piece of paper or plastic. The easiest method is to attach a catch pan (cardboard works nicely) under the spreader openings and catch the material in the catch pan during the test run to determine how much was applied.

6. Begin calibration at the lowest setting and proceed to progressively higher settings (larger openings). The more trials at a given setting, the better the average rate of application. Usually three trials at a given setting are sufficient to obtain a reliable application rate. Weigh the material and record the information on each trial run for future use.

7. One of the calibrated settings will approximate the correct rate of material. *Example:* You wish to calibrate a spreader to apply 1 pound of nitrogen per 1000 square feet using a 10-10-10 fertilizer. This calculates to 10 pounds of fertilizer per 1000 square feet since the material is 10 percent nitrogen (10% × 10 pounds = 1 pound nitrogen). Since the area for calibration trials is only 100 square feet, apply one-tenth of 10 pounds, or 1 pound of fertilizer, per 100 square feet. Complete calibration is suggested for the complete spreader range. Settings are not necessarily linear; i.e., half of a particular application range will not necessarily be obtained by using a setting number that is half of the original. Thus, it is necessary to calibrate the spreader over the entire range of application settings.

8. The same calibration procedure is used for any material you want to apply. Since the quantity applied depends on the physical properties of the material, the same settings cannot be used for different materials, even if the ratios are the same. Once the spreader is calibrated and set for the proper rate, an area of any size can be treated accurately.

Calibrating a Rotary (Centrifugal) Spreader

It is important that the "effective" width of application be determined first. To calibrate your rotary (centrifugal) spreader, follow these steps in the order given:

1. Check the spreader to make certain all parts are operating properly.
2. Fill the spreader about half-full with the material you plan to apply and

run it with the spreader setting about half-open (medium setting). Make the application on bare ground or on a hard surface where the width of the surface covered by the material can be measured.

3. Rotary spreaders do not apply a constant amount of material across the entire width of application. More material is applied toward the center and less at the edges. For this reason, the width of application is accurate for a constant application rate only at about two-thirds (60–70%) of the actual width measured. *Example:* If the application width is 12 feet, only about 8 feet, or 4 feet from the center on both sides of the spreader (within the band of application), is receiving approximately the same application rate. The other 2 feet on each edge receive much less material than the center area. Once this "effective" width is determined, calibration is fairly simple.

4. Mark off a distance which when multiplied by the effective width will give you a 1000-square-foot area. For this example, assume that the "effective" width is 10 feet. The test strip will then be 100 feet long, since the width times length is 10×100, or 1000 square feet. *Note:* This calculation is based on "effective" width of application and not the total width.

5. Determine the amount of material to be applied. *Example:* to apply 1 pound of nitrogen per 1000 square feet using a 16-4-8 fertilizer, 6¼ pounds of material should be applied per 1000 square feet.

6. Fill the hopper with a known weight of fertilizer and adjust the spreader to the lowest setting that will allow the material to flow. Push the spreader down the center of the test area, opening the hopper at the starting line and closing it at the finish. Weigh the material left in the spreader and subtract that amount from the starting weight to determine the amount used per 1000 square feet. The beginning weight minus the ending weight tells how much material was applied per 1000 square feet.

7. Repeat step 6 at successively greater settings (openings) and record the amount of material applied at each setting.

8. Select the spreader setting that most closely applies the desired rate of material, set the spreader accordingly, and use it on an area of any size. To obtain uniform spread of material, remember to set the spreader at half the desired rate of application and make two passes perpendicular to each other. Strive for proper spread overlap during application. *Example:* if the "effective" width is 10 feet after each pass, move the spreader 10 feet over from the center of the tire tracks. This will give a fairly constant rate of application over the entire area. Also, it should be remembered that each time you change the grade (or analysis) of the materials being applied, it is necessary to calibrate the spreader to the material being applied.

Soil Testing

Most people agree that a healthy, well-maintained turfgrass is a thing of beauty. However, many of these same people believe that beautiful turfgrass is a lot of trouble and hard work, possibly demanding an expertise that they do not possess. This is not necessarily true; however, a few basic facts concerning the nutritional requirements of turfgrasses and the properties of fertilizer and liming materials are essential. Water and pest infestation influence turfgrass growth, but more lawns suffer from nutritional deficiencies than from the former problems.

Florida soils are predominantly sandy and have a low capacity for nutrient retention. Thus, fertilizer nutrients must be supplied on a regular and continuing basis to satisfy the nutritional needs of the turfgrass. Except for the calcareous soils of south Florida, our soils are predominantly acidic. A liming material must be applied in many cases to neutralize a portion of this acidity to obtain optimum growth and color of turfgrasses. Nutritional requirements of turfgrasses and suggested soil test levels for the various nutrients are presented in the following sections.

Soil Test Philosophy

Soil testing is not an exact science, but it can be used as one of the tools in the maintenance of a healthy turfgrass. Soil testing should be used in conjunction with tissue testing to arrive at an optimum fertility maintenance program for your turfgrass. Many things influence the level of nutrients extracted from the soil sample, the quantity taken up by the plant, and the observed response. The soil test and resulting recommendations represent the turfgrass production area only as well as the sample itself; therefore, it is imperative that the soil sample be taken and handled properly. The quantity of a target nutrient extracted depends on several mostly uncontrollable soil factors, but the recommendations are based on plant growth responses that have been correlated with the levels of nutrients extracted. The levels of extracted P, K, and Mg are divided into five categories: very low, low, medium, high, and very high. Recommendations are based on the statistical probability of response to an application at the various levels of nutrient extracted, as follows: a very low level of nutrient implies that there is a 75 percent or less probability that a response will be observed if that nutrient is applied; a low level implies 50 percent or less probability; a medium level implies a 25 percent or less probability; and a high level implies that a response is not anticipated. Thus a response to the application of a recommended nutrient is not guaranteed. The anticipated response is based on a probability calculated on a large number of soils and conditions that may or may not be representative of your soil situation. This discussion is not meant to diminish your faith in using soil testing as a management tool for the health of your turfgrass and environmental stewardship, but to strengthen your understanding of soil testing and subsequent recommendations.

Soil Analysis Interpretation

One of the first steps in producing and maintaining beautiful turfgrass is to obtain an analysis of a representative soil sample from the turfgrass production area. The sample should be obtained by taking fifteen to twenty small plugs at random over the entire area, avoiding any unusual areas or areas with an identifying appearance. Ideally, one should sample any areas with special characteristics separately. Most turfgrass roots are located in the top 4 inches of soil; therefore, limit sampling depth to 4 inches.

Place the fifteen to twenty plugs in a plastic container, mix them thoroughly, and send approximately 1 pint of the mixed sample to the UF/IFAS Extension Soil Testing Laboratory (ESTL) for chemical analysis. The county Extension Service can also supply additional information on proper techniques for sampling and submitting a soil sample. The office address and phone number are listed in the appendix, or you may contact the ESTL on the internet at http://www.soilslab.ifas.ufl.edu or by e-mail at soilslab@mail.ifas.ufl.edu.

A soil analysis supplies a wealth of information concerning the nutritional status of a soil and can detect potential problems that could limit turfgrass growth. A routine soil analysis supplies information relative to soil acidity and the Mehlich I extractable phosphorus, potassium, calcium, and magnesium status of the soil (table 3.6). A lime requirement determination is included in the routine analysis if the soil pH is less than 6.0. Nitrogen is not determined because in most soils it is highly mobile, meaning that soil N status varies greatly with rainfall and irrigation events. Nitrogen recommendations are based on the nutritional requirements of the turfgrass being grown and the quality of turfgrass desired.

You will note from table 3.6 that there is no interpretation made for soil test Ca or Fe. No interpretation is made for Mehlich I extractable Ca levels because the extractant dissolves calcium compounds in the soil that are not readily plant-available; thus, an erroneous interpretation of the plant-available Ca could be made. In most cases, Ca levels are adequate for turfgrass growth because most Florida soils are inherently high in Ca, have a history of Ca fertilization, or receive Ca regularly through irrigation with high-Ca water. The soil test level for Mehlich I extractable Ca is used only to determine the type of limestone needed when lime is recommended. For most soils and crops, liming to insure an adequate soil pH for proper growth will insure a Ca level that is more than adequate. When the Mehlich I extractable Ca level is greater than 250 ppm, research has shown no crop response to added Ca, whether from liming or gypsum.

The ESTL does not analyze for extractable Fe because definitive interpretation data are lacking. Significant correlation of soil test Fe levels and plant tissue levels is lacking, and testing procedures tend to produce highly variable results. Most soils, except those having a pH greater than 7.0, generally contain adequate levels of Fe for optimum growth. Turfgrasses grown on soils with pH 6.5 or greater exhibit a greening response to Fe applied via foliar spray. Unfortunately, reapplication may be required to sustain the desired color.

Table 3.6. Suggested ranges for Mehlich I extractable soil nutrient levels for Florida turfgrasses

Macronutrients, ppm[a]			Micronutrients, ppm[b]		
P	K	Mg	Mn	Zn	Cu
16–30	36–60	20–30	3–9	0.5–3	0.1–0.5

a. The medium range of Mehlich I extractable nutrients in which a response to applied fertilization would be expected 25% of the time or less.
b. Soils testing below these levels of micronutrients are expected to respond to applied micronutrients. Interpretation of soil test micronutrient levels is based on soil pH. The smaller number is for soils with a pH of less than 6.0 and the larger number is for soils with a pH of 7.0 or greater. Mehlich I extractable micronutrient levels are determined only when requested and require an additional charge.

Table 3.7. Desirable pH ranges for turfgrasses

pH <5.5	pH 5.5–6.4	pH 6.5–7.4	pH >7.4
Bermudagrass	Bermudagrass	Bermudagrass	Bermudagrass
Carpetgrass	Carpetgrass	Fescuegrass	St. Augustinegrass
Centipedegrass	Centipedegrass	Italian Ryegrass	Zoysiagrass
Bahiagrass	Bahiagrass	St. Augustinegrass	
	Italian Ryegrass		

Liming recommendations are based on the Adams-Evans lime requirement test. This test is included in the routine soil analysis, but the test is run only if the soil pH is 6.0 or less. The quantity of lime recommended is based on the type of turfgrass being grown and the target pH desired.

Soil Acidity

Turfgrasses differ in their adaptability to soil acidity. For example, centipedegrass and bahiagrass grow better in an acid environment (pH 5.0–6.0) than St. Augustinegrass or zoysiagrass, which grow best in near-neutral or alkaline soils (pH 6.5–7.5) (table 3.7).

Adjusting the Soil Reaction (pH)

Soil reaction, or pH, is important because it influences several soil factors that affect plant growth. Soil bacteria that transform and release N from organic matter function best in the pH range 5.5–7.0; certain fertilizer materials also supply nutrients more efficiently in this range. Plant nutrients, particularly P, K, Ca, Mg, B, Cu, Fe, Mn, and Zn, are generally more available to plants in the pH range 5.5–6.5. Plant nutrients leach more rapidly at pH values less than 5.0 than in soils with reactions between 5.0 and 7.5. In certain soils, when the pH drops below 5.0, aluminum may become toxic to plant growth.

Normally, liming materials are used to increase soil pH and supply the essential nutrients Ca and Mg. The two most commonly available liming materials

Table 3.8. Chemical composition and calcium carbonate equivalents of liming materials

Material	Chemical Composition	C.C.E[a]
Burned Lime	CaO	56
Hydrated Lime	$Ca(OH)_2$	74
Dolomitic Limestone	$CaCO_3 \cdot MgCO_3$	92
Calcic Limestone	$CaCO_3$	100
Basic Slag	$CaSiO_3$	135

a. The number of pounds of the material required to give the same neutralizing value as pure calcium carbonate.

are calcitic and dolomitic limes (table 3.8). In instances where the soil tests low in Mg (less than 20 ppm Mehlich I extractable Mg), dolomitic lime should be used. Generally, about six months' reaction time is required for calcitic and dolomitic lime to have their maximum effect on soil acidity. If more immediate results are desired, hydrated lime can be used. However, hydrated lime is not recommended for use by the nonprofessional because this material can severely damage the turfgrass if improperly used. Lime recommendations are typically made on a calcitic limestone basis. If another liming material is used, adjust the application rate according to the calcium carbonate equivalents given in table 3.8. Basic slag is a slow-reacting product that also contains large amounts of phosphorus; however, cost and availability limit its use.

The amount of lime necessary to properly adjust the soil pH depends on the soil type. The greater the amount of organic matter or clay content of the soil and the lower the pH, the more lime required to increase the soil pH to a desired level. Soil lime requirement cannot be determined by soil pH alone. If the soil pH is less than 6.0, a lime requirement test will be run on the soil sample to determine how much lime is required to increase the soil pH to 6.5. The lime requirement test is included in the routine standard analysis of a soil sample.

Soil Alkalinity

If a soil is too alkaline, with a pH greater than 7.5, one must determine whether the excess alkalinity is due to an inherent soil characteristic or previous excessive application of liming materials. Soils having a pH of greater than 8.3 are not alkaline as a result of the presence of calcium carbonate materials, because calcium carbonate has an equilibrium pH of 8.3 in water. Thus, excessively high soil pH is mostly likely due to the presence of elevated levels of sodium. It is difficult and uneconomical to appreciably change the pH of naturally occurring alkaline soils (such as those found in coastal areas, or fill soil containing marl, shell, or limestone) by using sulfur, ammonium sulfate, or similar acid-forming materials; however, if a high pH is due to applied lime or other alkaline additives, then these acid-forming materials can effectively reduce soil pH when applied at the proper rate and frequency.

Granular, super-fine dust, or wettable sulfur can be used to decrease soil pH. Granular sulfur is preferred for turfgrass production systems because of its ease of application (with cyclone fertilizer spreaders) and the reduced possibility of foliar burn from the granules. Thoroughly water-in sulfur after application, taking care to wash off all aboveground turf parts. It takes approximately one-third the amount of sulfur to decrease the soil pH by 1 unit as it takes calcic lime to increase the soil pH by 1 unit. Do not apply more than 10 pounds of sulfur per 1000 square feet per application. Repeat applications of sulfur should not be made more often than once every three months. Remember that sulfur oxidizes in the soil and reacts with water to form sulfuric acid, which can severely damage plant roots, so it must be used cautiously.

General Fertilizer Recommendations

A soil analysis furnishes information about the P, K, Ca, and Mg status of the soil. Adjustments should be made in the fertilization and liming program to take advantage of the information derived from the soil test. A routine soil analysis does not include nitrogen, sulfur, or micronutrient analysis.

Nitrogen

Nitrogen is used in larger quantities than any of the other applied nutrients and needs to be applied on a regular basis. The actual quantity of N required depends on a number of factors: the type of turfgrass being grown, the turfgrass quality desired, the type of soil, and the quantity of water the turfgrass receives. Rates and frequency of N application should be closely monitored because excess N can pollute ground waters. Therefore, N should be applied only when needed, at the proper rate (never exceeding ½ pound soluble N per 1000 square feet per application), and when the turfgrass is actively growing. Turfgrasses take up N efficiently, but fertilizer N applied at rates that exceed the plant's ability for nutrient uptake or when the turfgrass is dormant may be lost through leaching.

Some turfgrass species, such as centipedegrass and bahiagrass, require relatively little N for optimum growth. In fact, high levels of N fertilization on centipedegrass can ultimately cause declines in turfgrass growth and quality. Bahiagrass can also survive under conditions of very low N application and without the benefit of irrigation, particularly in grazed pastures.

On the other hand, turfgrasses such as bermudagrass, St. Augustinegrass, and zoysiagrass require moderate to high levels of N fertilization for good performance. These turfgrasses will not survive on most sandy Florida soils for extended periods in the absence of N application. The level of turfgrass quality desired and the maintenance level one hopes to sustain determine the quantity and frequency of N application. As a general rule, N should be applied at least two times per year, and as many as six to eight applications per year can be necessary to sustain these turfgrasses, depending on your location within the state and the level of quality desired. Soluble N applications are not recommended on St. Augustinegrass during the hot summer months of May, June, July, and August because of excess growth production and the susceptibility of N-succulent St. Augustinegrass to chinch bugs and gray leaf spot during this period. For detailed N fertilizer guidelines for turfgrasses, see "Fertilizer Recommendations for Your Florida Lawn" at the beginning of this chapter.

Phosphorus

Phosphorus is used by turfgrasses in much smaller quantities than N; thus, less P should be applied to turf. As a result of their marine origin, Florida soils often test high in soil-extractable P. Additionally, many of our soils have received abundant fertilizer P in the past and have high soil-test levels of P. This means that turfgrass often does not require P for adequate growth and survival in Florida. A soil test is always recommended to determine the status of phosphorus for turfgrass.

Most mixed fertilizers contain a source of P because P materials are good conditioners and are added to blended fertilizers to enhance handling properties. If your soil test calls for no P, you may apply a fertilizer with 0–2 percent P, depending upon availability of the product.

As a general rule, P does not induce growth and color responses in turfgrass as N does. In fact, research has shown that, in most cases, established turfgrasses show little response to P application. Newly planted turfgrass areas are much more likely to respond to P application through enhanced rooting characteristics. A color response is almost never observed, except in extreme deficiency situations where the soil is composed of uncoated sands that retain very little P. If your soil is an uncoated sand (pure white sand with no iron staining), P should be applied with caution because it tends to leach through these soils freely and can contaminate surface water bodies.

Potassium

Potassium is used by turfgrasses in quantities second only to N. However, as with P, most turfgrasses do not exhibit growth or visible responses after K application. Only when soil test levels are very low is there a noticeable response to K application. Levels of K application are often tied to the rate of N application, since maintaining a high-quality turfgrass through high N fertilization requires more K for optimum growth and root production. The primary effects of K on growth of turfgrass include enhanced rooting and tolerance to water stress, heat stress, and cold stress.

Most Florida sandy soils contain low to very low levels of Mehlich I extractable K, so most turfgrass soils require K fertilization sometime during the year. The level and frequency of K application depends on the specific turfgrass being grown, the location in the state, and the soil-test level of K, as well as the level of N being applied. In general, K should be applied to home lawns at rates equal to or one-half the amount of N applied. For additional insights into the K fertilization requirements of turfgrasses, refer to "Fertilizer Recommendations for Your Florida Lawn" at the beginning of this chapter.

Micronutrients

Essential nutrients required in very small quantities for turfgrass growth are referred to as micronutrients, and include iron (Fe), manganese (Mn), zinc (Zn), copper (Cu), boron (B), chlorine (Cl), and molybdenum (Mo). Most low-maintenance turfgrasses do not require the addition of micronutrients, but if a micronutrient deficiency is suspected, the Extension Soil Testing Laboratory offers a soil test for Mn, Cu, and Zn. Interpretation of Mehlich I extractable Mn, Cu, and Zn depends on the soil pH. The critical soil levels for these nutrients increase with soil pH for turfgrasses grown on acid, sandy soils in Florida. The Mehlich I extractant is not recommended for alkaline soils; micronutrient availability in the alkaline pH range is better evaluated with a plant tissue test or with a soil test extractant developed especially for alkaline soils.

Manganese

In most cases, a turfgrass response to applied Mn, visible as greening, is likely if the soil pH is greater than 6.5. Soil tests and tissue analyses for Mn are more reliable in predicting a response than they are for Zn and Cu. Thus, if your soil pH is high and your turfgrass is not responding to macronutrient fertilization, a micronutrient soil test may be warranted. If the soil tests low or tissue analysis indicates an Mn deficiency, application of 30 pounds Mn per acre as manganese sulfate or manganous oxide is recommended. Turfgrasses growing on acidic soils (pH 6.0 or less) do not generally respond to Mn application.

Zinc

A turfgrass response to applied Zn has not been observed in Florida. Most responses to Zn application have occurred in tree crops, such as citrus and pecans. Bermudagrass did not respond positively to Zn application on soils testing low in Zn, nor did it respond negatively in soils testing high in Zn. This suggests that the apparent critical level for Zn is very low and that the toxicity level is very high. There appears to be very little reason to analyze for or to apply Zn to turfgrasses grown in Florida soils.

Copper

In Florida, Cu deficiencies are generally confined to soils high in organic matter and to "new ground" just coming into cultivation in the flatwoods areas. There is no documented research in Florida demonstrating a response to Cu applications on acid mineral soils. Turfgrasses produced for sod on organic soils often require an initial application of Cu, but a single application of Cu can suffice for several years. The application should not be repeated until soil or tissue tests indicate a need for Cu. Copper added to a soil is fixed and remains in the soil for a long time, so it should not be added until a need is clearly identified. If Cu is required, application of 5 pounds of elemental Cu per acre as either copper sulfate or finely ground copper oxide should meet turfgrass needs for Cu for several years.

Iron

Strong relationships among extractable soil Fe, tissue levels of Fe, and predictable responses to applied Fe do not exist, so the UF/IFAS Extension Soil Testing Laboratory does not analyze for extractable Fe. However, there are certain soil conditions warranting consideration of Fe application. In most Florida soils with a pH of 7.0 or greater, turfgrass greens in response to Fe application. Centipedegrass and bahiagrass are particularly sensitive to Fe deficiencies and typically respond to Fe application when grown on soils with an alkaline pH. St. Augustinegrass and bermudagrass growing on high-pH soils will also respond to Fe application by greening. Iron is often applied instead of N during the hot summer months to green the grass. This will provide deep green color without the shoot growth that typically results from N application. Turfgrass Fe needs can be met through various means. If the Fe deficiency occurs on acid soils, use 1 pound of iron sulfate per 1000 square feet. If the deficiency occurs on neutral or alkaline soils, use the container label recommended rate of iron chelate. If you wish to apply the Fe to leaves, spray on 2 ounces of iron sulfate in 3–5 gallons per 1000 square feet. Responses to foliar applications are usually temporary, and frequent reapplication may be required.

4

Cultural Practices for Your Florida Lawn

Mowing Your Florida Lawn

Mowing is one of the most important aspects of maintaining a good quality lawn. Mowing increases turfgrass density, producing a tighter lawn that is resistant to weeds. Proper mowing practices, along with fertilization and irrigation, can largely determine the success or failure of a lawn.

The two main components of mowing are cutting height and frequency. Both of these factors depend on the turfgrass species, cultivar, and the level of lawn quality desired. Several other practices involving the use of mowers are also important in creating a quality lawn.

Height of Mowing

The optimum cutting height is determined by the growth habit and leaf width of the turfgrass species. A grass that spreads horizontally can usually be mowed shorter than an upright-growing, bunch-type grass. Grasses with narrow blades can generally be mowed closer than grasses with wide blades. Bermudagrass is mowed at very low heights because of its numerous narrow leaf blades and low growth habit. On the other hand, bahiagrass needs to be mowed at higher heights because of its open, upright growth habit.

Turfgrass undergoes physiological stress with each mowing, particularly if too much leaf tissue is removed. Effects of "scalping," or removal of too much shoot tissue at one time, can produce long-term damage to the turf. This can leave turf susceptible to other stresses such as insects, disease, drought, and sunscald. Mowing also greatly influences rooting depth, with development of a deeper root system in response to higher mowing heights. Advantages of the deeper root system are greater tolerances to drought, insects, disease, nematodes, temperature stress, poor soil conditions, nutrient deficiencies, and traffic. Mowing below the recommended heights for each species is a primary cause of turf death and should be avoided (pl. H).

Table 4.1. Suggested mowing heights and mower types for Florida home lawns

Turfgrass Species	Optimal Mowing Height (inches)	Mowing Frequency (days)	Preferred Mower Type
Bahiagrass	3.0–4.0	7–17	Rotary/flail
Bermudagrass	0.5–1.5	3–5	Reel
Carpetgrass	1.5–2.0	10–14	Rotary
Centipedegrass	1.5–2.0	10–14	Rotary
Seashore Paspalum	1.0–2.0	5–10	Reel
St. Augustinegrass	2.5–4.0[a]	5–14	Rotary
Zoysiagrass	1.0–3.0	10–14	Reel/rotary

*Dwarf varieties of St. Augustinegrass ('Seville,' 'Jade,' 'Palmetto,' 'Delmar') are the only cultivars of this species that should be mowed at less than 3 inches (plate 23).

Frequency of Mowing

The growth rate of the lawn determines how frequently it needs to be mowed. The growth rate is influenced by grass species, weather conditions, time of year, and level of management. Slowest growth rates occur in the winter or under low fertility and irrigation, while fastest growth rates occur in the summer or under high fertility and watering practices. Bermudagrass is a rapidly growing grass compared to zoysiagrass. Low-maintenance grasses like bahiagrass and centipedegrass are frequently mowed just to remove seedheads, rather than to cut leaf blades. Mow often enough so that no more than one-quarter of the blade height is removed per mowing. For example, if your St. Augustinegrass lawn is mowed at a height of 3 inches, it should be mowed when it grows to a height of 4–4½ inches. Stress to the grass caused by mowing can be minimized by removing only one-third of the leaf blade at each mowing. It is important to always leave as much leaf surface as possible so that photosynthesis can occur.

Clipping Removal

On most lawns, grass clippings should be returned to help recycle nutrients to the soil. If the lawn is mowed frequently enough, clippings cause few problems. Although many people believe that clippings contribute to thatch, research has shown that clippings are readily decomposed by microbial action. Thatch is the intermingled layer of already dead and decomposing organic matter on top of the soil and below the leaf blades. Excessive thatch can cause many problems for lawns, including poor water infiltration, increased insect and disease infestation, and poor turf quality. The tougher shoot components such as stems, rhizomes, and stolons are not easily degraded and do contribute to thatch. Problems like clumping may also arise when turf is mowed infrequently and excess clippings result. When this happens, clippings can be raked to distribute them more evenly.

Mowing Equipment

Lawn mowers are available in a wide variety of sizes and styles with many features. The two basic types are the rotary mower and the reel mower (pls. I, J). Variations of these include mulching, flail, and string mowers. Most mowers can be obtained as push or self-propelled models. Front, side, and rear-clipping discharge models are also available. The choice of mower often depends on personal preference. Points to consider when purchasing a mower are lawn size, turfgrass species, and level of lawn maintenance. Rotary mowers are the most popular for home lawn maintenance because of their low cost, easy maneuverability, and simple maintenance. A large motor is required to turn the blade horizontally. The grass blade is cut on impact with the mower blade. Rotary mowers can pose a safety problem if improperly used. Most rotary mowers cannot mow lower than 1 inch and are best used for higher mowing heights. The blade needs to be sharpened and balanced frequently for the best possible cut.

Mulching mowers (pl. K) are modifications of rotary mowers. These are designed to cut leaf blades into very small pieces that decompose more quickly than leaf blades cut by conventional mowers. The mower blades are designed to create a mild vacuum in the mower deck until the leaf blades are cut into small pieces. Mulching mowers do not have the traditional discharge chute of most rotary mowers. Advantages and disadvantages of mulching mowers are listed below.

Advantages of Mulching Mowers

1. Clippings are returned to the turf, where they will be decomposed very rapidly. This reduces yard waste and recycles nutrients to the turf.
2. Mulching prevents yard waste from contributing to landfill overuse and eliminates clipping collection and disposal costs.

Disadvantages of Mulching Mowers

1. They are ineffective on wet or tall turf.
2. Blades must be kept sharp.
3. Current models are small and require higher horsepower.

Reel mowers are for highly maintained turf where appearance is important. Reel mowers cut with a scissorlike action to produce a very clean, even cut. They are used at cutting heights of 2 inches or less. The number of blades needed to produce a smooth, uniform cut will depend on the mowing height. Sharpening reel mowers is difficult and is best left to a professional mower repair service.

Flail mowers have numerous, loose-hanging small knives that are held out by centrifugal force as the shaft rotates at high speeds. The blades sever grass by impact. Flail mowers are used for low-maintenance utility sites that are cut infrequently. Mowing quality is inferior compared to that of a reel or rotary mower, and the time it takes to sharpen the many small blades limits flail mower use.

String mowers are similar to rotary mowers, except the blade is replaced with a monofilament line. This is a definite safety feature when operating the mower in some hard-to-mow areas such as hillsides or ditch banks. A high-speed motor is needed in these mowers to spin the line fast enough for a clean cut.

Good Mowing Practices

Follow these procedures and precautions for safe, good mowing:

- Pick up all stones, sticks, and other debris before mowing to avoid damaging the mower or injuring someone with flying objects.
- Never mow wet turf with a rotary mower because clippings can clog the machine. Mow only when the turf is dry.
- Sharpen the mower blade frequently enough to prevent a ragged appearance of the turf (pls. L, M).
- Mow in a different direction every time the lawn is cut. This helps prevent wear patterns, reduces the grain (grass lying in the same direction), and reduces the possibility of scalping.
- Do not remove clippings. If clumping occurs, distribute by removing or lightly raking. A leaf blower can also be used to distribute clippings.
- Check your mower every time it is used. Follow manufacturer's recommendations for service and adjustments.
- Adjust cutting height by setting the mower on a driveway or sidewalk and using a ruler to measure the distance between the ground and the blade.
- Never fill a hot mower with gasoline.
- Always wear heavy leather shoes when mowing the lawn.
- Wash the mower after use to reduce rusting and weed seed movement.

Watering Your Florida Lawn

All plants require water for metabolic and physiological functioning. Although some plant species are large consumers of water, other species can be maintained with relatively low quantities of water. Many people consider turfgrasses to be large water consumers, but many turf species have excellent drought tolerance mechanisms. Bahiagrass, for example, can survive for long periods of time with virtually no water. In drought periods, bahiagrass will go into a dormant stage and shoot tissue will become chlorotic or necrotic. Upon resumption of adequate rainfall, however, bahiagrass resumes growth and becomes green again (pl. N).

What Water Does in Plants

- Water combines with light and carbon dioxide in the process of photosynthesis, which provides the plant with carbon needed for growth and storage.

- Water flows from the roots to the top of plants in a process called transpiration, which provides the plant with a cooling mechanism.
- Water in the soil solution helps move mineral nutrients to the plant roots for absorption.
- Imbibing water is the first step in seed germination.
- A well-irrigated grass plant is better able to withstand pressure from weeds and insects.
- A well-irrigated grass plant is better able to withstand environmental stresses such as wear, high temperatures, soil problems, or nutrient deficiencies.

Although water is important in maintaining a healthy lawn, the majority of homeowners overirrigate or irrigate incorrectly. Too much water is damaging to turfgrass and is often the underlying cause of lawn failure. Problems with overwatering include:

- A less developed and shorter root system, which has reduced capacity to seek out water and nutrients at lower soil depths and lower overall stress resistance
- An overly succulent shoot system, susceptible to disease and insect infestation
- Weaker cell walls in the shoot tissue, reducing the strength of leaf tissue
- Buildup of excessive thatch, particularly in St. Augustinegrass

When developing an irrigation plan, it is essential to consider the following:

- How frequently to water
- How much to water
- Time of day to water
- How to uniformly apply water
- How your turf irrigation affects your landscape plants
- Any microenvironmental conditions in the landscape that affect irrigation requirements

How Frequently to Water

Irrigation of many Florida lawns is controlled by a preset automatic sprinkler system. While automation is becoming increasingly necessary in many areas of our lives, automatic sprinkler systems and improper watering practices are undoubtedly the biggest factors leading to decline of home lawns. It is important to remember that, on average, we receive 60 or more inches of annual rainfall in most parts of Florida, and that the majority of this rainfall occurs between June and October. When rainfall is adequate to meet the plant's transpiration needs, supplemental irrigation systems should be turned off. How do you know what the grass's transpiration needs are? University of Florida guidelines call for watering lawns on an "as-needed" basis. This can be determined by observing the grass for signs of drought, indicating that transpiration needs are not being met, including:

- Leaf blades are folded in half lengthwise to conserve water.
- The grass has taken on a blue gray tint.
- Footprints or tire tracks remain visible on the grass long after being made (pl. O).

When these signs of drought are seen on a large portion of the lawn, it's time to irrigate. The length of time needed between irrigations will vary depending on grass species, soil characteristics, location in the state, time of year, temperature, and particular microenvironmental conditions such as shade. If rain is forecast for the next two days, delay irrigation.

How Much to Water

The amount of water to apply at any one time varies with the amount of water present in the soil, water-holding capacity of the soil, and soil drainage characteristics. An efficient watering wets only the turfgrass root zone, does not saturate the soil, and does not allow water to run off.

Florida soils are typically sandy and hold 1 inch of water in the top 12 inches of soil. If the roots are in the top 12 inches of soil and the soil is dry, then ½–¾ inch of water is required to wet the area thoroughly. Generally, turfgrasses require no more than about ⅓ inch of water per day. Under extreme summer conditions, almost ½ inch of water can be used per day. During winter, when grasses are not actively growing, water use may be only a tiny fraction of an inch of water per day. *Light, frequent watering is inefficient and encourages shallow root systems. Excessive irrigation, which keeps the root system saturated with water, is also harmful to the lawn.*

A simple watering schedule would apply ½–¾ inch of water when the turfgrass shows water deficit symptoms as discussed earlier. Once this water is applied, do not apply any more until water symptoms are again noticeable. With no rainfall, two to three waterings per week in the summer and once every ten to fourteen days in the winter are adequate. If rainfall occurs, irrigation should be suspended until visible drought symptoms appear.

When to Water

The best time for lawn irrigation is in the early morning hours. Watering during the day wastes water as a result of excessive evaporation and can scald the lawn when temperatures are high. Watering in late afternoon or late morning may be detrimental if it extends the time the lawn is naturally wet from dew. This extended "dew period" can accelerate disease occurrence.

How to Uniformly Apply Water

Irrigation system installers are licensed in some Florida counties, while in other counties there is no regulation of installation at all. This may lead to inefficient or sloppy installation, resulting in water waste and nonuniform coverage of turf areas. Even with a professionally installed system, it is important to check coverage on a regular basis, as heads may become clogged, damaged, or off-center, and leaks in the line may occur. An easy way to routinely check your irrigation system is to place small cans in a straight line from your sprinkler to the edge of the watering pattern, and look for uniformity of coverage. If an area is not receiving water from one or more heads, or if a head is not providing complete coverage, dry spots can develop. This can lead to any of the problems associated with drought-stressed turf. While checking uniformity with the coffee can method, you can also easily determine how long it takes your system to apply ½–¾ inch of water. Turn the water on for fifteen minutes and calculate the average depth of water in the cans. Multiply this number by 4 to determine the irrigation rate in inches per hour.

While checking for damaged sprinkler heads, replace any that are leaking or not providing uniform coverage. Also, check to ensure that valves open and close properly.

How Turf Irrigation Affects Your Landscape Plants

It's important to remember that a sprinkler zone may be irrigating not only turf, but landscape plants as well. These plants may have different irrigation requirements and may be over- or underwatered if irrigation is based on turfgrass needs. This factor emphasizes the importance of good landscape design and irrigation planning, where all components of the system must be considered (pl. P).

Microenvironmental Effects in the Landscape That Affect Irrigation Requirements

Not every part of your lawn will have the same irrigation requirements. For instance, if grass is planted close to the house, it will be in shade for some portion of the day. Trees or large shrubbery can also cause shade, and some mature canopies actually shade a portion of the lawn for an entire day. In these cases, it may be very difficult to grow an acceptable stand of turf, and a different ground cover may be a better choice. If you choose to grow grass in the shade, you must reduce irrigation to this part of your lawn. For more information on this, see "Growing Turfgrass in the Shade" in chapter 6.

Soil conditions will also influence water requirements. Sandy soils do not hold water for long and dry out faster than soils with more mineral content. Climatic conditions such as wind, temperature, and humidity also alter water requirements.

How to Calibrate Your Sprinkler System

Knowing the amount of water your sprinkler system applies to your lawn is an important step in efficient water use. Most people irrigate their turf for a given number of minutes without knowing how much water they are really applying. This leads to over- or underwatering, neither of which will benefit the turf. In addition, water is becoming an increasingly scarce natural resource and should be utilized as efficiently as possible. Calibrating will help you to apply the correct amount of water to your yard (pl. Q). Whether you have an in-ground system or a hose and sprinkler, the following steps will calibrate your system:

1. Obtain five to ten coffee cans, tuna fish cans, or other straight-sided containers to catch the irrigation water. Containers that are 3–6 inches in diameter work best.
2. If you have an in-ground system, place the containers in one zone at a time. Scatter the cans at random within the zone. Repeat the entire procedure in every zone because there may be differences in the irrigation rates. If you use a hose-end sprinkler to water your turf, place the containers in a straight line from the sprinkler to the edge of the watering pattern. Space the containers evenly.
3. Turn the water on for fifteen minutes.
4. Use a ruler to measure the depth of water in each container. *Note:* The more precise the measurement, the better your calibration will be. For most cases, measurements to the nearest ⅛ inch are adequate.
5. Find the average depth of water collected in the containers (add up the depths and then divide by the number of containers).
6. To determine the irrigation rate in inches per hour, multiply the average depth of water by 4.

Now that you know your sprinkler system irrigation rate, you can more efficiently apply water to your turf. Use table 4.2 as a guide for sprinkler times. For example, if the sprinkler system applies water at the rate of 2 inches per hour and you wish to apply ¾ inch of water, then you would need to run your sprinklers for about twenty-three minutes.

To calculate time required for irrigating rates not listed in table 4.2, use the following equation:

Minutes required to run sprinklers in each zone = amount of water to be applied × 60

Calibration Pointers

- Try to calibrate the sprinkler system during the same time it is normally run so that water pressures are similar.
- Low water pressure can significantly reduce the amount and coverage of water applied by a sprinkler system.

Table 4.2. Average time required to apply water for a given irrigation rate[a]

| Total water to apply | Irrigation rate: amount of water applied per hour | | | |
	½"	1"	1½"	2"
	Minutes to run sprinklers in each zone			
½"	60	30	20	15
¾"	90	45	30	23
1"	120	60	40	30

a. Note that time may vary based on pipe and sprinkler head size, water pressure, and time of day.

- Application rates normally should not exceed ½–¾ inch of water per irrigation.
- Most irrigation controllers can be adjusted for accurate time settings. Consult your operating instructions or local sprinkler company for details.
- If you use a hose-end sprinkler, a mechanical timer and shutoff switch that attach to the faucet will help make watering more efficient.
- Avoid mixing sprinkler head types. Mist heads apply more water than impact heads. Match sprinkler heads for uniform coverage.
- Check the sprinkler system frequently. Replace broken sprinkler heads, clear clogged nozzles, and adjust the direction of spray as needed.
- Use water efficiently; do not waste it.
- For more specific information on turf irrigation, see "Watering Your Florida Lawn" in this chapter.

Overseeding Your Florida Lawn

In many parts of Florida, it is not possible to have an attractive, green lawn throughout the winter months because of low-temperature exposure. Permanent lawn grasses in north Florida (bahiagrass, bermudagrass, centipedegrass, St. Augustinegrass, and zoysiagrass) go dormant in late fall or winter. These grasses grow very slowly and lose color in the fall, then turn completely brown with the first frost. Brown lawns throughout the winter are unattractive and weeds are easily seen, so a practice called "overseeding" is sometimes used to provide a green winter turf cover. Grasses used for overseeding will not survive in Florida's warm weather; consequently, these grasses die out in the spring when warm weather returns and the warm-season grass comes out of dormancy. Overseeding is the practice of using a temporary grass that is seeded into the permanent lawn to provide winter color. While this practice is common on golf courses, athletic fields, and high-profile landscape areas, the principles also apply to homeowners who wish to have a green lawn year-round. It is important to remember, however, that this also entails year-round lawn maintenance (pls. R, S).

Which Grass To Use

Several cool-season grasses can be used for overseeding, including ryegrass, bluegrass, bentgrass, and tall fescue. The best choice for overseeding for home lawns is ryegrass. Annual, intermediate, and improved (perennial) ryegrasses are popular because of rapid seed germination, fast growth, adaptability, and reasonably low cost. Ryegrass is widely adapted, does well in either sun or shade, and tolerates close, frequent mowing. If seeded heavily and mowed closely, ryegrass can provide a very dense and beautiful lawn throughout the winter. By the time the ryegrass dies, the permanent lawn grass should be actively growing again and will provide color and cover the rest of the growing season. Of course, the ryegrass will have to be reseeded each fall to provide a green wintertime lawn.

Ryegrass for Winter Lawns

Establishment of winter ryegrass is a simple procedure. Seeding time varies from October to early November in north Florida to mid-November and early December in central Florida. It is best to wait until the daytime temperatures are consistently in the low- to mid-70°F range. If the seeds are planted during warmer periods, water stress and diseases may reduce the chance of seedling survival. In frost-free areas of south Florida, lawns generally do not go dormant, and overseeding is probably not needed for winter color.

Seedbed Preparation

The two most important steps in overseeding are proper seedbed preparation and proper watering. A seedbed where the overseeded grass contacts the soil is necessary for optimum performance. To prepare the lawn for overseeding, the grass should first be raked thoroughly to remove all debris. Next, mow the lawn closely, catching all clippings, or rake the grass afterwards. The lawn may need to be cut more than once to reduce it to the desired height.

A lawn with heavy thatch produces an overseeded lawn with irregular patches. In this case, dethatching with a power vertical mower or power rake (these can be rented) is advisable. Vertical mower blade spacing should be 3 inches for St. Augustinegrass and Bahiagrass, 1–2 inches for centipedegrass, and 1 inch for Bermudagrass and zoysiagrass. A final raking will remove additional material and loosen the soil somewhat so that the seed can come in contact with the soil.

The next step is seeding. There are no "magic" seeding rates. Rates listed in table 4.3 will produce reasonably good color and density. If a heavy thatch layer exists, increase seeding rates by 25–50 percent. If available, buy fungicide-treated seed. For best coverage, use a mechanical seeder and sow half the seed as you walk in one direction and the remaining half by walking at right angles to the first. A very uniform stand can be established this way. After seeding, rake

Table 4.3. Overseeding rates for home lawns

Overseed grass	Pounds of seed per 1000 sq ft
Bluegrass	3
Fescue	7
Ryegrass (annual)	10
Ryegrass (intermediate)	10
Ryegrass (perennial)	10–20

the ground with a stiff broom to ensure that the seed has gotten through the grass and is in contact with the soil.

Watering

Watering is the last but most important step in establishing the winter lawn. Water should be applied lightly and carefully to the seeded lawn once or twice a day until the seeds have germinated. Watering should continue until seedlings are well established. *Do not overwater,* as this will wash seed away and encourage disease development. Once the plants are well established (e.g., mowed several times), water on an as-needed basis to prevent wilting.

Maintenance of Winter Lawn

Once the winter lawn is established, it will require the same maintenance as the permanent lawn. This includes mowing, watering, fertilizing, and controlling pests. Begin mowing when the grass is tall enough to be cut (around 1–2 inches). Properly fertilized ryegrass grows very quickly, so weekly mowing will probably be required. Do not mow with a dull blade or the seedlings may be torn from the ground or develop a ragged appearance. Water as needed to keep the grass from wilting. Fertilization is needed to keep the ryegrass growing vigorously and to maintain a deep green color. To help prevent root burn, the first application should follow the second mowing. For the first application, apply ½ pound nitrogen per 1000 square feet, using a complete fertilizer such as 15-0-15. Thereafter, use a nitrogen fertilizer such as ammonium nitrate, ammonium sulfate, IBDU, or others monthly at ½ pound nitrogen per 1000 square feet.

Ryegrass is very susceptible to a disease called *Pythium* root rot (damping off, cottony blight). The disease appears to be most severe on overwatered, overfertilized ryegrass, especially during warm, humid weather. Use of fungicide-treated seed, along with cultural practices such as seeding during the coolest months, proper watering and fertilizing, and appropriate fungicide applications, may reduce disease pressure. If *Pythium* root rot occurs, a fungicide should be applied immediately because this disease can kill the entire winter lawn in twenty-four to forty-eight hours. For chemical disease control recommendations, refer to "Disease Management" in chapter 5.

Reestablishing Permanent Grass

To maintain good vigor in the permanent lawn grass, do not encourage the winter grass after temperatures warm up in the spring. The permanent lawn grass can be weakened by the highly competitive ryegrass during this overlapping (transition) season of growth. Ryegrass will normally die out in late spring, but if the weather is cool and the lawn is watered frequently, it can be very persistent. To discourage the ryegrass, discontinue fertilization in February (south Florida) and March (north Florida). Water as infrequently as possible, but make sure the permanent lawn grass does not suffer excessively. Continue to mow the ryegrass as closely as possible each week. These practices tend to weaken the winter grass and facilitate a faster transition back to the permanent lawn grass. Once the permanent lawn grass has resumed growth, begin your regular lawn maintenance program.

Thatch Control in Your Florida Lawn

Thatch is defined as an intermingled layer of dead and living shoots, stems, and roots that develops between the zone of green vegetation and the soil surface. Thatch consists of a loosely interwoven collection of plant matter that leaves the turf feeling spongy or puffy. When excessive (1 inch or more), thatch may cause serious problems in Florida lawns (pl. T).

Why is Thatch a Problem?

Thatch accumulations are undesirable for a variety of reasons:

- *Thatch can restrict water and air movement into the soil.* Dry thatch tends to repel water rather than allow infiltration, and wet thatch enhances disease problems. If your lawn has dry spots that are difficult to rewet (unless you almost flood the areas), these are probably dry thatch spots.
- *Thick thatch makes mowing very difficult.* As thatch builds up, mowing height actually increases above the soil line, and the turf becomes very spongy, allowing the mower to sink into the turf and scalp the lawn. This results in an uneven appearance and often a mottled brown and green surface.
- *Thatch provides an ideal habitat for insects and disease.* Thatch accumulation is associated with an increased incidence of many insects and diseases.
- *A thatchy condition elevates the growing points (crowns), runners (rhizomes and stolons), and roots above the soil surface.* As a result, the lawn is prone to damage from mowing too low and from environmental stresses such as winter injury because elevated plant parts are exposed to

greater extremes in temperature. Centipedegrass is especially sensitive to winter kill because the stolons are elevated and are more prone to cold temperatures in thatchy lawns. Heavily thatched lawns also go dormant following the first exposure to cold weather and green up more slowly in spring (pl. U).

- *Thatch can interrupt and restrict the downward movement of pesticides and fertilizers into soil.* This reduces the effectiveness of these materials, making pest control difficult and producing a nonuniform, erratic response to fertilization.

Causes of Thatch Buildup

Thatch is basically a residue problem that occurs in most turfgrasses. Thatch buildup has been attributed to numerous factors. Excessive plant growth (when vegetative production exceeds decay) results in the accumulation of thatch. Grasses depend on constant regeneration for survival, and new growth of creeping grasses covers the old, causing residue accumulation.

St. Augustinegrass, hybrid bermudagrass, seashore paspalum, and zoysiagrass often accumulate excessive thatch. Likewise, improper management practices such as overfertilizing, overwatering, and infrequent mowing often increase thatch buildup. In addition, failure to keep the soil environment favorable for bacterial and fungal growth by pH control, adequate irrigation, and aeration decreases the rate of decomposition of thatch residues, since these organisms are responsible for decay of organic matter. Failure to remove clippings after mowing has been cited as a cause of thatch buildup, but research findings do not support this concept. If properly mowed, leaf clippings decompose readily and *do not* contribute to thatch.

Thatch Control

Effective control of thatch requires a combination of several management practices. These include reducing the buildup rate by reducing plant growth and increasing microbial decomposition as well as periodic physical removal through scalping and/or vertical mowing.

Cultural Practices

Excessive fertilization and irrigation are two of the primary causes of thatch buildup over time. Fertilizer should be applied as necessary to maintain reasonable growth and density. This will minimize weed invasion. Excessive succulent growth caused by overfertilization increases thatch and susceptibility to pests and reduces the turf's overall tolerance to environmental stresses. Mowing practices can help control thatch buildup. Lawns should always be mowed at the recommended height and frequency. Thatch seldom increases if no more than one-third of the leaf blade is removed at each mowing.

Liming of acid soils may help increase decomposition of thatch residues and thus retard buildup. A soil pH of 7.0 is ideal for maximum microbial activity and decomposition.

Mechanical Thatch Removal

Scalping

Close mowing or scalping entails mowing the turf to a much shorter height than normal in an attempt to remove thatch. *We do not advise homeowners to attempt this without consulting a turfgrass professional or county extension agent.* Damage done to the lawn from scalping may kill St. Augustinegrass or centipedegrass and can severely injure other turf species.

Vertical Mowing

The most common method of mechanical thatch removal is the use of a heavy-duty vertical mower. This specialized piece of equipment has evenly spaced, knifelike blades revolving perpendicularly to the turf that slice into the thatch to mechanically remove it (pl. V). This process removes both thatch and mat and simultaneously cultivates the soil and topdresses the turf. It is very important to use proper blade spacing when vertically mowing different turfgrasses. Use a blade spacing of 1–2 inches for bermudagrass and zoysiagrass, 2–3 inches for centipedegrass, and 3 inches for bahiagrass and St. Augustinegrass. Because of their underground rhizomes, zoysiagrass, bermudagrass, and bahiagrass may be vertically mowed down to soil level in several directions without killing the lawn; however, if all of the aboveground stolons are removed from centipedegrass and St. Augustinegrass, these turfgrasses may die. If thatch accumulation exceeds 2–3 inches, lawns should be vertically mowed carefully more than once, but the lawns should be allowed to fully recover between mowings.

Vertical mowing is an effective means of removing thatch, but if not done properly, the grass can be so severely damaged that it may not survive. Experience with the method and equipment as well as knowledge of the type of grass being renovated are essential. In many cases it may be advantageous to have a reputable commercial lawn maintenance company remove thatch.

Thatch removal should be considered necessary when thatch thickness exceeds 1 inch. Frequency of thatch removal will vary, depending on intensity of management. The best time to vertically mow grasses south of Orlando is March through August; for grasses north of Orlando, the best time is April through July. Vertical mowing at these times ensures quick recovery since warm-season grasses grow rapidly during these periods.

After dethatching, cleanup is necessary. Thatch removed from an average-sized lawn may fill several pickup trucks. This debris must be raked, swept, or vacuumed, and removed from the lawn. Following cleanup, the lawn should be conventionally mowed closely to remove further debris. The lawn should then be thoroughly watered (e.g., with ¾ inch of water) to prevent drying of exposed roots. Approximately one week following dethatching, nitrogen fertilizer should be applied to encourage turf recovery. Apply ½–1 pound of actual nitrogen per 1000 square feet in a quick-release soluble form (e.g., ammonium nitrate or ammonium sulfate). Be sure to irrigate after nitrogen application in order to minimize turf burn. This type of renovation places the turf under a considerable amount of stress, so it is important to minimize any other stresses. Do not subject the grass to traffic, over- or underwatering, or chemical applications until normal growth has resumed.

Power Raking

This specialized machine uses evenly spaced, flexible, spring steel tines that revolve at high speeds to strip through turf and loosen debris for subsequent removal. The machine and procedures are often confused with vertical mowing. Power raking does not involve a cutting action, as does vertical mowing. Therefore, it is not a substitute for vertical mowing and thatch removal, but is used most often to remove a mat layer.

Cultivation and Soil Topdressing

Periodic cultivation by coring (aerification) and soil topdressing (application of soil to the turf surface) are sometimes used for control of thatch on highly managed turf areas (pls. W, X). Mechanical cultivation removes small plugs of thatch and soil, thus leaving small holes in the soil that allow penetration by air, water, fertilizers, and pesticides. Coring does not remove substantial amounts of thatch, but does provide a more favorable environment for microbial activity. It also improves drainage in some soils and provides increased oxygen to the roots. Topdressing increases decomposition by bringing soil microbes and moisture into contact with thatch. When beginning a topdressing program, it is important to realize that this is a long-term approach to improving soil conditions and a single treatment will not produce good-quality results. Frequent, light soil topdressings have been repeatedly shown to be the most effective and consistent method to reduce thatch. Thick applications of topdressing or sand are not recommended and will only compound the problem by causing a layering effect and possibly increasing disease incidence. This results in restricted water and air movement and encourages shallow root systems. Topdressing soil should be free of weeds and nematodes (sterilized is ideal) and should be of the same type as that on which the turf is growing. Topdressing should begin in early spring when turf begins active growth. Light, frequent topdressings provide quicker results than infrequent, heavier ones.

While the above practices are common on highly managed turf, they are not always needed in home lawns. Homeowners are sometimes convinced that buying these services will improve the condition of their lawn and may spend unnecessary money on unneeded practices. Thatch is seldom a problem in younger lawns, but can sometimes become a problem in older lawns, particularly ones that have been overfertilized and overirrigated.

Table 4.4. Approximate soil volumes needed to topdress

Topdressing depth (inches)	Soil volume (cu yd/5000 sq ft)
0.03	½
0.06	1
0.12	2
0.25	4
0.50	8

Summary

The following steps should be followed to control thatch formation.
- Mow at recommended height and frequency.
- Avoid indiscriminate use of fertilizer. Use minimal amounts of nitrogen, and soil test for phosphorus levels.
- Maintain a soil environment conducive to rapid decomposition. This includes adequate aeration, irrigation, and soil pH control.
- Core cultivation (aerification) can help control thatch formation and soil layering.
- Topdressing with sand provides the best biological control of thatch. Proper timing and rates are necessary to provide the best thatch control with least chance of disease occurrence.
- Use vertical mowers if mechanical removal of thatch becomes necessary. Follow this with irrigation.

5

Pest Management

Integrated Pest Management Strategies

One of the most appealing aspects of a landscape is the beauty of the lawn (plate 12). The responsibility for maintaining this beauty in acceptable condition usually falls on the homeowner and/or contracted lawn maintenance firm. One method for meeting this objective is to incorporate a commonsense approach to turf management through information gathering, analysis, and knowledgeable decision making. Integrated Pest Management (IPM) utilizes the most appropriate cultural, biological, and chemical strategies for managing plant pests. Unfortunately, attempts to maintain perfect conditions throughout the year often force homeowners and lawn care managers to abandon sound agronomic practices for quick fixes to get them through the current crisis. For example, too-close mowing heights, requests for perfect lawns with no blemishes, and attempts to grow grasses outside their natural range of adaptability require the increased use of fertilizer, water, and pesticides. At the same time, public concerns over these inputs and restrictions on the availability of natural resources, especially water, should lead many homeowners to incorporate IPM programs into their total management scheme.

IPM Beginnings

Modern IPM concepts and practices began to emerge in the late 1950s in apple production systems and were vastly expanded with cotton production in the 1960s. This movement was in response to the greatly increased use of pesticides that began after World War II. At that time, many felt that pesticides were the "silver bullet" needed to control all pest problems. Many traditional pest and plant ecological studies were abandoned, as were nonchemical control alternatives. This led to a new generation of producers and scientists who had little experience with nonchemical approaches to pest or plant management. However, resistance to pesticides, especially insecticides, forced researchers and growers to seek alternative methods of pest control—thus, IPM was born.

In recent years, turf managers have realized that their escalating dependence on pesticides and the lack of research and training in the pest management arena are now affecting their industry. For example, in the early 1980s, several very effective and relatively inexpensive pesticides were removed from the market. Two such pesticides were EDB (ethylene dibromide), a soil-injected nematicide, and chlordane, an insecticide. When these chemicals were available, turfgrass management did not include adjusting cultural practices to reduce insect populations. However, since the loss of these materials, nematodes, grubs, and mole crickets have become very serious turf pest problems in many areas. Researchers are currently trying to find alternative methods of management and control for these pests based on pest life cycle and use of biological control agents. Obviously, additional time and research will be necessary to solve problems that were basically ignored for more than forty years.

Strategies of IPM

Strategy Development

Developing IPM strategies requires integration of information. Three main areas are:

- *Knowledge concerning all normal inputs required for growing turf—not only what the inputs are, but also why they are required.* This is supplemented by knowledge of pest life cycles and the management practices that disrupt or influence them to reduce pest numbers. Understanding the logic behind a management practice, rather than just doing it "because that is the way we have always done it," allows the homeowner to make decisions to alter these practices to reduce pest problems or encourage turf growth to overcome or tolerate the pest.
- Use of a monitoring system to carefully follow pest trends to determine if a pesticide will be necessary and, if so, when it would be most effectively applied. Ideally, monitoring systems are based on known economic or aesthetic threshold levels. Unfortunately, in many cases, these thresholds are not specifically known; thus, they are determined to reflect local conditions and threshold levels tolerated by clientele.

Some landscape maintenance firms employ a professional scout, who, while visiting several areas, can easily recognize pest trends. Useful information from one area can easily be used to assist other sites.

Tools required for scouting vary with pest problems, scout training, and clientele budget. A good set of eyes and an inquisitive mind are essential. These are supported by a standard 10× hand or pocket lens, soil profile probe, spade, cup cutter, pocketknife, tweezers, scalpel, collection vials and paper bags, and field identification guides. Soap and water are also necessary for insect monitoring.

- Monitoring lawns includes scouting turf areas, adjacent ornamental plantings, flowerbeds, and trees. Frequency of scouting is determined by pest trends, desired level of aesthetics, and, of course, economics. During periods of active turf growth or suspected pest activity, weekly scouting may be justified. During periods of inactive growth, scouting frequency can be reduced. Scouting begins by simply walking around the area to observe insect and disease activity as well as other pest and noninfectious symptoms. In order to better recognize specific pest damage such as disease symptoms and nocturnal insect feeding, early morning scouting is suggested.

- *Maintenance of careful records measures effectiveness of the IPM strategies.* It is important to understand that 100 percent elimination of pests is not ecologically or economically desirable and that some tolerance to pests in your landscape is needed. However, if necessary, the decision to apply a pesticide will be supported by carefully maintained records should regulatory officials or the public question it. In addition, an IPM program will constantly evolve as new control strategies, monitoring techniques, and threshold information become available.

IPM Control Tactics

Tactics in IPM embrace cultural, biological, and chemical control strategies. All are equally important in implementing a successful IPM program.

Cultural Controls

The following are integral features of a good cultural control strategy for pest management:

Host-plant Resistance

Until recently, turfgrass breeders have been concerned primarily with improving the appearance and recreational value of grasses, including their texture, density, and growth habit. Breeding for pest resistance has been a secondary concern. However, one of the oldest means of pest control has been through careful breeding and selection of resistant or tolerant plants. For example, 'Floratam' St. Augustinegrass was initially selected for its resistance to chinch bugs (although this is no longer the case).

Pest-free Propagating Material

Another easy but often overlooked means of preventing pest establishment in turf is the use of planting materials (seed or vegetative sprigs/sod) that are free of pests. Every state has a program for certification of pest-free propagation material. Each bag of certified seed must provide information on purity and germination percentages. In addition, a weed seed listing must be provided, and no noxious weed seeds are allowed. If vegetative material such as sprigs or sod is being planted, inspect the turf for weeds, fire ants, and other pests. One should also ask to see results from a nematode assay of the planting material before purchasing. Remember, these steps will help to prevent or reduce pest problems during and after establishment.

Site Preparation

Proper preparation of a planting site is an important step in pest management, primarily because of its effects on the health and viability of the turf. For turf managers, this includes planning and constructing highly utilized areas with irrigation and drainage systems capable of providing precise water management. If the soil remains saturated for too long, diseases and soil compaction will eventually occur.

Basic Agronomic Practices

Probably the best defense against pest invasion is a dense, healthy, competitive turf (plate 12). This is achieved after establishment by providing cultural practices that favor turf growth over pest occurrence. Important cultural practices in IPM programs include proper irrigation, fertilization, mowing, aerification, verticutting, and topdressing. Prolonged use of incorrect cultural practices and lack of understanding of the interrelationships among these practices weaken the turf, encourage pest activity or invasion, and quite often lead to excess thatch development. Thatch harbors many insects and disease pathogens. It also binds pesticides and reduces the efficiency of an irrigation program.

Biological Controls

Pests in their native areas are usually regulated by predators and parasites that help keep populations at a constant level. Problems occur when pests, but not their natural enemies, are introduced into new areas and the pest populations increase unchecked. Biological pest control involves the use of natural enemies to reduce pest populations, both indigenous and introduced, to aesthetically acceptable levels.

One inherent principle concerning classic biological pest control, where the agent is introduced only once or on a limited basis for permanent establishment, is accepting that a minimum level of the target pest will always be present. This low pest population ensures that the biological control agent will continue to have a food source after the target pest has been reduced to an acceptable level. Thus, complete elimination of the pest is not feasible when integrating biological control measures into the overall pest management scheme. Homeowners must understand this fact and be willing to accept minor levels of pest pressure.

Various success stories have occurred using biological control agents such as parasites, predators, or diseases to control another organism. However, only a few biological control measures are currently being used in commercial turf production. *Bacillus popilliae,* a bacterium that causes milky spore disease, has been used with variable success in the control of Japanese beetle grubs. Other potential agents for biological control of turf pests include endophytic fungi for insect control, various rust fungi (*Puccinia* spp.) for nutsedge control, predaceous nematodes such as *Steinernema scapterisci* and the so-called Brazilian red-eyed fly (*Ormia depleta*) for mole cricket control, and possibly parasitic fungi and bacteria for turf nematode control. Research on antagonistic fungi and bacteria for biocontrol of diseases and fire ants also shows promise.

Biological control agents are complex, not totally effective, and not always predictable. The concept of biological control has been so widely publicized that the general public views it as a viable and readily available alternative to all pesticides. Unfortunately, this is not always the case, but this area is currently receiving much-needed attention and hopefully will provide additional control agents in the future. The public must be informed that biological controls are not the answer to all pest problems, but may be a useful component of a good IPM program.

Chemical Controls

Not all pest problems can be solved by manipulating cultural practices in the plant environment or by the use of biological control agents. In these cases, pesticides become the second or third line of defense. In the IPM scheme, indiscriminate spraying is eliminated and only judicious use of pesticides is employed, thus minimizing damage to biological control agents and the environment. This requires knowledge of the ecological interrelationships among the pest, the host plant, and the biological control agent. Judicious pesticide use involves making management decisions.

- The pest must be properly identified and monitored with reliable techniques to establish aesthetic thresholds. A determination must then must be made as to when or whether further action is necessary. IPM programs in vegetable and horticultural crops refer to economic, damage, or action thresholds, but in turf management, economic and related threshold-level terms mean little since an acceptable aesthetic level, not crop yield, is the ultimate goal. The term "aesthetic threshold level" refers to the amount of visual damage a particular turf area can withstand before action is required. Obviously, the aesthetic threshold level of a highly manicured lawn is lower, requiring action sooner, than that of a more casual lawn.
- The most effective control of many insects and weeds occurs at a particular stage in their life cycle, usually during the early stages of development. For example, mole crickets are most susceptible to chemical control when they are small, usually during the months of May or June. Chemical applications at other times are less effective.
- If use of a pesticide is necessary, select the one that is most effective but least toxic to nontarget organisms or least persistent in the environment, whichever is more important in that location. Read the label completely and thoroughly. Spot-treat if possible, instead of applying blanket or wall-to-wall treatments. This requires effective scouting techniques and proper recording or mapping of pest outbreaks.
  Nonsynthetic pesticides include soap flush for mole cricket control, natural pyrethroids derived from chrysanthemums for foliage-feeding insects, and a mixture of copper and sulfur (Bordeaux Mixture) for foliar diseases.

Starting an IPM Program

Pest problems are going to occur in turf, and even the best management program cannot guarantee that pest damage will not occur. The following steps have proven successful in developing IPM programs and should provide a good starting point for those who are innovative enough to try such an approach.

Determine management objectives for specific areas of the landscape, and correct all practices that favor pest development or place undue stress on the turf. Before implementing the IPM program, inspect and map each area. This will provide the foundation on which all management decisions can be based. Information that should be obtained includes:

- turf species
- mowing height and schedule
- irrigation amount and frequency
- soil drainage
- complete soil analysis
- fertilizer program
- traffic patterns
- shade and air circulation concerns

A field history form can be used to record such foundation data. Be prepared to improve the existing problems that weaken turf, such as a poor irrigation or drainage system or severe tree effects. Improve these conditions before the IPM program is implemented. Otherwise, the potential for success of the IPM program will be greatly reduced.

- Monitor local weather patterns closely. This will provide detailed, localized data on rainfall, soil temperatures, humidity, sunlight indexes, and evapotranspiration rates. Climatic conditions usually play the most important role in creating specific turf growth patterns and pest problems.
- Establish aesthetic or action threshold levels and begin monitoring and recording pest levels. Threshold levels will vary according to the specific pest being scouted, use of the turf area, expectations, and budget constraints. Table 5.1 lists suggested aesthetic or action thresholds for several common turf insects. It may be useful to create a map of the lawn area and then note on the map where the problem areas occur. For example, mole crickets usually lay eggs in the same location each year. This may allow for spot treatment rather than a blanket pesticide application. Over time, these maps can indicate where pest problems annually occur and possibly allow management or environmental variables influencing this occurrence to be corrected.
- Use pesticides correctly and only when threshold limits are reached. One of the goals of IPM is intelligent and prudent pesticide use. Pesticide use will not necessarily be reduced by an IPM program, although it often is; generally speaking, the method allows for more efficient and effective

Table 5.1. Common turf insects, their aesthetic thresholds, and inspection/detection methods

Insect	Aesthetic Threshold for Lawns	Inspection/Detection Method
Armyworms	3–4 per sq ft	Visual + soap flush
Billbugs	6 per sq ft	Visual
Chinch Bugs	20 per sq ft	Water float
Cutworms	1 per sq ft	Visual + soap flush
June Beetle grubs	3–4 per sq ft	Visual + soil inspection
Masked Chafer Beetle grubs	4 per sq ft	Visual + soil inspection
Mole Crickets	2–4 per sq ft	Visual + soap flush
Sod Webworms	10–12 per sq ft	Visual + soap flush

use of pesticides. For example, by monitoring pest development, the pesticide can be used during the most susceptible stage of the life cycle. Use the safest, most effective pesticide available for the particular pest. Spot-treat whenever possible.

- Evaluate the results of the cultural modifications and pesticide treatments by periodically monitoring the site environment and pest populations. Keep written records of site pest management objectives, monitoring methods, data collected, actions taken, and the results obtained.

Weed Management

Weeds can be defined simply as unwanted plants or plants growing out of place. The proper identification of weeds and some understanding of how and why weeds are present in a lawn are important in selecting the best control strategy. Knowledge of whether or not weeds were previously present in a particular area will also help the homeowner prepare for control procedures in the future. Weed control should be a carefully planned and coordinated program instead of a hit-or-miss operation.

Types of Weeds

Knowledge of weed growth habit is important for developing an effective weed management program.

Broadleaves

Broadleaves, or dicotyledonous plants, have two cotyledons (seed leaves) when the weed seed germinates. Their true leaves have net-like veins and usually have showy flowers. Examples include clovers, lespedeza, plantain, henbit, chickweed, Florida pusley, beggarweed, matchweed, and many others. Broadleaves illustrated in this book:

Hairy Beggarticks (*Bidens alba*) (plate 13)
Red Spiderling (*Boerhavia diffusa*) (plate 14)
Shepherds Purse (*Capsella bursa pastoris*) (plate 15)
Spotted Spurge *Chamaesyce maculata* (plate 16)
Pinnate Tansymustard (*Descurainia pinnata*) (plate 17)
Dichondra (*Dichondra repens*) (plate 18)
Virginia Buttonweed (*Diodia virginiana*) (plate 19)
Rough Fleabane (*Erigeron strigosus*) (plate 20)
Dogfennel (*Eupatorium capillifolium*) (plate 21)
Catchweed Bedstraw (*Galium aparine*) (plate 22)
Carolina Geranium (*Geranium carolinianum*) (plate 23)
Wandering Cudweed (*Gnaphalium pensylvanicum*) (plate 24)
Oldworld Diamondflower (*Hedyotis corymbosa*) (plate 25)
Pennywort (Dollarweed) (*Hydrocotyle spp.*) (plate 26)
Henbit (*Lamium amplexicaule*) (plate 27)
Virginia Pepperweed (*Lepidium virginicum*) (plate 28)
Black Medic (*Medicago lupulina*) (plate 29)
Cuban Purple Woodsorrel (*Oxalis intermedia*) (plate 30)
Yellow Woodsorrel (*Oxalis stricta*) (plate 31)
Longstalked Phyllanthus (*Phyllanthus tenellus*) (plate 32)
Chamberbitter (*Phyllanthus urinaria*) (plate 33)
Buckhorn Plantain (*Plantago lanceolata*) (plate 34)
Broadleaf Plantain (*Plantago major*) (plate 35)
Florida Pusley (*Richardia scabra*) (plate 36)
Eastern Blue-eyed Grass (*Sisyrinchium angustifolium*) (plate 37)
Greenbriar (*Smilax* spp.) (plate 38)
Spiny sowthistle (*Sonchus asper*) (plate 39)
Common Sowthistle (*Sonchus oleraceus*) (plate 40)
Florida Betony (*Stachys floridana*) (plate 41)
Common Chickweed (*Stellaria media*) (plate 42)
Large Hop Clover (*Trifolium campestre*) (plate 43)
White Clover (*Trifolium repens*) (plate 44)
Narrowleaf Vetch (*Vicia sativa* subsp. *nigra*) (plate 45)
Asiatic Hawksbeard (*Youngia japonica*) (plate 46)

Grasses

Grasses are monocotyledonous plants, with only one cotyledon, or seed leaf, present when seedlings emerge from the soil. Grasses have hollow, rounded stems with nodes (joints) and parallel veins in their true leaves. Examples include crabgrass, goosegrass, crowfootgrass, dallisgrass, bullgrass, annual bluegrass, alexandergrass, cogongrass, torpedograss, and smutgrass. Grasses illustrated in this book:

Blanket Crabgrass (seedling) (*Digitaria serotina*) (plate 47)
Blanket Crabgrass (mature) (*Digitaria serotina*) (plate 48)

Goosegrass (*Eleusine indica*) (plate 49)

Annual Bluegrass (*Poa annua*) (plate 50)

Sedges/Rushes

Sedges have stems that are triangular in shape and solid, while rush stems are round. Both sedges and rushes favor a moist habitat. Economically important weed species include yellow and purple nutsedge, globe, Texas, annual, and water sedge, and perennial kyllinga as well as path and beak rush.

Kyllinga rhizomes (*Cyperus brevifolia*) (plate 51)

Purple nutsedge (*Cyperus rotundus*) (plate 52)

Globe Sedge (*Cyperus globulosus*) (plate 53)

Proper Management First

The first and best method of weed control begins with proper management practices that encourage a dense, thriving turf. Healthy turf shades the soil so sunlight can't reach weed seeds that are ready to germinate. A thick turf also minimizes the physical space available for weeds to become established. There are several management practices that will promote a healthy, dense grass.

Proper Turfgrass Selection

The first management decision is selection of the best turf species or variety for a particular area. For example, heavily shaded areas will support only a few turfgrass species. Growing bermudagrass or bahiagrass in shaded areas will result in thin, weak turf that is very susceptible to weed invasion. Alternate grass choices for shady conditions include certain cultivars of St. Augustinegrass, zoysiagrass, and, to a lesser degree, centipedegrass.

Proper Cultural Practices

Proper fertilization, watering, mowing, and control of other pests are required to produce a dense turf that will prevent weed infestation (plate 54). If turf is over- or underwatered, over- or underfertilized, or mowed too low or too infrequently, the turf will be weakened and unable to compete with weeds. The use of mowers with unsharpened blades results in damaged areas and increases the time needed for turf recovery, allowing for weed invasion. It is very important to understand that weeds don't *create* a void—they *fill* a void.

Traffic Control

Turf damaged by foot or vehicle traffic invites weeds (plate 55). Turf growing in areas compacted by excess traffic, especially when the soil is water saturated, cannot extract oxygen as well as turf under noncompacted conditions. Goosegrass, annual bluegrass, and certain sedges are weeds that grow well in compacted and/or continuously wet soil. The first step to managing weeds in such a situation is to alleviate soil compaction and/or the saturated condition.

Other Pest Control

Turf damaged by pests such as insects or diseases does not always recuperate quickly enough to outcompete germinating weeds. For example, tunneling from mole crickets disrupts the soil surface, enabling weeds to germinate and become established. Other insects and diseases can severely damage turf, resulting in bare areas. These open areas are usually slow to recover, thus enabling weeds to become established. High nematode populations also thin the turf and make it less able to recuperate from environmental stresses. Weeds that often become established in nematode-infested soil include spotted spurge and Florida pusley.

Sanitation

It is extremely important to prevent the introduction of weeds into lawn areas. If one can prevent weed establishment, there will be no need for control practices. Areas adjacent to fine turf that are hard to mow, such as fencerows or ditch banks, often serve as a source of weed seed that infests the nearby turf. These areas should receive weed management attention.

Another good practice is to wash mowers and trimmers used in weed-infested areas before mowing or trimming in weed-free areas. Similarly, rototillers should be thoroughly cleaned prior to and after use to minimize dispersal of weed seeds found in the soil. Yard clippings that contain weeds should be properly disposed of or composted to reduce the possibility of unwanted contamination.

It is important to use weed-free soil during construction or renovation. To minimize weed invasion during planting, use only certified seed or weed-free sod. It is not unreasonable to request a tour of the sod farm where the sod will be purchased in order to inspect the quality of the grass.

Weed Biology and Control

Weeds complete their life cycles in one growing season (annuals), two growing seasons (biennials), or three or more years (perennials). Annuals that complete their life cycles between spring to fall are generally referred to as summer annuals, and those that complete their life cycles between fall to spring are winter annuals. Summer annual grasses, as a class, are generally the most troublesome weeds in turf. A weed identification guide, *Weeds of Southern Turfgrasses* (SP-79) can be obtained through your local county Extension Service office.

Methods

As previously stated, it is essential that turf be properly maintained in order to minimize weed invasion. If weeds become established, several methods of control are available.

Mowing

If proper mowing height and frequency are maintained, many annual weeds will be eliminated. Mowing prior to weed seedhead formation will also reduce weed seed reserves. Some weeds, however, will readily establish below the optimum mowing height for the turfgrass. Control of these weeds will require additional control methods.

Hand Pulling

If only a few weeds are present, it is easier and less time-consuming to physically remove the plant. If weeds are a major problem, however, other alternatives should be considered.

Mulch

Smothering with a mulch of nonliving material to exclude light is effective in certain areas, such as flowerbeds, footpaths, or nurseries, where turf is not grown. Materials used in such a manner include straw, sawdust, hay, wood chips, and plastic film. Care must be taken to prevent mowing accidents resulting from movement of these materials into a maintained turf area. To be effective, a minimum of 2 inches is required when using natural mulch materials. Synthetic mats impregnated with herbicides are an alternative available for use in the landscape. These provide long-term weed control when properly used, but care must be taken to keep desirable plant roots from encountering these layers.

Herbicides

An herbicide is any chemical that injures or kills a plant. Herbicides are safe and effective if product label instructions are followed. For best results, herbicides should be applied at the proper time, at the labeled rate, utilizing the appropriate application method. Timing of postemergence herbicide application during the plant's growth cycle is important. For example, weeds not treated prior to seedhead formation are harder to control and are able to deposit new seeds for future problems. Herbicides are classified based on how and when they control weeds.

Herbicide Types

Selective: A selective herbicide controls certain plant species without seriously affecting the growth of other plant species. The majority of herbicides used are selective herbicides.

Nonselective: Nonselective herbicides control green plants regardless of species. These are generally used to kill all plants, such as in the renovation or establishment of a new turf area, for spot treatment, or as a trimming material along sidewalks, etc. Glyphosate (Roundup), glufosinate (Finale), and diquat (Reward) are examples of nonselective herbicides.

Contact: Contact herbicides affect only the portion of green plant tissue that is contacted by the herbicide spray. These herbicides are not translocated or moved in the vascular system of plants. Therefore, these will not kill underground plant parts, such as rhizomes or tubers, and often require repeat applications to kill regrowth from these underground parts. Examples of contact herbicides include the organic arsenicals (MSMA, DSMA), bentazon (Basagran), glufosinate (Finale), and diquat (Reward).

Systemic: Systemic herbicides are moved through the plant in the plant's vascular system, which transports the nutrients and water necessary for normal growth and development. Systemic herbicides are generally slower acting and kill plants over a period of days. Examples of systemic herbicides include glyphosate (Roundup), 2,4-D, dicamba (Banvel), imazaquin (Image), and sethoxydim (Vantage).

Timing of Application

Herbicides can also be classified by application timing.

Preemergence: Preemergence herbicides form the basis for a chemical weed control program in turfgrass and are used primarily to control annual grasses (e.g., crabgrass, goosegrass, and annual bluegrass) and certain annual broadleaf weeds (e.g., common chickweed, henbit, and lawn burweed). Preemergence herbicides are applied prior to weed seed germination. Knowledge of weed life cycles is important, especially when herbicide application is timed to attempt preemergence control. If the chemical is applied after weed emergence, preemergence herbicides will have little or no effect. This narrow window of application timing is a potential disadvantage for many lawn care companies and homeowners, who often wait until too late in the spring to apply the preemergence herbicide. A general rule of thumb for application of preemergence herbicide is February 1 in south Florida, February 15 in central Florida, and March 1 in north Florida (when day temperatures reach 65–70°F for four or five consecutive days). These application timings generally coincide with blooming of landscape plants such as azalea and dogwood. If goosegrass is the primary weed species expected, perform preemergence application two to three weeks later than these suggested application dates, since goosegrass germinates later than most summer annual grasses.

For preemergence control of winter annual weeds such as annual bluegrass, apply an herbicide when nighttime temperatures drop to 55–60°F for several consecutive days (early October for north Florida, late October to early November for central and south Florida).

Adequate soil moisture before and after application is necessary to activate most preemergence herbicides. Preemergence herbicides are generally effective in controlling weeds from six to twelve weeks following application. Most herbicides begin to degrade soon after application when exposed to the environment. Therefore, to obtain season-long control, an additional application should follow six to nine weeks after the initial one.

Note: On those areas where turf is to be established (including winter overseeded areas), most preemergence herbicides should not be used in the two to four months preceding planting. Otherwise, root damage and germination reduction of the turf seed may result.

Postemergence: Postemergence herbicides are active on emerged weeds. Normally, *the younger the weed seedling, the easier it is to control.* Postemergence herbicide effectiveness is reduced when the weed is under drought stress, has begun to produce seeds, or is mowed before the chemical has time to work. Avoid application when these detrimental growing conditions exist, and avoid mowing for several days after application.

Fertilizer/Herbicide Mixtures

Many herbicides are formulated with a granular fertilizer as the carrier. Fertilizer/herbicide mixtures enable a "weed-n-feed" treatment in the same application. These materials should be used only when a lawn has a uniform weed population. If weeds exist only on a portion of the lawn, *do not* apply a weed-n-feed product to the entire lawn. If the situation warrants the use of a weed-n-feed product, it is important to determine if the manufacturer's recommended rate of application supplies the amount of fertilizer needed by the turfgrass and the amount of herbicide that is required for weed control. Supplemental applications of fertilizer or herbicide may be required if the fertilizer/herbicide product does not supply enough fertilizer to meet the fertility needs of the turfgrass or the amount of herbicide needed for weed control. Turfgrass fertilizer/herbicide products should be used with caution near ornamentals. Products that contain dicamba, metsulfuron, or atrazine can be absorbed by the roots of ornamentals and cause severe injury. Do not apply products that contain these ingredients near the root zone of ornamental trees and shrubs.

Adjuvants

An adjuvant is a spray additive that enhances the performance or handling characteristic of an herbicide. Adjuvants include surfactants, crop oils, crop oil concentrates, antifoaming agents, drift control agents, and compatibility agents. Surfactants, crop oils, and crop oil concentrates should be added according to label directions, since indiscriminate use may result in severe turfgrass injury or decreased herbicide performance. These additives do not improve the performance of preemergence herbicides and are used only with postemergence herbicides. Surfactants, crop oils, and crop oil concentrates are not always added to postemergence herbicides. Some herbicide formulations have premixed surfactants, and no additional surfactant is necessary. The herbicide label will indicate whether a spray additive is required.

Weed Control Prior to Turf Establishment

A nonselective herbicide should be used to kill existing weeds such as bermudagrass or nutsedge prior to grass establishment. Only emerged plants will be controlled with this type of herbicide. For best results, apply two treatments of a nonselective herbicide fourteen days after the first application or when weed regrowth has occurred.

Seeded Areas

Do not apply preemergence herbicides prior to or immediately following the seeding of grasses such as common bermudagrass, bahiagrass, centipedegrass, or overseeded winter ryegrass. Because of their root-pruning or seedling-kill mode of action, preemergence herbicides may be applied only after seeded grasses have emerged and are well established. Follow label directions for proper interval between seeding and herbicide application.

Sprigged, Sodded, or Plugged Areas

After planting, preemergence herbicides should not be applied until the turfgrass is established, in order to prevent damage to the turf. Postemergence herbicides, in general, should not be applied until the grass is visibly growing and spreading. Mowing will help control most broadleaf weeds until the lawn is well established. Spot spraying of weeds should be practiced until turf establishment occurs.

Weed Control in Established Turf

Preemergence Weed Control

Broadleaf Weed Control

Broadleaf weeds in turf have traditionally been controlled with members of the phenoxy herbicide family (e.g., 2,4-D, MPlateA, and mecoprop) and benzoic acid herbicide family (e.g., dicamba). All are selective, systemic, foliar-applied herbicides, and few broadleaf weeds, especially perennials, are controlled with just one of these materials. Therefore, these materials are commonly found in three-way herbicide mixtures such as Trimec, Ortho's Weed-B-Gon, and Spectracide Weed Stop. Additionally, repeat applications spaced ten to fourteen days apart are usually necessary for satisfactory weed control.

Grass Weed Control

Traditionally, for tolerant turfgrass species, postemergence grass weed control has been through single and repeat applications of the organic arsenicals (e.g., MSMA), which are often found in retail products such as Fertilome Crabgrass,

Nutgrass, and Dallisgrass Killer and Drexel MSMA 6 Plus. Two to four applications spaced seven to ten days apart are generally required for complete control. The rate and number of applications necessary for weed control usually increase as weeds mature.

Postemergence control of grassy weeds in centipedegrass can be achieved with sethoxydim, an herbicide sold under the trade name Vantage. Additionally, atrazine-containing materials (e.g., Scotts Bonus Type S, Hi-Yield Atrazine Weed Killer, and Ortho's Atrazine Plus) will provide good control of young grassy weeds with the added benefit of controlling many young broadleaf weeds.

Nutsedge Control

The predominant nutsedge (often inappropriately called nutgrass) weed species in turfgrasses are yellow and purple nutsedge. Other, more local members of the *Cyperus* genus include annual or water sedge, perennial and annual kyllinga, globe sedge, Texas sedge, flathead sedge, and cylindrical sedge. Path or slender rush, a member of the rush (Juncus) family, also can occur in some turf situations.

These weeds generally thrive in soils that remain wet for extended periods of time as the result of poor drainage or excessive irrigation. The first step in nutsedge control is therefore to correct the problem of continuously wet sites. Do not overirrigate an area and, if necessary, provide surface and subsurface drainage.

Historically, chemical control of most sedges was with repeat applications of the organic arsenicals (e.g., MSMA). Although effective, the treatments are slow to kill the weeds and repeat applications are generally necessary, resulting in extensive damage to certain turf species.

Selective yellow nutsedge control is possible with bentazon, an herbicide found in products such as Basagran T/O and Hi-Yield Basagran. Bentazon is a contact material, meaning it will control only those portions of the weeds treated. Complete coverage of weeds is therefore necessary for greatest bentazon activity. Even with good herbicide coverage, regrowth will normally occur from the roots and tubers, and repeat applications will be necessary.

Purple nutsedge can be controlled with herbicides containing either halosulfuron or imazaquin, sold as Manage and Image, respectively. As with bentazon, repeat applications—possibly over several years—will be required to control all the underground reproductive parts of purple nutsedge.

Application Procedures

Proper Rates

To avoid injury to turfgrasses and ornamentals, apply the proper rate of herbicide. Mark off areas of 1000 square feet and apply herbicides in ½–1 gallon of water per area (approximately 20–40 gallons per acre).

Applicators

For increased application accuracy, air-pressure sprayers are preferred over hose-end sprayers. For herbicides formulated as granulars, use a spreader and calibrate properly.

Vapor Drift

Volatile vapor drift from 2,4-D ester or spray drift from 2,4-D amine, dicamba, or other phenoxy or benzoic acid compounds may damage sensitive plants such as ornamentals, trees, vegetables, or fruits. Amine forms of phenoxys can be used with greater safety near sensitive plants, but caution should still be exercised.

Equipment

Do not apply insecticides, fungicides, or other herbicides with equipment used for 2,4-D because of the difficulty of removing this herbicide from most sprayers.

General Pesticide Information

Labels

Observe all directions, restrictions, and precautions on pesticide labels. It is dangerous, wasteful, and illegal to do otherwise.

Table 5.2. Herbicides for homeowner lawn weed management

Herbicide	St. Augustinegrass	Bahiagrass	Centipedegrass	Zoysiagrass
atrazine	Yes	No	Yes	Yes
atrazine + bentazon	Yes	No	Yes	Yes
benefin	Yes	Yes	Yes	Yes
benefin + trifluralin	Yes	Yes	Yes	Yes
bensulide	Yes	Yes	Yes	Yes
bentazon	Yes	Yes	Yes	Yes
dicamba	Yes	Yes	Yes	Yes
dithiopyr	Yes	Yes	Yes	Yes
ethofumesate	Yes	No	No	No
fenoxaprop	No	No	No	Yes
halosulfuron	Yes	Yes	Yes	Yes
imazaquin	Yes	No	Yes	Yes
metolachlor	Yes	Yes	Yes	Yes
MSMA	No	No	No	Yes
oryzalin	Yes	Yes	Yes	Yes
oxadiazon	Yes	No	No	Yes
pendimethalin	Yes	Yes	Yes	Yes
simazine	Yes	No	Yes	Yes
2,4-D + dicamba + MCPP, MCPA, and/or 2,4-DP	Yes	Yes	Yes	Yes

Table 5.3. Common and brand names of herbicides

Common Name	Brand Name
atrazine	many brands
atrazine + bentazon	Prompt
bentazon	Basagran T/O
Hi-Yield	Basagran
benefin	Balan
benefin + trifluralin	Team
benefin + oryzalin	XL
bensulide	Betasan
	Bensumec
	Pro Turf Weedgrass Preventer
	Pre-San
	Lescogran
CAMA	Ortho Weed-B-Gon Crabgrass Killer
dicamba	Banvel
dithiopyr	Dimension
diquat	Spectracide Systemic Grass and Weed Killer
ethofumesate	Prograss
fenoxaprop	Acclaim Extra
fluazifop	Grass Away
	Grass Out
	Grass-B-Gone
	Fertilome Over-the-Top Grass Killer
	Spectracide Grass and Weed Killer 2
glyphosate	RoundUp
	Real Kill Weed and Grass Killer
halosulfuron	Manage
imazaquin	Image
metolachlor	Pennant
metsulfuron	Manor
	Blade
MSMA	many brands
oryzalin	Surflan
pendimethalin	Pendulum
	Pre-M
	Turf Weedgrass Control
	Halts Crabgrass Preventer
prodiamine	Sam's Choice Crabgrass Preventer
sethoxydim	Vantage T/O
simazine	Princep
triclopyr	Ortho Brush-B-Gon
2,4-D + dicamba + MCPP, MCPA, and/or 2,4-DP	many brands
2,4-D + MCPP + dicamba + carfentrazone	SpeedZone for St. Augustinegrass
	SpeedZone
MCPA + MCPP + dicamba + carfentrazone	PowerZone

Storage

Store pesticides behind locked doors in original containers with label intact, separate from seed and fertilizer.

Dosage

Use pesticides at correct dosage and intervals between applications to avoid illegal residues or injury to plants and animals.

Rinsing

Triple-rinse empty containers into the spray tank. Never pour pesticides down a drain or into an area exposed to humans, animals, or water.

Disposal

Dispose of used containers in compliance with label directions so that water contamination or other hazards do not result.

Clothing

Always wear protective clothing when applying pesticides. At a minimum, wear a long-sleeved shirt, long-legged pants, rubber gloves, boots (never go barefoot or wear sandals), eye protection, and a wide-brimmed hat. Additional protective gear may be listed on the pesticide label.

Handling

Never eat, drink, or smoke when handling pesticides, and always wash with soap and water after use.

Insect Management

Several insects and insect relatives live in Florida lawns, but not all of them hurt the grass. Many are harmless, some are beneficial, and some are pests. Only a few cause significant damage and need immediate control. For example, chinch bugs, spittlebugs, and grass scales live on plant foliage and suck plant juices. Other pests, including sod webworms, grass loopers, and armyworms, eat grass leaves. Mole crickets, white grubs, and billbugs live in the soil and primarily damage grass roots, in addition to creating tunnels and/or mounds. Other insects and related pests (e.g., fleas, ticks, millipedes, chiggers, sowbugs, and snails) are nuisances because they may bite people or pets or invade houses, garages, or swimming pools.

Sometimes it's easy to confuse beneficial insects with pests. For example, certain insects (e.g., big-eyed bugs, anthocorids, and nabids) look like chinch bugs, but are actually predators and feed on chinch bug eggs and nymphs. Earwigs, ground beetles, and spiders search through the grass and feed on chinch bugs, webworms, and several other lawn pests. The presence of beneficial organisms likely prevents the insect pests from increasing to damaging levels.

However, such natural enemies can't kill all of the pests. A small pest population needs to survive to maintain these beneficial organisms. Preventive or by-the-calendar treatments (pesticide applications made every four to eight weeks) may kill many beneficial organisms and contribute to a persistent pest problem. Thus, pesticides should be applied only when damage is apparent.

Research has demonstrated that the need for pesticide applications to control insect outbreaks can be reduced by following these management practices:

Monitoring

Early detection of insects is vital to any management program. Check the lawn for pest activity every fourteen days in the winter and every seven to ten days in the spring, summer, and fall, especially in "hot spots" where damage tends to recur.

Factors other than insect outbreaks can also result in thin or brown grass, including diseases, nematodes, drought, and nutritional disorders. Correct identification of the problem can save money, prevent excessive damage to the grass and forestall unnecessary pesticide applications. Specific monitoring tips will be discussed for each insect in this chapter.

Cultural Practices

The way grass is grown and maintained often affects insect survival and development. In general, healthy turf is less vulnerable to pests and can recover faster from an infestation. Attention to the following practices can reduce the need for pesticide use:

Nutrition

Overfertilization generally increases plant susceptibility to sap-feeding insects. Some insects tend to feed more on actively growing plant parts, rather than the older, slower-growing ones. The incidence of damage from these pests can be reduced with applications of minimum amounts of slow-release nitrogen fertilizers in combination with other macro- and micronutrients. Contact your local county Extension Service office or refer to the appropriate sections in this book for fertility recommendations.

Mowing

Improper mowing coupled with excessive watering and improper fertilization can cause lawn grasses to develop a thick, spongy mat of live, dead, and dying shoots, stems and roots that accumulate in a layer above the soil surface. This spongy mat, called thatch, is an excellent habitat for chinch bugs and caterpillars and chemically ties up insecticides, thereby reducing their effectiveness. When a serious thatch problem exists, it may be necessary to remove the thatch mechanically (vertical mowing, power raking, etc.). Proper mowing practices can make the grass more tolerant to pests and greatly improve the appearance of a lawn. Mow often enough so that no more than one-third of the leaf blade is removed each time.

Insects in Your Florida Lawn

Because of Florida's varied climatic and environmental conditions, many different insects can become problematic in your Florida lawn. The following sections describe a number of these destructive pests.

Armyworms, Cutworms, and Loopers

Description: Armyworms (plate 56), cutworms (plate 57), and loopers are brown to greenish in color and have stripes along their sides. Adults of the fall armyworm are light brown moths with a wingspan of about 1½ inches. The armyworm caterpillar is greenish when small and dark brown when mature. It has a light midstripe on its back with darker bands on either side. The midstripe ends in an inverted Y on the head. Cutworm caterpillars are mostly hairless. Armyworms, cutworms, and loopers grow to about 1½ inches in length.

Life Cycle: Armyworms and loopers may be present during the spring, summer, or fall. Armyworms and loopers differ from sod webworms in size and feeding habits. Moths lay eggs on grass or almost any object near lawns; they hatch within two weeks.

Monitoring: Monitor by mixing 1 tablespoon of liquid dishwashing soap in 1 gallon of water; pour the solution onto 4 square feet near the damage. Insects will crawl to the surface if present. Examine several suspected areas. Adults can be seen flying to lights at night.

Damage: Armyworm injury is similar to that of webworms, but the damage is often more scattered and not confined to patches. Populations of armyworms, webworms, and other lawn caterpillars often feed at the same time in the same location. Armyworms and loopers feed during the day and do not rest in a curled position. Cutworm caterpillars usually dig a burrow in the ground or thatch (or use an aeration hole) and emerge at night to chew off grass blades and shoots. This damage may appear as circular spots of dead grass or depressed spots that look like ball marks on golf greens.

Billbugs

Description: An adult billbug is a beetle (weevil) that has a "bill" or snout. It is black, and about ⅜ inch long (plate 58). The chewing mouthparts are at the end of the snout. Hunting billbug adults have a raised Y-shaped area surrounded by curved lines on the prothorax (behind the head) and rows of large and small pits on the wing covers (elytra). Billbug larvae are white, legless grubs with brown heads.

Life Cycle: Hunting billbugs appear to have one generation each year, but all life stages may be present at a time. Eggs are laid in the leaf sheaths or top of the crown and hatch within about ten days. Young larvae feed on the inner leaves and chew down to the roots. Pupation occurs in the soil or roots and may last up to seven days.

Monitoring: Billbugs are found throughout Florida and have become more of a problem in recent years. If grass consistently wilts in an area of the turf despite proper irrigation, an infestation of root-feeding billbugs should be suspected. Monitor off-color areas by cutting 1 square foot of sod 2 inches deep. Lay back the sod and examine roots for chewing damage, and check the soil and thatch for larvae. Replace the strip of sod and irrigate it. Check several places in the turf area.

Damage: Zoysiagrass and bermudagrass are preferred hosts for the hunting billbug. Most damage occurs in the fall, when populations are high, and may be misdiagnosed as dormancy. Dead patches or areas that green up slowly may also be noticed in the spring. Stems and rhizomes will break easily and have irregular feeding marks, and turf will not hold together if cut. Most damage occurs on infertile or dry soil. Adults also make small mounds when exiting the soil.

Control: Treatment may be necessary if ten to twelve billbugs are found per square foot. The soil should be moist at the time of insecticide application. Immediately irrigate with about ½ inch of water after applying the insecticide to move it into the soil where the insects are feeding. Parasitic nematodes (*Steinernema* and *Heterorhabditis*) and *Beauveria* fungus can also effectively control billbug larvae and adults.

Chinch Bugs

Description: The southern chinch bug (plate 59) is the most important insect pest of St. Augustinegrass in Florida, but may also feed on other turfgrasses and weeds. Adults are about ¹/₅ inch long and are black with white patches on the wings. The young (nymphs) range from ¹/₂₀ inch long to nearly adult size. Small nymphs are reddish orange with a white band across the back, but older nymphs and adults have black bodies.

Life Cycle: Sometimes adults hibernate during the winter in northern Florida, but all stages are present year-round in most of the state. Eggs are laid in grass sheaths or pushed into soft soil and protected places. In summer, eggs hatch in ten days and nymphs become adults in three weeks. There are three to four generations per year in northern Florida and seven to ten in southern Florida.

Monitoring: Chinch bugs can be found by several methods. First, part the grass near yellowed areas and look at the soil surface and base of the turf. Examine several different areas if chinch bugs aren't immediately found. In heavy infestations, chinch bugs can be seen crawling over grass blades, sidewalks, and outside walls of houses.

Another option is the flotation method. Cut both ends out of a metal can, such as a 3-pound coffee can. Push or twist one end 2–3 inches into the soil on green or yellowing grass (not dead grass). Cut the grass runners around the bottom edge of the can with a knife, if necessary. Slowly fill with water and count the number of chinch bugs that float to the top within five minutes.

Keep the water level above the grass surface during the five-minute period. If nothing emerges in the first area, examine three or four other areas.

Another, less labor-intensive option is to vacuum near a damaged area for about two minutes using a handheld vacuum cleaner. Remove the filter, dump the contents on the sidewalk, and look for nymphs and adults. Repeat in several damaged areas.

Damage: Southern chinch bugs prefer open, sunny areas of St. Augustinegrass, especially areas that are drought stressed, such as those near sidewalks and driveways. They live in the thatch and suck fluids from the crowns, stems, and stolons with their needlelike mouthparts. This causes the grass to turn yellow and die. Chinch bugs tend to feed in groups, so dead patches of grass appear and seem to get larger as they spread through the grass. Severe damage tends to occur from March through October in southern Florida and from April through September in northern Florida.

Control:

Resistant Varieties. Several varieties of St. Augustinegrass are used in Florida lawns, but the most common is 'Floratam.' Floratam was once very resistant to chinch bug damage, but some chinch bugs can now develop on and damage this variety. Other varieties such as 'Bitterblue,' 'Floratine,' 'Floralawn,' and 'Seville' are somewhat chinch bug resistant. 'Common,' 'Roselawn,' 'Raleigh,' 'Delmar,' and 'Jade' are very susceptible.

Beneficial Insects. Common predators of the southern chinch bug are big-eyed bugs (*Geocoris* spp.), earwigs (*Labidura* spp.), and anthocorids. A small wasp, *Eumicrosoma benefica,* parasitizes chinch bug eggs. Big-eyed bugs and anthocorids are similar to chinch bugs in size and shape and are often mistaken for them (plate 60). Unnecessary insecticide use can reduce these natural enemies and their ability to suppress pest populations.

Control with Pesticides. If twenty to twenty-five chinch bugs per square foot are detected, an insecticide application may be needed. Buy an insecticide that is specifically labeled for chinch bug control. Read and understand all directions on the container label regarding dosage rates, application information, and precautions. Spot-treat with a 5-foot buffer area when infestations are first noticed and damage is minimal, but treat the entire area if damage is widespread. Irrigate afterwards with ¼ inch of water to move the insecticide into the thatch. Inspect two to three times over the following four to six weeks to ensure that the infestation has been controlled. A correctly applied treatment should control chinch bugs for eight to ten weeks, but because many insecticides do not kill the eggs, repeated applications may be needed.

Ground Pearls

Description: Ground pearls (plate 61) are scale insects that live in the soil. They will suck fluids from the roots of most turfgrasses, but prefer centipedegrass. The "pearls" resemble some fertilizer granules. They occur throughout Florida, but are more abundant in the northern part of the state.

Life Cycle: Clusters of pinkish white eggs covered in a white waxy sac are laid in the soil from March to June. Tiny crawlers hatch from eggs, find a root, insert their piercing-sucking mouthparts, and cover themselves with a hard, yellowish to purple globular shell. These round "pearls" range in size from a grain of sand to about $1/16$ inch in diameter. They may occur as deep as 10 inches in the soil. After emerging from the "pearl," the adult female is $1/16$ inch long, pink colored, with well-developed forelegs and claws. Adult males are rare, tiny, gnatlike insects. One generation may last from one to two years or longer.

Damage: Symptoms attributed to ground pearl injury are first yellowing and then browning of the grass. Stressed grass is most susceptible to injury and may not be able to outgrow or survive ground pearl feeding damage. Properly watered and well-managed lawns often lack symptoms despite being heavily infested. Other factors such as disease, nutritional unbalances, drought, and nematodes (especially in centipedegrass) may cause off-color areas in lawns. The lawn should be carefully examined to determine which corrective measures may be needed. Weeds also tend to invade areas infested with ground pearls.

Control: Minimize plant stress and maintain proper fertility and soil moisture to help grass tolerate the damage. No insecticides are currently available for ground pearl control.

Mole Crickets

Description: Three exotic species of mole crickets occur in Florida, including the tawny (plate 62), southern, and shortwinged mole crickets. Adults are about 1½ inches long and light brown, with enlarged forelegs that they use to dig in soil. The forelegs have large blade-like projections called dactyls, and the number and arrangement of dactyls, as well as the pattern on the pronotum (area behind the head), are used to identify different species (plate 63). Nymphs look like adults, but their wings (wing pads) are not completely developed and they can't reproduce. Shortwinged mole cricket adults have short wings and cannot fly.

Life Cycle: In northern Florida, egg laying by tawny and southern mole crickets usually begins in late March and peaks in May through mid-June. Because of warmer temperatures, adult southern and tawny mole crickets emerge one to two weeks earlier in southern Florida. However, the shortwinged mole cricket can produce eggs throughout the year in southern Florida (this species doesn't occur in northern Florida). Mole crickets lay their eggs in chambers 2–12 inches below the soil surface. Egg chambers are closer to the surface in moist soil and deeper in dry conditions. Females may lay up to four or five clutches of eggs containing about twenty-five to sixty eggs per clutch. Eggs develop in about three weeks and most hatch during early June in northern Florida and through August in southern Florida. Some adults occur in August or September, but both nymphs and adults overwinter. Overwintering nymphs become adults by April, and adults fly and mate. One generation per year is normal, though southern mole crickets have two generations and fly three times (spring, summer, and autumn) in southern Florida.

Monitoring: Several methods are used to estimate mole cricket populations and to assist in timing pesticide applications, if they are needed. First, look at the soil and count the number of tunnels that are visible. Tunneling is easier to see in low-cut grass, but may be hard to see in St. Augustinegrass. Tunnels are most visible in early morning when the dew is on the grass and the soil is moist. To actually find the mole crickets, use the soap flush described in the armyworm section. Check several places in the lawn; if there are more than two to three large mole crickets per square foot, a treatment should be applied. In addition, watch for adult tawny and southern mole crickets near lights during their spring and fall dispersal flights.

Damage: Mole crickets damage turfgrass in several ways. Nymphs and adults feed on grass roots and blades at night after rain or irrigation during warm weather. Their tunneling near the soil surface dislodges plants or causes them to dry out. Small mounds of soil are also pushed up. More than 20 feet of tunneling per night has been observed. Tunneling and root-feeding reduce turfgrass density and create patches of bare soil.

Control:

Beneficial Insects. When mole crickets come to the soil surface, they are subject to predators, including fire ants, ground beetles, *Labidura* earwigs, and *Lycosa* spiders. Larger animals including raccoons, skunks, red foxes, armadillos, birds, and several toads also feed on mole crickets, but often damage turf areas when searching for them. Natural enemies, such as a parasitic wasp (*Larra bicolor*) and the Brazilian red-eyed fly (*Ormia depleta*), have been released by University of Florida researchers to suppress mole cricket populations. Nematodes, such as *Steinernema scapterisci*, can also effectively suppress mole crickets.

Control with Pesticides. If damage occurred the previous year or if excessive tunneling was noticed in the spring, a pesticide application may be needed. The optimum times to control mole crickets are in mid- to late June in northern Florida, and in late May in southern Florida. However, the nymphs will be small at this time, and damage may not be very noticeable. Using a soap flush, determine if mole crickets are present and treat accordingly.

Mole crickets can be controlled by sprays, granules, or baits. Use an insecticide specifically labeled for mole cricket control in home lawns. For best results, make sure the soil is moist (not soaked) when the treatment is applied. This helps the insecticide to penetrate into the soil, or, in the case of baits, encourages mole crickets to come to the surface to feed on the bait. Immediately following application (except for baits), apply ½ inch of water to move the insecticide into the top 1–2 inches of the soil. Bait formulations are useful against larger nymphs in late summer. Because mole crickets feed at night, baits should be applied in late afternoon or early evening. It is very important to scatter the bait evenly over the soil surface. Do not irrigate after application or apply a bait if rain is expected.

Spittlebugs

Description: Two-lined spittlebug nymphs may be yellow, orange, or white and are covered by a frothy mass of spittle. Adults (plate 64) are about ¼–½ inch long and black, with two reddish orange lines across the wings. Their eyes are dark red.

Life Cycle: Spittlebugs occur throughout the entire state, but are more numerous in northern and northwestern Florida. Although they prefer centipedegrass, they will attack all turfgrass species, many crops and weeds, and ornamental plants, especially hollies. Eggs are laid at the base of the grass in the thatch, in hollow grass stems, or behind the leaf sheaths. One generation may last 2–2½ months, and there are two generations per year. Eggs laid by the second generation overwinter and hatch the following spring, from late March to late April. The first generation adults are abundant in June. The adult population peaks again in early August to early September.

Monitoring: Most spittle masses are not obvious because they are located near the soil surface or in the thatch, but they may be more visible in the morning. Adults are most active during the early morning hours, but retreat to the soil surface during the heat of the day. They often jump from the leaf surfaces if the turf is disturbed.

Damage: Nymphs and adults suck plant juices through their piercing-sucking mouthparts. Adults, who inject a phytotoxic substance into the plants while feeding, cause most of the damage. Infested turf wilts, and the tips turn yellow, eventually brown, and then curl.

Control: Spittlebugs are rarely a problem on well-managed turf. They require high humidity for optimum development, and excess thatch provides good habitat. Follow approved practices regarding mowing, fertilization, and irrigation to reduce thatch buildup, and dethatch if necessary. If greater control is needed, purchase an insecticide specifically labeled for spittlebugs. Mow, dispose of clippings, and irrigate before an insecticide is applied so the insecticide effectively reaches the thatch layer.

Tropical Sod Webworm

Description: The most damaging caterpillar is the tropical sod webworm (plate 65). Larvae are gray green and have brown spots on each segment. Mature larvae reach about ¾–1 inch in length. Sod webworm adults are small tan to gray moths with a wingspan of ¾–1 inch.

Life Cycle: Eggs are deposited on the grass blades and hatch after about one week. Larvae feed on the grass blades and cause noticeable injury within two weeks. There may be rather extensive damage within the next 1–1½ weeks until pupation. Adults appear about one week later. Moths fly low to the grass when disturbed and hide in shrubs and other sheltered areas during the day. Three generations occur in northern Florida and four generations occur in southern Florida. Most activity occurs from April through November, but may occur year-round in southern Florida.

Monitoring: Part the grass in suspect areas and closely examine the soil surface. Look for chewed leaves, silken webs, green frass (excrement), and larvae. A flashlight used at night will reveal the caterpillars feeding in the grass foliage. Soap flushes (2 tablespoons of liquid dishwashing soap mixed in 2 gallons of water) also help by drenching larvae and other potential pests out of the ground. Pour the mixture on 1 square yard of damaged grass, and see what emerges within five minutes. If nothing emerges in the first area, examine at least three or four other places.

Damage: Sod webworm damage becomes visible from June through August. The webworms feed primarily at night and remain in a curled position on or near the soil surface during the day. This habit makes them difficult to find. Newly hatched caterpillars cause little visible damage to grass, although they can skeletonize grass blades. Older caterpillars chew notches along the sides of the blades, and serious damage seems to occur almost overnight. The foliage may be almost completely stripped off in patches, and these close-cropped areas soon become yellowish to brownish. Adults do not cause damage.

White Grubs

Description: Several species of white grubs damage grass, including May or June beetles (*Phyllophaga* spp.) and masked chafers (*Cyclocephala* spp.). White grubs (plate 66) are the creamy white, C-shaped larvae of scarab beetles. They have brownish heads and six legs (unlike legless billbug larvae). Mature grubs vary in length from ¼ to 2 inches, depending on the species. The grubs also have a pattern of hairs (raster) on the tip of their abdomen, which is important in identification.

Life Cycle: Masked chafers have a one-year life cycle. Adults are tan, about ⅝ inch long, and often present from May to July. Adults lay their eggs in the top inch or two of soil, often in small clusters. Small grubs hatch from the eggs and begin feeding on grass roots. Second or third instar grubs may move deeper in the soil as the weather cools and come up again in the spring to feed on the grass roots. They pupate in earthen cells and emerge as adults to begin a new cycle.

May or June beetles have mostly one-year life cycles. Adults are dark brown, may be hairy, and are less than 1 inch long. They emerge from April through July, mate, and lay eggs in the soil. They may feed on tree leaves. Little is known about their larval habits.

Monitoring: If grubs are suspected, cut 2 inches deep into a 1-foot-square area near damaged grass. Lay the grass back, check the quality of the roots, and look for grubs in the soil. If grubs are present, they may be in the upper 4–6 inches of soil or in the thatch. In addition, frass or tunneling may be visible, and grass roots will look pruned. Check several places in the turf. If grubs are commonly a problem in an area, examine all turf in May and again in August. Don't wait for brown patches to appear before inspecting the soil. It is normal to find a couple of small white grubs per square foot in turfgrass. The mere presence of a grub is not necessarily a problem because healthy turf can easily outgrow minor root loss, but certain grubs (e.g., *Ligyrus subtropicus*) can be damaging in low numbers. Also look for adult scarab beetles flying at night around windows or porch lights in the spring and early summer to determine when adults are laying eggs in moist turfgrass.

When grubs are found, examine their raster (hair) patterns, located on the bottom of the last abdominal segment, with a 10- or 15-power hand lens (plate 67). May or June beetle grubs have two very distinct rows of short hairs, whereas chafer larvae have no distinct raster pattern.

Damage: White grubs occur throughout Florida but tend to cause more damage along the Gulf Coast. When white grubs feed on grass roots, the grass gradually thins, yellows, wilts, and dies. Scattered, irregular, brown patches of grass appear and increase in size over time. The root injury reduces the turf's ability to take up water and nutrients and to withstand the stress of hot, dry weather. Heavily infested grass may either roll back like a carpet because the root system is gone or be kicked around like hay. Grubs usually feed for several months before any turf damage becomes visible, and areas tend to be reinvaded year after year. Feeding by second and third instar grubs can be severe. Adult beetles usually do not feed on grass, but may feed on flowers and foliage of ornamental plants.

Control: Minimize conditions that attract beetles and favor grub development, such as irrigation during adult flights (especially if surrounding areas are dry) and the use of organic fertilizers.

Curative treatments are usually applied in late summer after the eggs have hatched and grubs are feeding. Because most insecticides used on turf have relatively short residuals (less than three weeks), a curative application needs to be timed correctly. The best time is when grubs are small and their feeding damage is relatively light. As they grow, they become progressively harder to control, and root damage may be severe. Monitor infestations to be sure of accurate timing, and irrigate with about ½ inch of water after the application to keep the grubs near the soil surface and to wash in the pesticide.

White grubs tend to occur in localized populations, so an application "just in case" grubs are present is not advised. But in those spots where grubs do reoccur, preventive applications may help. Preventive treatments increase flexibility in application timing, are easier to schedule and implement than curative treatments, and require less sampling and monitoring of grub populations. Such insecticides have a longer residual in the soil and give good control of newly hatched white grubs when applied weeks or even months before grub hatch. But the optimum timing is during the month or so before egg hatch until the time when very young grubs are present.

Notes on Control

Apply insecticides properly. Read and understand all directions on the container label regarding dosage rates, application information, and precautions. When a spray is applied for controlling insects, it is important to apply the insecticide in a large amount of water. The jar attachment to a garden hose is the suggested application device for lawns. The type that requires 15–20 gallons of water passing through the hose to empty the quart size jars is recommended. Put the amount of insecticide in the jar as directed on the label for 1000 square feet. Fill the jar the rest of the way with water. Spray the contents over 1000 square feet. To insure even coverage, spray back and forth across the measured area, then turn at right angles and spray back and forth across the same area.

When spraying for control of soil insects (mole crickets, white grubs, and billbugs), the turf should be moist at the time of application. Immediately after spraying the insecticide, irrigate with about ½ inch of water to move the insecticide into the soil where the insects are feeding. For control of surface feeders (chinch bugs, lawn caterpillars, bermudagrass mites, grass scales, and spittlebugs), do not irrigate after application.

Granular formulations for the recommended insecticides may be substituted for sprays in controlling chinch bugs, webworms, mole crickets, white grubs, or billbugs. If applied for soil insects (mole crickets, white grubs, or billbugs), irrigate with about ¾ inch of water immediately after applying.

To help prevent unnecessary environmental contamination and reduction of beneficial insects, spot treatments can be applied when infestations are new and the damaged area is small. Treat the off-color area and about a 5–10-foot buffer area surrounding it. If damage is widespread over the yard or if many infested areas are detected, the entire yard should be treated. Inspect the area two to three times at biweekly intervals to determine if infestation is under control.

Precautions

Insecticides are poisons and should be handled as such. Read the manufacturer's label carefully before opening the container, and observe all instructions and precautions. Wear rubber gloves when handling and applying insecticides. Do not spill sprays on skin or clothing. Do not breathe mists or fumes. Wash exposed parts of the body with soap and water immediately after using insecticides.

Store pesticides locked up in original labeled containers and out of reach of children. Rinse empty containers and put rinse water in spray tank. To dispose of the empty container (1 gallon or smaller), wrap in newspaper, crush or puncture to prevent reuse, and put in garbage can for disposal in an approved sanitary landfill.

Disease Management

Turfgrass diseases are difficult to understand because the biological organisms (plant pathogens) causing the problems are rarely observed. Fortunately, grasses maintained using proper cultural practices (water, mowing, and fertility) are not as likely to become diseased or be as severely damaged as grasses not receiving proper care. The following section discusses turfgrass diseases, their causal agents, diagnosis, and management.

What Is a Disease?

Diseases are the exception and not the rule for lawns. Observing spots and patches of yellow or brown turfgrass does not necessarily mean your lawn has a disease. Because diseases are difficult to diagnose, it is often faster to rule out involvement of *other* factors than to verify the presence of disease. By determining if other factors are causing the turf to look "sick," you will solve the problem more quickly and avoid applying unnecessary fungicides.

An *injury* to turfgrass is a destructive physical occurrence such as pesticide damage (plate 68), mowing the grass too short (plate 69), or a fuel leak. A turfgrass *disorder* is associated with imbalances of physical or chemical requirements for turfgrass growth. Examples would be nutritional deficiencies, cold temperatures, drought (plate 70), or excessive rainfall.

A *disease* is an interaction between the plant and a pathogen that disrupts the normal growth and appearance of the plant. While turfgrasses may be affected by diseases all year, individual turf diseases are active for only a few months each year, usually because of weather patterns and resulting environmental effects. However, any stress (environmental or manmade) placed on the turf will weaken it, making it more susceptible to diseases.

Turfgrass diseases in Florida are caused by fungi (molds in your bathroom are fungi; the green stuff on an old orange or old bread is fungi). Most fungi living in lawns are totally harmless. In fact, they are beneficial because they decompose (break down) the grass clippings and old roots. A very small number of fungi cause plant diseases. It is important to know that when a fungal pathogen is not actively attacking the plant, it has not disappeared from the turfgrass area. It is simply surviving in the environment in a state of dormancy (like a bear in hibernation) or as a saprophyte (nonpathogenic phase), living off dead organic materials in the thatch and soil layers.

Disease Symptoms

There are two common patterns of turfgrass disease symptoms. One is a circular patch of turfgrass, either small or large, that is no longer uniformly green. The second is turf that has "spots" on the leaves. If disease patches are present, examine the leaves and roots in these patches for characteristic symptoms of a disease and signs (actual fungal structures) of the pathogen (see key and description of individual diseases that follow). The best time to observe fungal mycelia is in the early morning when dew is still present. Early afternoon is a good time to look for localized patches of wilt or drought symptoms that may indicate root or crown diseases. For turf with spots, note the color and shape of the spots.

Disease Control Is Not Simple or Easy!

Disease control recommendations are aimed at: (1) altering the environment so it is less favorable for disease development, (2) suppressing growth of the pathogen, and (3) decreasing stress on turfgrass. An integrated management program that includes cultural and chemical methods is the key to preventing and controlling turfgrass diseases.

There are three steps to disease management. First, correctly identify the disease. Second, identify the conditions promoting disease development. Third, identify the management techniques that will alter or eliminate these conducive conditions.

Cultural Control Practices

Cultural practices should create an environment that does *not* promote disease development. We realize you cannot change weather patterns (the overall environment), but you can change localized environments. Water-saturated soils due to excessive irrigation are a local environmental condition created by humans. The north side of the house is cooler and receives less sun than the south side. A big oak or *Ficus* tree creates a local environment that is much different than that under a palm tree or in an area with no trees. *Remember that every maintenance practice, fertilizer application, and chemical (especially herbicide) application has an impact on turfgrass health.*

The cultural practices discussed below are all designed to alter the turfgrass environment to prevent diseases or at least lessen their severity. For more specific details on each topic, see the relevant chapters in this book.

Turfgrass Selection

The selection of turfgrass species (St. Augustinegrass, centipedegrass, bahiagrass, etc.) and cultivars within that species (example: 'Floratam' vs. 'Raleigh' St. Augustinegrass) should be based on your location and how the turf will be used and maintained. Selections that are not suited for a particular area will be continually stressed and more susceptible to diseases (and other pests) and will require increased maintenance costs in terms of labor and pesticides. For example, it is difficult to grow St. Augustinegrass without supplemental irrigation. Centipedegrass should be grown on soils with low pH (less than 6.0). Check with your county Extension Service office for local recommendations.

Mowing Practices

Mowing is the most common turfgrass maintenance practice and the most damaging when done improperly. Mowers must be sharp so they cut rather than tear the turf leaves. Turfgrasses that are cut below their optimum height will become stressed and more susceptible to diseases, especially root rots. Be sure to mow as frequently as necessary so that *no more* than half of the leaf is being removed at any one time. The actual recommended turf height depends on the turfgrass species being grown. It is especially important not to mow St. Augustinegrass too low. A lawn is not a golf course, so don't mow your lawn to look like one.

Mulching mowers do not increase diseases. However, if an area of your lawn has an active leaf disease, this area should be mowed *last* to prevent the spread of the disease. Likewise, wash the mower with water after mowing the diseased area to remove diseased leaf clippings.

Water Management

Irrigate only when drought stress is observed (as evidenced by curled leaf blades), and then apply enough water to saturate the root zone of the turfgrass. Make sure the irrigation system is applying the water uniformly across the lawn. Irrigating every day for a few minutes is not beneficial for the turfgrass because it does not provide enough water to the root zone, but it *is* beneficial for the turfgrass pathogens. It is always best to apply the water in the early morning hours (after 2:00 a.m.). This saves water and helps to reduce disease development.

Nutrition (Fertilizer) Management

Both excessively high and excessively low nitrogen fertility contribute to turfgrass diseases. Excessive nitrogen applications encourage brown patch and gray leaf spot diseases. Very low nitrogen levels encourage dollar spot disease. Remember, it is easy to add nitrogen but impossible to remove it. Therefore, apply the minimal amount of nitrogen required for your particular turfgrass lawn.

Potassium (K) seems to be an important component in the prevention of diseases, perhaps because it prevents plant stress. To maintain healthy turfgrass, the amount of elemental potassium applied should be either the same or greater than the amount of nitrogen. Refer to "Fertilizer Recommendations for Your Florida Lawn" in chapter 3. In an area prone to disease, it would be beneficial to increase the amount of potassium applied. It is important to remember that potassium will leach just as readily as nitrogen. The use of both nitrogen and potassium from slow-release sources is highly encouraged. If it is not possible to obtain slow-release potassium, apply smaller amounts of quick-release potassium more frequently. This is especially useful during the rainy season.

When turfgrass roots are damaged or not functioning properly, whether from diseases, nematodes or water-saturated soils, it is beneficial to apply nutrients in a liquid solution sprayed on the leaf tissue. Damaged roots will have a difficult time absorbing nutrients from the soil. Frequent applications of small amounts of nutrients to the leaves will help keep the plant alive until new roots are produced.

Thatch Management

Thatch is the tightly bound layer of living and dead stems and roots that develops between the zone of green vegetation and the soil surface. It is a natural component of turfgrass. When excessive thatch accumulates, it means plant tissue is being produced more quickly than it is being decomposed. Bacteria, fungi, earthworms, and other organisms that naturally live in the soil decompose thatch.

Excessive thatch often causes the mower to sink because the turfgrass is "spongy." This produces a lower cutting height than desired and potential scalping of St. Augustinegrass, which will result in stressed turf. Physical removal is the best way to eliminate excessive thatch. To prevent excessive thatch from occurring again, review your maintenance practices. Are you applying too much nitrogen? Are you applying too much, or not enough, water when you irrigate? Correct those practices that may be promoting excess thatch development.

Soil Physical and Chemical Status

Compacted soils will prevent proper drainage, causing areas to remain excessively wet. Turfgrass in these areas may have root systems that are deprived of oxygen, resulting in a weak plant. This is also an ideal situation for root rots to develop. High soil pH may affect nutrient uptake and weaken the plant. High salt concentrations will impact turfgrass health, making a plant more susceptible to diseases.

If you have areas in the lawn or landscape that appear to dry out first or are the first to appear "sick," use a metal rod to be sure that there is nothing buried at that location. It is not uncommon to find discarded building materials buried in the landscape. If you have an area that is water-logged for long periods, build that area up and make it level with the rest of the lawn.

Chemical Control Practices

What Is a Fungicide?

Fungicides are pesticides used to manage fungal diseases. Fungicides suppress or slow down fungal growth or prevent the fungus from reproducing. Most fungicides are active against a limited group of fungi. This is why it is important to know what disease you need to control.

Fungicides do *not* promote the growth of the turfgrass. The only way healthy turfgrass will reappear is when new growth occurs. For example, a leaf spot will remain on the leaf, even after a fungicide is applied. This diseased leaf area will remain until it is removed by mowing and a new leaf replaces it. Since many of the turfgrass diseases to be described later occur when the grass is not growing actively, complete recovery may be very slow. You may think you are seeing no response to the fungicide application when in fact the fungicide has been effective against the fungal target. It is simply that the turfgrass has not grown enough to replace the diseased tissue.

When to Use a Fungicide

It is acceptable to use fungicides on a preventive basis (prior to disease development) as long as you really understand what diseases/pathogens you are protecting the grass from at any given time of the year. For example: why apply a fungicide to protect against *Pythium* blight on St. Augustinegrass when this is an extremely rare disease? Why apply a fungicide to prevent take-all root rot when you have never observed this problem in your lawn?

Use fungicides only when absolutely necessary. Just because your neighbor has a lawn disease, it does not mean it will occur on your lawn, as your management techniques or turfgrass cultivar may be different. Remember that the primary factor for turfgrass disease development in Florida is the environment—not just the overall environment, but also the microenvironment created by placement of the buildings in your landscape site or by your management practices. In fact, each side of the house may have its own microenvironment, influenced by trees, other buildings, bodies of water, soil type, and so on.

Read Labels!

You would not or should not give a family member any medication without following the instructions on the label. Turfgrass pesticides deserve the same amount of respect. Almost all pesticide failures are due to misapplication, including misidentification of the problem! Don't waste your money, become a safety risk, or pollute the environment by using a product incorrectly. Remember that *following labels is the law*; they are considered legal documents!

Turfgrass Disease Samples

County extension agents and the Plant Disease Clinic at the University of Florida in Gainesville cannot diagnose a problem if all they are sent is dead grass. Samples *must* be adequate in both quality and quantity in order to make a proper analysis. The best samples brought to the county extension office represent various stages of disease development: beginning symptoms, moderately severe symptoms, and severe symptoms. For turfgrass diseases, there is no reason to test water or soil for plant pathogens. Why? Because the presence or absence of pathogens in these types of samples is not necessarily indicative of a disease problem. In addition, some pathogens cannot be isolated from water or soil (*Gaeumannomyces* spp.), whereas other pathogens are always present (*Pythium* spp.).

Many of the fungi that cause turfgrass diseases have the ability to survive on plants or in soil all year. The recovery of a particular pathogen from unhealthy turfgrass is not always sufficient evidence of a disease. The person collecting the sample must provide as much background information as possible in order for a final diagnosis to be made. Include pictures of the problem area with the sample!

Diseases are the exception and not the rule for most turfgrass plantings. Not every turfgrass problem is automatically a disease problem. Because diseases are difficult to diagnose, it is often faster to rule out involvement of other factors than to verify the presence of disease. A plant disease diagnosis only indicates what *potential* turfgrass pathogens are present—all of them. Without knowing the entire situation surrounding the problem, it is extremely difficult to pinpoint the actual pathogen.

Key for Identification of Landscape Turfgrass Diseases

The following is a general key that may help in making a preliminary diagnosis. Symptoms are presented as a series of choices in pairs of statements (four choices in one case); each choice in the pair leads either to another choice or to an identification of the disease. Please see the section following the key for more specific diagnostic characteristics and information concerning the time of year the disease is most likely to occur.

1a. Distinct patches of yellow to brown grass are present 2

1b. No distinct patches are present 5

2a. Patch areas are less than 3 inches in diameter. Leaf spot lesions are present
Dollar Spot

2b. Patch areas are greater than 3 inches in diameter. Leaf spot lesions are not present 3

3a. Ring or arc of lush growth or dead grass; mushrooms may be present
Fairy Ring

3b. No rings or arc of lush growth 4

4a. Affected areas are distinct circular patches. Leaf pulls out of leaf sheath easily .... Brown Patch

4b. Affected areas are irregular patches 8–24 inches in diameter or larger, with a mixture of yellow and dead grass. Roots are short and black. Stolons may be rotted also .... Take-all Root Rot

5a. Orange "spots" are present on leaves; "spots" rub off easily .... Rust

5b. Orange "spots" are not present on leaves 6

6a. Leaf spots are present 7

6b. No leaf spots are present 8

7a. Primarily on bermudagrass and ryegrass. Leaf spots have a wide range of sizes .... *Helminthosporium* Leaf Spot

7b. Primarily on St. Augustinegrass in summer. Leaf spots oval to irregular with brown borders and tan to gray centers .... Gray Leaf Spot

7c. Primarily on St. Augustinegrass in late spring and summer. Narrow, dark brown leaf spots initially, becoming oblong irregular spots with dark tan centers and brown borders .... *Cercospora* Leaf Spot

7d. Primarily on centipedegrass. Reddish brown to brown spots surrounded by a yellow halo .... Anthracnose

8a. Grass is covered with an easily removed slimy or crusty growth ....
.... Slime Mold

8b. Grass is chlorotic (yellow) or has mottled leaves associated with general decline ....*Pythium* Root Rot *or* Nematodes

Diagnostic Features and Control of Turfgrass Diseases

The following section will describe the common diseases found on turfgrasses used in the landscape in Florida, primarily on St. Augustinegrass. It is set up in the following format:

Disease: This is the correct name for the problem.

Pathogen: This is the Latin name of the fungus that causes the disease. The first word is the genus name, and the second word is the species name.

Occurrence: The exact time when a disease will occur is dependent on the environment. The time of year when the disease is most likely to occur is indicated. Since there are distinct climatic variations in Florida (north vs. south; coastal vs. inland), these variations should be considered when diagnosing a disease problem. The situations (ex: rain or fog) or stresses (ex: nitrogen deficiency) that will cause the disease to occur or make it worse are stated.

Symptoms/Signs: This section describes the appearance of the turf when diseased.

Cultural Controls: This section describes the cultural controls you can employ to prevent the disease or to help the turfgrass recover from the disease.

Chemical Controls: Chemical control treatments (fungicides) are listed by common name only. Since an active ingredient (common name) may have multiple trade names, only one example of a corresponding trade name is provided in table 5.4. Fungicide labels change frequently, so read the label to determine if the product is still legal to use on the turfgrass site. Many fungicides for lawns are available only through specialty outlet stores; for example, Lesco (look under Landscaping Equipment and Supplies in the yellow pages of your phone book). Alternatively, you can have them applied by a certified pesticide applicator. Note that mancozeb fungicides can be applied only by a certified pesticide applicator.

Fungicides suppress or inhibit fungal growth. They do not stimulate turfgrass growth. In many cases, diseases occur when the turf is not growing rapidly, usually because of suboptimal temperatures. Under these circumstances, recovery from a disease will be slow. After all, to replace diseased leaf tissue the grass plant must produce new leaves.

Disease: Anthracnose
Pathogen: Colletotrichum graminicola
Occurrence: This disease primarily affects centipedegrass. It is normally ob-

Table 5.4. Common names of chemical fungicides with examples of trade name products

Fungicide Common Name	Trade Name Example
azoxystrobin	Heritage
chloroneb	Terraneb
etridiazole (ethazol)	Koban, Terrazole
flutolanil	ProStar
fosetyl-al	Aliette
fludioxonil	Medallion
mancozeb	Dithane T/O
mefenoxam	Subdue MAXX
myclobutanil	Eagle
polyoxin D	Endorse
propamocarb	Banol
propiconazole	Banner MAXX
quintozene (PCNB)	Terraclor
thiophanate methyl	Fungo, Cleary 3336
triadimefon	Bayleton
trifloxystrobin	Compass

served in the spring during periods of high moisture (rain or heavy fog) and warm temperatures. Disease severity is often greater on stressed turfgrass, especially during springs following cold winters.

Symptoms/Signs: Leaf infection appears as reddish brown to brown spots that are often surrounded by a narrow yellow halo. Single spots may span the blade width, causing leaf yellowing and then death of the leaf. Tiller infection results in death of stems and the development of small, yellow patches of turfgrass (plate 71).

Cultural Controls: Avoid potassium deficiency. Do not apply excessive nitrogen during potential disease development periods. Do not use readily available forms of nitrogen such as soluble liquids or quick-release nitrogen sources just prior to or during these periods. Instead, use slow-release nitrogen sources. Apply a balanced fertilizer containing equivalent amounts of potassium, preferably a slow-release potassium form.

Avoid drought stress. Irrigate deeply to saturate the root zone. Irrigate only in the early morning hours (between 2:00 and 8:00 a.m.) when dew is already present. If the diseased areas are associated with compacted soils, alleviate the compaction. If thatch is excessive, renovate.

Chemical Controls: Azoxystrobin, myclobutanil, propiconazole, thiophanate methyl, triadimefon, and trifloxystrobin

Disease: Brown Patch (also called *Rhizoctonia* Blight)
Pathogen: Rhizoctonia solani
Occurrence: This disease is most likely to be observed from November through May when temperatures are below 80°F. It is normally *not* observed in the summer. Infection is triggered by rainfall, excessive irrigation, or extended

periods of high humidity resulting in the leaves being continuously wet for forty-eight hours or more.

Symptoms/Signs: The fungus infects the leaf area closest to the soil, eventually killing the leaf. A soft, dark rot will occur at the base of the leaf, and you can easily pull a leaf off the stem (plate 72). The base of this pulled leaf will smell rotted. Roots are not affected by this pathogen.

This disease usually begins as small patches (about 1 foot in diameter) that turn yellow and then reddish brown, brown, or straw colored as the leaves start to die. Patches can expand to several feet in diameter (plate 73). It is not uncommon to see rings of yellow/brown turf with apparently healthy turf in the center. Turf at the outer margin of a patch may appear dark and wilted (plate 74).

This disease is often confused with herbicide damage on St. Augustinegrass. Herbicide damage may cause the same overall symptoms of yellow or brown patches. The leaf may still pull out of the leaf sheath, but the base of the leaf is *not* dark and rotted (plate 75). Instead, the leaf base is dry with a tan discoloration, and there is no distinct "rotten" smell.

Cultural Controls: Avoid excess nitrogen during potential disease development periods. Do not use readily available forms of nitrogen such as soluble liquids or quick-release nitrogen sources just prior to or during these periods. Instead, use slow-release nitrogen sources. Apply a balanced fertilizer containing equivalent amounts of potassium, preferably a slow-release potassium form.

Irrigate only when necessary and do so only in the early morning hours (between 2:00 and 8:00 a.m.) when dew is already present. Since mowers can spread this disease, mow diseased areas last, and wash turf clippings off the mower before proceeding to the next site.

Chemical Controls: Azoxystrobin, fludioxonil, flutolanil, mancozeb, myclobutanil, PCNB, polyoxin D, propiconazole, thiophanate methyl, triadimefon, and trifloxystrobin.

Many of these products are effective for Brown Patch *only* as preventive applications. In other words, they need to be used *prior* to disease development. Read the labels carefully before selecting a product. Mancozeb can be applied to a residential lawn *only* by a certified pesticide applicator.

Disease: Cercospora Leaf Spot
Pathogen: Cercospora fusimaculans
Occurrence: This disease is observed between the late spring and summer seasons, especially during periods of frequent rainfall. Areas of St. Augustinegrass that are under cultural or environmental stresses are more susceptible to disease development. Areas of turf under low fertility or suboptimal light conditions seem to develop this disease.

Symptoms/Signs: Initial symptoms are narrow, dark brown leaf spots that enlarge over time into oblong to irregularly shaped lesions with dark tan centers and dark brown to purple margins (plate 76). Under humid conditions, the abundant sporulation of the pathogen in the lesion centers may confer a whitish sheen to the spots.

Numerous spots on multiple leaves can cause extensive yellowing and withering of the canopy. This disease is very similar in lawn pattern and symptoms to that of Gray Leaf Spot, but management is very different.

Cultural Controls: Prevent the disease by fertilizing adequately, using slow-release nitrogen sources balanced with potassium (preferably, a slow-release potassium form). Examine the irrigation cycle for timing, frequency, and amount. Time irrigation so as not to extend the dew period (between 2:00 and 8:00 a.m.). Water only when the turf exhibits moisture stress. Avoid daily, frequent irrigation cycles that promote foliar disease.

If *Cercospora* leaf spot is already present, the disease can be managed with the application of quick-release nitrogen in a fertilizer blend balanced with potassium (N:K ratio of 1:1). Apply ½ pound N per 1000 square feet, using an ammonium nitrate, ammonium sulfate, or quick-release urea formulation.

Where *Cercospora* leaf spot is persistent, St. Augustinegrass cultivars derived from 'Bitterblue' types offer more resistance to this disease.

Chemical Controls: Mancozeb, myclobutanil, thiophanate methyl, or triadimefon. Mancozeb can be applied to a residential lawn only by a certified pesticide applicator.

Disease: Dollar Spot
Pathogen: Sclerotinia homoeocarpa
Occurrence: This disease is most likely to be observed from fall through spring, and only on turfgrass areas with suboptimal nitrogen levels. Other factors associated with the disease are a dry root system combined with a humid leaf canopy. The humid leaf canopy may be due to high air humidity, light rainfall, or too little irrigation applied too frequently at the wrong time. See information on water and disease development.

Symptoms/Signs: Small (1–3 inches in diameter), brown to straw colored patches of dead grass will develop (plate 77). Irregular, light tan lesions with distinct brown borders will be present on the leaves at the outside edge of the patch (plate 78). The small individual patches do not expand in size, but as the number of patches increase, they may merge together to form larger patches. White, cottony mycelia may be observed in the early morning hours when dew is present.

Cultural Controls: Prevent the disease by avoiding extreme nitrogen deficiency. Use slow-release nitrogen fertilizers, and balance the nitrogen with potassium, preferably a slow-release potassium form. During dry weather, apply adequate water so the root zone is fully saturated each time you irrigate. Irrigate during the early morning hours (2:00 to 8:00 a.m.) when dew is already present.

If the disease is already present, apply a quick-release source of nitrogen (½ pound N per 1000 square feet) (plate 79) such as ammonium sulfate, ammonium nitrate, or quick-release urea (uncoated urea). Follow up with an application of slow-release nitrogen, balanced with potassium. This is just as effective as fungicides. If the soil is dry, irrigate to fully saturate the root zone.

Chemical Controls: Mancozeb, myclobutanil, PCNB, propiconazole, thiophanate methyl, and triadimefon. Mancozeb can be applied to a residential lawn only by a certified pesticide applicator.

Disease: Fairy Rings
Causal Agent(s): Chlorophyllum, Marasmius, Lepiota, Lycoperdon, and other basidiomycete fungi
Occurrence: Fairy rings, especially the mushrooms, are most commonly observed during the summer months, when Florida receives the majority of its rainfall. Fairy rings occur when large quantities of organic matter, such as lumber, tree stumps, logs, etc., are naturally located or have been buried in a lawn. The fungi are nourished and develop on this material. The mushrooms, which are all sizes and shapes, are the fruiting stages of these fungi.
Symptoms/Signs: There are three types of fairy rings: Type I rings have a zone of dead grass just inside a zone of dark green grass. Type II rings have only a band of dark green turf, with or without mushrooms present in the band (plate 80). Type III rings do not exhibit a dead zone or a dark green zone, but have simply a ring of mushrooms present (plate 81).

Rings may be very small initially, perhaps less than 1 foot, but they normally expand each year. It is not uncommon for rings to be 6 feet or more in diameter. The size and completeness (circular, semicircular, quarter circles) of the bands varies considerably. Mushrooms will normally be produced during rainy weather. Since some of the mushrooms (e.g., *Chlorophyllum* spp., plate 82) are poisonous, mushrooms should be removed or destroyed. Chopping them up with the mower is adequate.
Cultural Controls: If necessary for aesthetic purposes, mask the dark green ring symptoms with nitrogen fertilizers. Although it is possible to excavate and fumigate the fairy ring sites, it is quite likely the rings will return if the food source for the fungi is still present underground. The rings will disappear naturally, but it may take up to five years.
Chemical Controls: Azoxystrobin, flutolanil

Disease: Gray Leaf Spot
Pathogen: Pyricularia grisea
Occurrence: This disease of St. Augustinegrass is most often observed from late spring to early fall, especially during prolonged periods of rainfall. Excessive applications of quick-release nitrogen sources enhance disease severity, as does compacted soil. Application of the herbicide atrazine increases the susceptibility of St. Augustinegrass to this disease.
Symptoms/Signs: Initial symptoms include small pinhead-sized spots that are olive green to brown in color. These enlarge and form circular to oblong spots that are tan to brown colored with distinctive dark brown margins (plates 83,

84). Under humid conditions, the fungus produces abundant spores in the center of these spots, giving them a velvety gray appearance.

Many spots can occur on a single leaf, such that severely affected leaves wither and turn brown. No distinct patches are observed, but areas may appear thin. A severely affected turfgrass area may appear as though suffering from drought.

Once St. Augustinegrass is established in the landscape, the disease is chronic but not severe. During the summer months, individual St. Augustinegrass plants will always have a few spots on the leaf blades, but the overall health of the turfgrass is not affected unless the grass is placed under severe stress.

Cultural Controls: Avoid excess nitrogen during potential disease development periods. Do not use readily available forms of nitrogen such as soluble liquids or quick-release nitrogen sources just prior to or during these periods. Instead, use slow-release nitrogen sources. Apply a balanced fertilizer containing equivalent amounts of potassium, preferably a slow-release potassium form.

If soils are compacted (walking paths, for example), alleviate the compaction or reduce traffic in those areas.

Limit atrazine herbicide applications. If it is necessary to use atrazine, apply it only to weed-infested areas and not the entire lawn. Before and after atrazine applications, be sure the turfgrass is being managed correctly and that optimal fertility, mowing, and watering practices are in place. Monitor the turfgrass area for disease development. Avoid herbicides by learning how to manage the turfgrass to limit weeds.

Chemical Controls: Azoxystrobin, mancozeb, propiconazole, thiophanate methyl, triadimefon, and trifloxystrobin. Mancozeb can be applied to a residential lawn *only* by a certified pesticide applicator.

Disease: Helminthosporium Leaf Spot
Pathogen(s): Bipolaris, Drechslera, and *Exserohilum* spp. (previously classified as *Helminthosporium* fungi)
Occurrence: These diseases occur most frequently on bermudagrass and include a group of fungi that are active over a wide range of temperatures. Thus, diseases caused by these fungi can occur at any time of year. However, as a general rule, the leaf spot disease occurs during mild, wet periods in fall through winter.
Symptoms/Signs: Leaf spot symptoms tend to vary with each pathogen/host pair from very small (pinhead size), solid brown to purple colored lesions or spots to expanded lesions with bleached centers that girdle the leaf blade (plate 85). Severely infected leaves turn purple or reddish brown in color, giving the turf an overall purple cast. Severely infected leaves will eventually wither and dry to a light tan color. Distinct patches or patterns to the disease are usually not obvious. "Melting-out" occurs under severe infections as turf areas thin and die. Lesions on stolons are dark purple to black.

Cultural Controls: Avoid excess nitrogen during potential disease development periods. The nitrogen level must be balanced with potassium; a ratio of 1:2 (N:K) is recommended. In areas that are affected routinely by this disease, increase the potassium level *before* the disease normally occurs. Use slow-release potassium sources or apply quick-release potassium sources more frequently.

Overuse of certain herbicides (MPlateP, 2,4-D and dicamba) has been shown to enhance *Helminthosporium* disease development on cool-season grasses. Note if there is a correlation between disease outbreaks and the use of certain pesticides. If a correlation is determined, then avoid using that particular pesticide or treat preventively for *Helminthosporium* disease prior to the use of that pesticide.

Chemical Controls: Azoxystrobin, fludioxonil, mancozeb, myclobutanil, PCNB, propiconazole, trifloxystrobin. Mancozeb can be applied to a residential lawn *only* by a professional pesticide applicator.

Disease: Pythium Root Rot
Pathogen: Pythium spp.
Occurrence: Symptoms may appear at any time of the year, but they will always be associated with wet soil conditions, either from excessive rainfall or from irrigation. Poor drainage conditions will compound this problem.
Symptoms/Signs: This is a root rot disease. The symptoms observed on the leaves are the result of fungal activity on the root system. Aboveground symptoms are typically a nonspecific decline in turf quality. Small or large turf areas will become a general yellow, light green, or brown color and display thinning, a gradual decrease in density. However, the turf seldom dies from *Pythium* root rot, and no distinct patches are observed.

Roots appear thin with few root hairs and have a general discoloration, but are not black and rotted as they are with take-all root rot. Microscopic examination of affected roots will determine if *Pythium* spp. are associated with the symptoms.
Cultural Controls: Pythium spp. are naturally present on warm-season turfgrass roots. The triggers for disease are wet soil conditions and stressed turfgrass. To prevent the disease, especially during low-rainfall periods, improve drainage and reduce irrigation. Avoid irrigation management that maintains constantly wet soil.

During periods of high rainfall, incorporate the following techniques into your management program:

Mow the turfgrass at the correct height and frequency so that only one-third of the leaf tissue is removed during any one mowing event. It may be necessary to raise the mowing height during periods of conducive weather. Improper mowing is a major stress on turfgrass.

Balance nitrogen applications with equal amounts of potassium. Extra potassium may be useful in late summer and early fall for those areas that are routinely affected by *Pythium* root rot. Either use a slow-release potassium source, or apply a quick-release source more frequently. If the disease does occur, it may be beneficial to apply nutrients to the leaves since the roots are not functioning efficiently.

Chemical Controls: Azoxystrobin, chloroneb, ethazol, fosetylAl, and propamocarb hydrochloride

To increase effectiveness, these fungicides (except for fosetylAl) should be either lightly watered into the root zone or applied in 5–10 gallons water per 1000 square feet. At least two applications will probably be required. Please note that, except for azoxystrobin, these fungicides are specific for *Pythium* spp. only. They are not useful against any other pathogens that attack turfgrass.

Disease: Rust
Pathogen: Puccinia spp.
Occurrence: This disease primarily occurs on St. Augustinegrass and zoysiagrass. It can occur from late fall to early spring when the turfgrass growth is slowed as a result of cool weather. It will be more severe on turfgrass areas that are stressed from nutrient deficiencies or shade (ex: under trees or on the north side of a building). The leaves must be wet for infection to occur. This wetness may be from dew, high humidity, rain, or irrigation.
Symptoms/Signs: Initially, light yellow flecks will appear on the leaves. If the disease progresses, these flecks will enlarge into spots that are parallel to the leaf vein. Eventually, orange pustules (spots) will form containing spores (plate 86). These pustules will also be parallel to the leaf vein. The spores will rub off on your fingers (plate 87). Heavily infected areas will appear thin and chlorotic (yellow to light brown).
Cultural Controls: Maintain an adequate, balanced fertility program using slow-release nutrient sources. In shady areas, monitor irrigation closely to keep the leaves as dry as possible. In most situations, the disease will disappear as soon as the weather warms and the turfgrass starts to grow vigorously again. The disease may cause the turfgrass to look ugly, but it will not kill the turfgrass.
Chemical Controls: Azoxystrobin, mancozeb, myclobutanil, propiconazole, triadimefon, and trifloxystrobin. Mancozeb can be applied to a residential lawn *only* by a certified pesticide applicator.

Disease: Slime Mold
Pathogen: Physarum and *Fuligo* spp.
Occurrence: Slime molds will appear suddenly during wet weather. These fungi do not harm the turf, so they are not really pathogens. However, their sudden appearance alarms homeowners.
Symptoms/Signs: Leaves will be covered with a white, gray, or darker colored slime (spore mass) or soot.
Cultural Controls: Remove slime molds by mowing or washing off with a strong stream of water. Again, they do not harm the turfgrass.

Chemical Controls: None are required

Disease: Take-all Root Rot
Pathogen: Gaeumannomyces graminis var. *graminis*
Occurrence: The pathogen is naturally present on warm-season turfgrass roots. The trigger for disease is high rainfall and stressed turfgrass, so it is observed during the summer and early fall months when Florida receives the majority of its rainfall. Prolonged periods of rainfall are most conducive to this disease. *Any* stress placed on the turfgrass will encourage or worsen the disease.
Symptoms/Signs: This is a root rot disease (plate 88). Symptoms observed on the leaves are the result of pathogen activity on the root system. The fungus does not attack leaves.

Initial symptoms aboveground are irregular, yellow (chlorotic) or light green patches ranging in diameter from a few inches to a few feet. Roots will initially be thin and off-white in color with isolated black lesions. Eventually, roots will become very short, black, and rotted. Stolons and rhizomes may have black lesions and, under severe disease conditions, begin to rot. Entire plants may die resulting in irregular patches of thinning grass, and if the rot is not controlled, bare patches may develop (plates 89, 90).
Cultural Controls: This disease is very difficult to control once the aboveground symptoms are observed. Therefore, measures that prevent or alleviate stress are the best methods for completely controlling the disease or at least decreasing the potential damage. Stress on turfgrass can result from many factors, addressed below.

The turfgrass *must* be mowed at the correct height during the summer (plate 91). Turfgrass must be mowed as frequently as necessary so that only one-third of the leaf tissue is removed during any one mowing event. Scalping the grass damages the growing point.

Balance nitrogen applications with equal amounts of potassium. For every pound of nitrogen applied, an equal amount of elemental potassium should be applied. Slow-release nitrogen and slow-release potassium sources should be used. Avoid nitrate-nitrogen products and quick-release urea products (e.g., uncoated urea). If slow-release potassium is not readily available, then apply quick-release potassium to the turfgrass between nitrogen applications. Extra potassium may be useful in late summer and early fall.

Frequent foliar (leaf) feeding of all nutrients (N, P, K, and micronutrients) in small amounts will be necessary if the root system is severely damaged; the roots will not be functioning properly and will be unable to obtain nutrients efficiently from the soil. Apply micronutrients, especially manganese. Micronutrients should be applied in the sulfate form as foliar applications.

Do not apply lime to the turfgrass. If you are growing centipedegrass, it is acceptable to apply elemental sulfur or iron sulfate to lower the soil pH below 5.5, but do not do this with other turfgrasses.

Apply herbicides only as needed and according to the label. St. Augustinegrass is especially sensitive to herbicides. Even when herbicides are applied correctly, there will be some stress placed on St. Augustinegrass. Avoid herbicides by learning how to manage the turfgrass to limit weeds!

Chemical Controls: Azoxystrobin, myclobutanil, propiconazole, thiophanate methyl, and triadimefon.

These systemic fungicides are not as effective as the use of cultural controls once the disease symptoms are observed. These fungicides *may* be useful when used preventively. This means they must be applied *prior* to symptom development. Start applying the fungicides at least one month prior to the time when you normally observe aboveground symptoms. Continue applying once a month until the weather is no longer conducive to disease development. It is beneficial to lightly water-in these fungicides, but this must be done immediately after application.

Nematode Management

A well-maintained lawn can help beautify our environment, reduce water run-off, and reduce water and air pollution. In 1991–92 there were 3.3 million acres of grass grown in home lawns in Florida, making home lawns the largest agricultural crop in the Sunshine State. As with any other crop, pest management is key to growing healthy grass in a home lawn. Plant-parasitic nematodes are probably the least understood and most difficult to manage of the turfgrass pests in Florida (plate 92).

What are Nematodes?

Nematodes are unsegmented roundworms, distinguishing them from earthworms, which are segmented worms. Nematodes living in soil are very small, and most can be seen only with a microscope (plate 93). There are many kinds of nematodes found in the soil under any home lawn. Most of these are beneficial, feeding on bacteria, fungi, or other microscopic organisms (more detailed information on these nematodes is available online at the University of Florida Entomology and Nematology Department's Featured Creatures website: http://creatures.ifas.ufl.edu/nematode/soil_nematode.htm). There are even nematodes that can be used as biological control organisms to help manage certain insect pests (more detailed information on beneficial nematodes is available online at the University of Florida Entomology and Nematology Department's Featured Creatures website at http://creatures.ifas.ufl.edu/nematode/mole_cricket_nematode.htm). Unfortunately for us, there is also a group of nematodes that feeds on plants. These are called plant-parasitic nematodes.

All plant-parasitic nematodes have a stylet or mouth-spear that is similar in structure and function to a hypodermic needle (plate 94). The stylet is used to puncture plant cells so that the nematode can inject digestive juices and ingest plant fluids through it. All of the plant-parasitic nematodes that are important turfgrass pests feed on roots. Some plant-parasitic nematodes remain in the soil and feed by inserting only their stylet into the root (plate 95). These are called ectoparasitic nematodes. Others use their stylet to puncture a hole in the root in order to enter and feed inside the tissue; these are called endoparasitic nematodes (plate 96). For more detailed information on the biology of plant-parasitic nematodes affecting turfgrasses, see "Nematode Management in Residential Lawns," a publication of the Florida Extension Service, available at your county extension office or online at http://edis.ifas.ufl.edu/NG039.

How Do Nematodes Damage Grass?

As plant-parasitic nematodes feed, they damage the root system and reduce the grass's ability to obtain water and nutrients from the soil. Roots may be abnormally short and appear darkened or rotten when damaged by plant-parasitic nematodes (plate 97). Root galls or knots associated with certain nematode damage to other crops are usually not evident on grasses. When nematode population densities get high enough, or when environmental stresses such as high temperatures or drought occur, aboveground symptoms may become evident. Symptoms include yellowing, wilting, browning, thinning out, or death (plate 98). Often, weeds such as spurge, sedges, or Florida pusley become prominent as the grass thins out (plates 99, 100, 101). Nematode damage usually occurs in irregularly shaped patches that may enlarge slowly over time. Be aware that similar conditions may be caused by other factors such as localized soil conditions, fungi, or insects.

How Do I Know if Nematodes are a Problem?

With any plant problem, having an accurate diagnosis is important to address the problem and to avoid wasting effort and unnecessary pesticide applications. The only reliable way to determine if plant-parasitic nematodes are involved in a grass problem is by having a nematode assay conducted by a professional nematode diagnostic lab. The University of Florida has such a facility and will assay nematode samples for a nominal cost. Nematode sample kits containing everything needed to collect and submit a sample, along with instructions, are available at your local county Extension Service office.

Nematode analysis is a separate procedure and requires different sampling guidelines than those required for soil analysis or plant disease samples. Be aware that when a plant disease sample is submitted to most labs, a nematode analysis is not normally performed unless you specifically request it. Nematode analysis often requires separate payment and may even be sent to a different address. Familiarize yourself with the procedures required by the lab where you intend to submit the sample. The accuracy of the diagnosis depends on the quality of the sample that you submit. If you are taking a sample for submission to another lab, or if you are submitting a sample to the University of Florida lab without the university sample kits, follow the guidelines below to ensure an accurate diagnosis.

1. A sample must consist of multiple soil cores. Nematodes are not evenly distributed in soil, but rather congregate in "hot spots." Nematode populations may be high at one spot and low just a few feet way. By collecting multiple cores with a device such as a T-type soil sample tube (plate 102), an average population density can be measured. A good rule of thumb is to have a minimum of twenty cores per field. Cores should be taken to a depth of 3 inches.

2. If damage is evident, sample near the margin of the affected area (plate 103). Nematode populations will decline in severely damaged areas because they have nothing left to eat. Therefore, populations tend to be highest near the edges of a declining area, where the grass is still alive. If damage is occurring in a number of areas in one field, take a few cores from the border of several affected areas to make the twenty cores. When taking samples from turf that is not showing symptoms, or if sampling before planting, sample in a zig-zag pattern across the area (plate 104).

3. Put the soil from each sampled area into a plastic bag and seal it. Nematodes require moisture to survive, so drying the soil will kill them. This is different than submitting a sample for nutrient analysis where dry soil is preferred. Make sure that each bag is labeled with a permanent marker so that the diagnosis can be assigned to the correct area. If using a self-sealing bag, seal it with tape, because the zippers often come open in transit.

4. Handle samples carefully. Do not expose samples to direct sunlight or heat. Nematodes are sensitive to high temperatures and UV light. Leaving samples on the dashboard or in the back of a vehicle can kill them quickly and negatively affect the accuracy of the diagnosis. Keeping the nematode sample in a cooler is best. The nematodes will be sandwiched between soil particles, so rough handling will destroy them. For shipping and transport, pack the samples well to minimize shifting.

5. Submit the sample right away. Next-day delivery is best. One study found greatest nematode recovery from hand-delivered samples, the next highest from next-day delivery, and the lowest from regular postal delivery.

The staff at the University of Florida Nematode Assay Lab will make a determination as to whether nematodes are a problem based on which nematodes are found and how many of them there are. Not all plant-parasitic nematodes are equal in their ability to harm grass. For example, one sting nematode can cause as much damage as hundreds of individuals of some other types of plant-parasitic nematodes. The number of each type of nematode in 100 cc of soil from the sample that you submit will be compared to established "thresholds" for these nematodes. If nematode numbers are below the thresholds, your results form will state "Nematodes are below levels believed to be damaging." If nematode numbers exceed thresholds, statements such as "Nematode levels may be high enough to injure the crop indicated under some conditions" or "Numbers of nematodes are high enough to cause serious injury to the crop under normal circumstances" will be made.

Be aware that different diagnostic labs may use different extraction techniques, different quantities of soil, or different thresholds. Because of this, samples submitted to separate labs may report different quantities of nematodes. Do not be alarmed by this, as in most cases the different thresholds used are adjusted to account for the differences in methodology and local conditions. However, if you are using a lab in a distant location, your local conditions or regional variations in nematode aggressiveness may not be taken into account. Usually your local labs will provide the most accurate assessments.

What Can I Do About Nematodes in My Lawn?

Because plant-parasitic nematodes live in soil or roots, the pesticides used to kill them tend to be very toxic and they are also water-soluble. Because of health risks and environmental concerns, there are currently no toxic nematicides that are labeled for use on established home lawns. There are a number of products available for use on home lawns that are marketed as "organic," "biological," or "nontoxic" that claim to be suppressive of plant parasitic nematodes. Be aware that in order to be labeled for home use, these types of products need to be safe, but do not need to be proven effective. Nematologists at the University of Florida have tested many of these products for efficacy, generally with disappointing results.

Adding soil amendments can help the grass tolerate nematode damage or possibly suppress nematode population densities. Remember that anything that can be done to improve root health is good. Colloidal phosphate incorporated into fine sand has been shown to help bermudagrass withstand attack by certain nematodes. Organic materials such as composted municipal sludge or manures can also promote grass health, and at the same time may stimulate fungi that attack nematodes.

Some of the best practices for managing nematode damage in home lawns include avoiding other stresses on the grass. Grass that is given proper watering and fertilization can often withstand higher levels of nematode infestation than grass suffering from drought or nutrient deficiencies (see "Fertilizing your Florida Lawn," a publication of the Florida Extension Service available at your county extension office or online at http://edis.ifas.ufl.edu/EP055, and "Watering your Florida Lawn," a publication of the Florida Extension Service available at your county extension office or online at http://edis.ifas.ufl.edu/LH025). Over-fertilization should also be avoided; too much nitrogen can stimulate the production of succulent roots that are more susceptible to nematode damage. Grass that is mowed too low or allowed to grow too tall between mowing is also more likely to succumb to nematodes. Frequent mowing at moderate height is best (see "Mowing your Florida Lawn," a publication of the Florida Extension Service available at your county extension office or online at http://edis.ifas. ufl.edu/LH028). While minimizing these stresses can help, even the best-managed lawns can suffer from nematode damage from time to time.

If you are considering replanting your home lawn and have had a history of nematode problems, choosing a different type of grass can sometimes help. Bahiagrass is generally more tolerant of plant-parasitic nematodes than other common lawn grasses and is often a good choice, but even bahiagrass may suffer under extreme nematode pressure or drought conditions. Generally, centipedegrass is the only common lawn grass damaged by ring nematodes. Therefore, if you have a centipedegrass lawn where ring nematodes have been problematic, replanting with centipedegrass might be a poor choice.

Another option available when replanting a home lawn is soil fumigation to decrease nematode population densities before planting. The only fumigant currently labeled for use in establishment of home lawns is dazomet; this chemical is manufactured by BASF and is sold under the trade name Basamid. This is a granular product that when incorporated into the soil releases gases that are toxic to nematodes. This can be helpful in getting grass to establish in nematode-infested soils. However, Basamid will not kill all of the nematodes, and they may build back up to damaging levels over time. Basamid is a very toxic poison, so only professional pesticide applicators with a special license may apply it. Instructions on the product label must be strictly followed in order to ensure the safety of the applicator and of nontarget organisms (plants, animals, children).

Summary

At present, the best management strategies for nematodes in the home lawn are aimed at increasing the grass's ability to tolerate nematode damage. These strategies include avoiding stress, promoting root vigor, and choosing tolerant grasses. Researchers at the University of Florida are continually looking at new management options. Some of the options being investigated are new, safer products that are effective and can be used on home lawns, screening of turfgrass varieties for better resistance or tolerance to nematodes, and finding ways to use the nematodes' natural enemies to suppress them below damaging levels. For updated information on nematodes and other aspects of lawn care, visit your county Extension Service office, or view the University of Florida's Electronic Document Information System (EDIS) website at http://edis.ifas. ufl.edu/.

6

Environmental Stresses and Your Florida Lawn

Stresses

Florida lawns are subjected to many stresses. These include shade, drought, nutrient deficiency, traffic, salinity, and occasional cold temperatures. There are also biotic stresses resulting from living organisms such as insects, pathogens, or nematodes. Management of environmental stresses falls into two primary categories: (1) selection of the most stress tolerant species or cultivar for a particular area, and (2) proper cultural and management practices to alleviate effects of the stress. Proper fertility, irrigation, and mowing practices are the primary tools for maintaining a healthy lawn, and can greatly reduce the need for curative pesticides after the turf is already stressed.

Carbohydrates

Through the process of photosynthesis, plants intercept sunlight in green leaf tissue and convert that sunlight into energy for use by the plant for growth or storage. In combination with nutrient fertilization, this provides the plant with the building blocks for new root or shoot tissue growth. It also supplies the plant with excess carbohydrates, which are stored for use at a later time. In warm-season turfgrasses that are grown in Florida, these reserve carbon supplies are commonly stored in rhizomes, stolons, and roots. An ample supply of carbon reserves helps the turfgrass plant begin regrowth processes in the spring, aids in recovery from stresses, and ensures that continued growth and health can be maintained.

What Depletes Carbohydrates?

Our management and cultural practices greatly influence the reserve carbohydrate status of a turfgrass plant. Depletion of these carbohydrate reserves will occur with the following practices:

1. Excess nitrogen fertility. Nitrogen encourages the plant to form new tissue and grow. When nitrogen is applied in excess of amounts recommended in this book, the growth surge following the nitrogen applica-

tion will generally consume stored carbohydrates. This leaves the grass more vulnerable to stresses, as less reserve material is now available for recovery from, or avoidance of, other problems. If this carbohydrate depletion occurs late in the growing season, particularly in a part of the state where dormancy is likely to occur, spring regrowth can be delayed or reduced, which will decrease turf density and may increase the opportunity for weed invasion (plate 105).

2. Mowing at low heights. Mowing below recommended heights removes a large portion of the shoot tissue available for photosynthesis. This results in reduced photosynthesis and less accumulated carbon. The grass plant must then use up the carbohydrate reserves to outgrow the damage from low mowing. It is therefore advised that all landscape turfgrass species be maintained at their maximum mowing heights (plate 106).

3. Environmental stresses that influence turfgrass growth. If a turfgrass plant is under any type of stress, the growth and functioning of the plant will be altered. This results in greater energy requirements for maintenance of the plant, with much of that energy being supplied by stored carbohydrates. For example, a plant growing in a drought- or shade-stressed environment will suffer from reduced growth, but it still needs to consume energy to support life in that environment (plate 107).

The Root System

One way to enhance stress tolerance of turfgrass plants is to encourage maximum root growth. A vigorously growing root system is better able to penetrate deep into the soil for water and nutrients and will maintain a larger supply of carbon to help in recovery from stress. Maximum root growth can be achieved with the following management practices:

1. Moderate nitrogen fertility. Excess nitrogen can reduce tolerance to many stresses and will also reduce the growth of roots relative to shoots.

2. Mowing at the correct height. Mowing too low favors shoot regrowth, with a resulting reduction in root growth.

3. Proper irrigation. Irrigating turf on an as-needed basis, with less frequent but longer waterings, will encourage roots to grow downward deep into the soil. This will promote greater health and stress tolerance of the grass. Irrigating on a daily basis will cause the roots to remain in the upper few inches of the soil, rather than promote the deep rooting needed during any reduction in available water.

Fertility

In addition to nitrogen, other nutrients can also influence overall stress tolerance in turfgrass. In particular, potassium has been shown to enhance tolerance to numerous stresses, including cold temperatures, drought, and heavy traffic. Fall application of potassium also encourages earlier and faster spring green-up. Application of ½–1 pound of potassium per 1000 square feet with each fertilizer application can provide these stress protection benefits.

For newly established turf areas, adequate phosphorous is needed to enhance and quicken the root growth needed during establishment. See "Establishing Your Florida Lawn" in chapter 2 for more information on this.

A Stress-Free Lawn

Following the guidelines in this section of the *Florida Lawn Handbook* will help you to maintain a stress-free, healthy lawn that will be better able to withstand drought, traffic, cold temperatures, and invasion of weeds, insects, and diseases. This will not only give you a more attractive lawn, it will also require fewer applications of herbicides, insecticides, and fungicides.

Preparing Your Lawn for Drought

Turfgrass plants, like all green plants, require water for growth. During times of inadequate rainfall, application of supplemental irrigation will help maintain a higher-quality lawn. Although droughts are usually thought of as lasting for long periods, such as months or years, sandy Florida soils can experience drought conditions after only a few days without rain. Without adequate water from either rainfall or irrigation, turfgrasses will adopt a water-conserving habit. Under these conditions, grasses roll their leaf blades to stop transpiration (the loss of water from the leaves), they defer any new shoot growth until conditions are more suitable for growth, and they send their roots deeper into the soil in search of water. During periods of drought, leaves may die and drop from the plant, although grasses will generally recuperate upon receiving adequate irrigation. During the recovery period from drought, grasses will be more susceptible to other stresses (cold temperatures, traffic, insects, or diseases). Because of increased incidents of mandatory watering restrictions during extended periods of dry weather, management practices that will help enhance persistence of grass during times of drought should be considered (plates 108, 109).

Objective of Drought Conditioning

To condition a lawn successfully, the objective is to grow a good quality lawn that will survive on little or no supplemental irrigation. A conditioned lawn can withstand more stress than a lawn that is not conditioned. A properly conditioned lawn will have a deep and extensive root system that is better able to seek out water.

Irrigation Practices

Proper irrigation is the first step in conditioning a lawn for drought. Many people tend to rely on their automatic sprinkler systems to apply small amounts of water several times weekly to their lawn, regardless of any rainfall received. This practice is detrimental to the grass and actually promotes a lawn that requires more water and cannot withstand drought stress. *Less frequent, longer irrigations will assist in establishing a deeper, more viable root system.*

Frequent (e.g., daily), light waterings promote shallow root systems that do not result in healthy turf. To develop a deep root system, lawns should only be watered when the first signs of wilt occur. Spots in the lawn that turn bluish gray, footprints that remain in the grass long after being made, and the presence of many leaf blades folded in half lengthwise are all indications that the lawn needs water. Apply only enough water to wet the soil in the root zone. For most of Florida's sandy soils, ½–¾ inch of water is generally sufficient. Irrigation should then be withheld until signs of wilt occur again. This technique works regardless of turfgrass species, soil type, season, or other environmental conditions. It may take up to six weeks to condition a turf to survive several days or more without wilting between irrigations or rainfalls. During this time the root system is developing and growing deeper into the soil. In time, the lawn will establish a more uniform appearance, with less thatch and a deeper root system.

Mowing Practices

Proper mowing practices are essential for healthy, drought-resistant turf. Every time a lawn is mowed, the metabolic activities of the grass are stressed, reducing root growth. Mowing frequency and cutting height need to be carefully considered for a healthy lawn. Use of the highest cutting height on the mower will facilitate turfgrass drought conditioning. This will increase grass leaf area, allowing for more photosynthesis. This results in more stored carbohydrate, which are then available for use in recovery from stresses such as drought. The higher the mowing height, the deeper and more extensive the root system will be. Although transpiration (water loss through leaves) will be slightly greater with turf mowed at a higher height, the benefits of an expanded root system outweigh this loss. Mowing should be done often enough to minimize the shock of cutting. Never mow off more than one-third the height of the leaf blade at any one time. Adjust the frequency of mowing to the growth of the turf. In the summer, it may be necessary to mow more than once a week, but in the winter, once a month or less may be enough. Keeping mower blades sharp and properly balanced is also important. A leaf cut by a sharp blade will heal over more quickly and lose less water than a leaf blade shredded by a dull mower blade.

Fertilization Practices

Proper fertilization practices can enhance drought tolerance of turfgrasses. Understanding plant responses to nitrogen and potassium fertilization is helpful in developing a beneficial program, as well as for providing a well-balanced nutritional program. All of the drought conditioning accomplished by proper irrigation and mowing practices can be eliminated by excessive nitrogen fertilization, because shoot growth is enhanced and root growth reduced by excessive nitrogen. Leaf blades become more lush as nitrogen fertilization increases. Drought conditioning can best be accomplished by applying just enough nitrogen to obtain a small but continuous amount of growth.

Potassium fertilization, however, can help turfgrasses increase their tolerance to many stresses, including drought. Potassium promotes increased root growth and thicker cell walls and functions in control of water loss through leaves. Turfgrasses require nearly the same amounts of potassium as nitrogen, especially in sandy soils where both can readily leach out. Other macro- and micronutrients, as well as soil pH, should be kept at recommended levels for optimal growth. Supplemental iron application can provide desirable green turf without promoting succulent shoot growth. Iron applications have also been shown to increase turfgrass rooting. Soil testing is helpful in monitoring nutrient levels and determining turfgrass fertility requirements. Contact your county extension office for more information on this.

Pest Control

Chemical use should be minimized during drought stress. A healthy, vigorously growing turfgrass is the best defense against weeds, insects, and diseases. Following the irrigation, mowing, and fertility practices outlined above will promote a healthy, dense turf and reduce the need for pest control measures. However, if a pest problem has been diagnosed, it should be promptly treated following recommendations from your county extension office. Spot treatment of a pest problem is usually as effective as treating the whole lawn. Be particularly watchful for insects and diseases that attack turfgrass root systems.

Turfgrass Species

Drought tolerance varies greatly with turfgrass species and cultivars (plate 110). Bahiagrass and zoysiagrass generally have the best drought tolerance of the southern turfgrasses, while St. Augustinegrass and carpetgrass have the worst. Drought tolerance does not mean that grass will remain green without irrigation or rainfall, but that they will go into dormancy to wait until conditions become favorable for regrowth. After soil moisture becomes adequate, new growth will emerge from buds on rhizomes (underground stems) or stolons (aboveground stems). Bermudagrass, zoysiagrass, seashore paspalum, and bahiagrass can usually recover from drought-induced dormancy because they have rhizomes in the soil that are protected from desiccation (drying out). St. Augustinegrass and centipedegrass do not have rhizomes, which decreases their ability to recover from stresses such as drought. Deep root systems will enhance recovery from drought.

Choosing a grass to plant for drought tolerance in Florida is difficult, because each species has particular pest problems. Bermudagrass and zoysiagrass tend to have trouble with nematodes, although both provide good quality turf when nematodes are controlled. Bahiagrass has mole cricket problems, but these pests are easier to control than nematodes. If a person can accept an open growth habit and not overmanage the turf, then bahiagrass may be a good selection. Bahiagrass is adapted to a wide range of soils and can survive under minimum management. Centipedegrass has a slow growth habit and low water and nutrient requirements, but has a light green color that is objectionable to some people.

Alternatives to Turfgrass

People often attempt to grow turf where it will not survive without extraordinary care. High-quality turf cannot be maintained without supplemental irrigation, although a lower-quality turf may persist. In landscapes where poor-quality turf may detract from the design, alternatives to turf should be considered. Mulched beds or ground covers may be more suitable. Plant materials that do not require supplemental irrigation should be chosen. Consult your County Extension office for the plants that grow best in your area.

Low-Temperature Stress

Injury to warm-season turfgrasses often occurs when temperatures drop below 20°F(–6.7°C) (plate 111). In general, major winter injury to turfgrass is caused by the following: (1) tissue desiccation, (2) direct low-temperature kill, (3) diseases, and (4) traffic effects. For example, damage from the 1989–90 freeze can probably be attributed to poor cultural practices that weakened turf and made it more susceptible to injury or death from low temperatures. Subsequent damage may also have resulted from effects of traffic on frozen turf.

Reasons for Low-Temperature Damage

Most warm-season grasses have very poor cold tolerance ratings when compared to cool-season grasses. Because of lower fall temperatures and reduced day lengths, warm-season grasses enter a state of dormancy, evidenced by brown, dead shoot tissue, which is maintained throughout the winter in north Florida. In central Florida, a growth and metabolism reduction, rather than an actual dormancy, may be seen unless the winter is extremely cold. This death of shoot tissue or lack of growth does not generally indicate that the grass is not going to recover; rather, this is a natural state that provides protection for the grass when it is faced with cold temperatures. In cases of severe freezing temperatures, some grasses may suffer irreversible damage, and use of these grasses should be limited to warmer climates. For instance, St. Augustinegrass, which generally exhibits poor cold tolerance, is not used as extensively in north Florida as other grasses, and is used less as you progress into Georgia.

Cultural factors that tend to promote cold injury include: poor drainage (soil compaction), excessive thatch, reduced lighting, excessive fall nitrogen fertilization, and a close mowing height. The weather pattern preceding a severe and sudden cold wave also influences a turf's low-temperature tolerance. In general, if turf has had several frosts prior to a drastic temperature drop, it has been better "conditioned" to survive. The 1989–90 cold snap in much of north and central Florida was preceded by three to five frosts. These helped increase carbohydrate and protein levels in plants, enabling crown tissue to withstand cold temperatures without severe membrane disruption. The freezes that occurred in the early 1980s did not have these preconditioning periods, resulting in severe damage. In that case, grasses were still green, and protective crown tissue was succulent and therefore susceptible to cold temperatures.

Shaded areas may suffer more intense cold damage. Shade (low light intensity) prevents normal daytime soil warming; therefore, these areas stay colder for longer periods of time, and more low-temperature damage may occur. Shade also reduces the plant's ability to produce the carbohydrates needed for increased cold tolerance.

Traffic (foot or vehicular) may further increase injury to cold-damaged turf. Traffic should not be allowed on frozen turf until the soil and plants have completely thawed. Syringing the area lightly prior to allowing traffic will help reduce frozen turf injury associated with traffic.

Assessing the Extent of Injury

Symptoms of direct low-temperature damage include leaves that initially appear wilted. They may subsequently take on a water-soaked look, turning whitish brown and progressing to a dark brown. Damaged leaves are not turgid and tend to mat over the soil, often emitting a distinct putrid odor. Areas hardest hit are usually poorly drained, such as soil depressions. If you suspect your grass has experienced cold damage, take several 4–5-inch-diameter plugs from suspected areas and place them in a warm area for regrowth. A greenhouse or warm windowsill should suffice. Observe these for thirty days or until growth resumes. If good regrowth occurs, then little damage is assumed. If regrowth is absent or sporadic, then some degree of damage was sustained.

Selection of Cold-Hardy Grasses

Among the warm-season grasses, the most cold-hardy species is zoysiagrass, followed in descending order by bermudagrass, bahiagrass, centipedegrass, seashore paspalum, carpetgrass, and St. Augustinegrass. Within these species, there are different degrees of cold tolerance among cultivars. For instance, centipede-grass cultivars 'Oklawn,' 'TifBlair,' and especially 'TennTurf' have good cold tolerance. In St. Augustinegrasses, 'Raleigh,' 'Bitterblue,' 'Seville,' and 'Jade' generally exhibit the best cold tolerance, while 'Floratam,' 'Floralawn,' and 'Floratine' are more susceptible to cold temperatures.

Management Practices to Minimize Cold Damage

Regardless of the turfgrass species selected, management practices can help minimize cold temperature damage.

Recently planted (sprigged, sodded, or seeded) grasses can be expected to be more severely damaged by cold. As a result of incomplete root development and more tender and succulent shoot tissue, overall stress tolerance is reduced in grasses undergoing establishment. Therefore, particularly in north Florida, de-lay fall planting of grasses until spring or early summer. In south Florida, year-round establishment may be practiced, but care should be taken to protect im-mature turf from occasional cold temperatures.

Fertility can also influence cold tolerance. Late season application (late Sep-tember in northern Florida, after mid-October in the central and southern re-gions) of nitrogen will promote shoot growth in the fall, when grass growth and metabolism are slowing down. This will deplete carbohydrate reserves, which help the grass regrow from any stress, and will also produce new, tender shoot growth that is less able to tolerate adverse conditions such as cold. Therefore, late-season application of nitrogen is not recommended.

Potassium fertility in the fall may enhance cold tolerance and promote earlier spring green-up of grass. Application of potassium at the rate of ½–1 pound per 1000 square feet is recommended for the last fertilization of the year.

Effects of shade can increase cold damage. Because shaded areas do not be-come as warm as areas in full sun, injury in these areas may be more severe. Compacted soils also remain cooler than well-drained areas, which increases the probability of cold temperature damage. See chapter 4, "Cultural Practices for Your Florida Lawn," for information on relieving soil compaction.

Increasing mowing height can reduce cold injury in a number of ways. First, it will promote deeper rooting, which is one factor always associated with greater stress tolerance. It will also allow for production and storage of more carbohydrates late in the summer. In addition, higher mowing heights can create a warmer microenvironment as a result of extra canopy cover provided by longer leaf tissue.

Because cold damage may initially resemble drought stress, people sometimes feel that additional water may be needed. Overall, correct irrigation practices as described throughout this book can alleviate many stresses faced by turf, but as the grass goes into dormancy, there is no need to apply water. In many cases, roots may not even be able to take up water during dormancy.

Spring Green-up

Unless your turfgrass has been subjected to unusually cold or freezing temperatures for long periods, or your management practices have augmented the effects of cool temperatures, your grass should begin to green up as temperatures and day lengths increase in the spring. At this time, the recommended fertility, irrigation, and mowing practices should be resumed for best health of your lawn all season.

Growing Turfgrass in the Shade

Turfgrass requires a minimum amount of light for growth. Both intensity (brightness) and duration of light are important factors affecting turfgrass growth. In many landscape settings, grass will receive a minimum amount of light during enough of the day for adequate growth, even if the area is shaded for other portions of the day. However, in some situations, a grassed area may be shaded for most or all of the day, making it difficult for the grass to obtain either intensity or duration of light adequate for growth. Under shaded conditions, grasses will have elongated leaf blades and stems as they attempt to obtain sunlight by outgrowing their neighbors. This tissue elongation depletes carbohydrates, causes shoot tissue to be weakened, and reduces the overall health and vigor of the turfgrass plant. Turf ground cover is also reduced and the resulting bare ground is conducive to weed growth. It is not advisable to grow turfgrass under conditions of heavy shade. Other ground cover plants or mulch should be used on these sites. For areas receiving moderate amounts of shade, however, there are certain species and cultivars that are able to maintain suitable growth. There are also specific management practices that will encourage better turfgrass health under shaded conditions (plate 112).

Species Suitable for Use in Shade

Some species are particularly well suited for use in shaded areas. Within these species, certain cultivars sometimes maintain considerable advantages when grown in a shaded environment. Included in these species are:

St. Augustinegrass: This species is among the best overall for growth in shade, although it will also perform well in full sunlight. St. Augustinegrass cultivars that exhibit best shade tolerance include cultivars 'Seville' and 'Delmar.' 'Floratam,' 'Floratine,' and 'Floralawn' exhibit moderate shade tolerance.

Zoysiagrass: This is another good choice for shaded areas. Like St. Augustinegrass, it will also do well in full sunlight. Generally, any cultivar of zoysiagrass will perform well in shade.

Bahiagrass is not recommended for use in shaded conditions, but centipedegrass will tolerate moderate shade. Seashore paspalum and bermudagrass do not do well in shaded conditions.

Management Practices for Growing Turfgrass in Shade

Because the turfgrass is already suffering from effects of a stress (lack of sufficient light), it is important to follow specific management practices for turf growth in the shade. Included in these practices are the following:

1. Increase the mowing height for grasses growing in the shade. For instance, if you normally cut St. Augustinegrass at a 3-inch height, increase the cutting height to 4 inches. The increased mowing height allows for more leaf area, thus intercepting as much available light as possible. In addition, leaf blades will be longer and narrower in the shade, and a lower cutting height will cause an excessive reduction in leaf length, which is not good for the grass. Higher mowing heights will also promote deeper rooting, which is one of the key mechanisms of stress tolerance for turfgrasses.

2. Reduce fertilizer applications to turf growing in shade. The grass grows more slowly in a shaded environment, which reduces fertility needs (plate 113). Too much nitrogen fertilizer depletes carbohydrates and produces a weaker turf system. If you normally apply 4 pounds of nitrogen per 1000 square feet yearly, apply 2H–3 pounds to turf growing in the shade. Limit any single fertility application to no more than H pound of nitrogen per 1000 square feet at any one time.

3. Irrigation. Water usage is reduced under shaded conditions, so irrigate only on an as-needed basis. This would be when the leaves begin to roll up lengthwise, take on a blue gray color, or when impressions from foot or vehicular traffic remain on the grass. If the irrigation system covers an area that is partially shaded and partially in sun, consider removing the sprinkler heads from the shaded areas and irrigating by hand instead.

4. Avoid effects of traffic. The grass will be more easily injured by traffic if growing in shade and may not be able to recover adequately. Also, if trees cause shade, traffic may damage tree roots, resulting in decline or death of the tree.

5. Monitor for weed pressure. Weeds are able to outcompete turf in certain situations, and will seek out those opportunities. In a shaded environment, lateral turfgrass growth and ground cover may be sparse, leaving bare ground suitable for certain weeds. Treatment with a pre- or postemergence herbicide may be necessary. Use caution, however, when applying any chemical treatment to a shaded lawn, as there is a greater chance of phytotoxicity when a grass is under stress. Addition-

ally, many herbicides are potentially damaging to landscape trees and shrubs.

6. Monitor for disease pressure. In many shaded environments, there will be decreased air movement and higher humidity, which may increase the possibility of disease. Again, use caution if applying pesticides to a turf that is already under environmental stress.

Watch for Competition from Trees

Grasses growing under trees are subjected to further stresses in addition to reduced light. These include competition with tree roots for soil space, water, oxygen, and nutrients. Tree roots may extend far from the canopy line, so these competitive effects may occur at some distance from the tree.

Consider Alternatives to Grass

Attempting to grow grass in shaded environments may be time-consuming, frustrating, costly, and damaging to the environment. In areas that receive shade all day or for much of the day, an alternative ground cover or mulch may be the best choice. Consult your county extension office for information on alternative ground covers for shaded environments.

Traffic Stress

Vehicular or foot traffic can cause injury to turfgrass in two ways. The first type of injury is to shoot tissue, where physical damage to leaf blades is manifested by abrasion, tearing, or stripping of the leaf tissue. This injury results in death of the leaves and a reduction in photosynthetic capacity. The second type of damage from traffic is to root systems, and results from soil compaction due to the weight of the traffic. Root growth and viability are greatly reduced, resulting in reduced capacity for roots to seek out water or nutrients. Often, damage from traffic will cause both types of injury simultaneously. Rates of recovery of the grass vary based on the capacity of the grass to tolerate traffic injury, the growth rate of the turf, which will determine how long it will take the grass to grow out of the injury, and the degree of severity of the injury. In addition, there are specific management and cultural practices that will improve the wear tolerance of your grass (plates 114, 115).

Wear Tolerance of Warm-Season Grasses

The warm-season grasses grown throughout Florida are generally more wear tolerant than cool-season grasses grown in northern climates. A typical ranking of wear tolerance of our warm-season grasses is as follows:

1. Zoysiagrass
2. Seashore paspalum, bermudagrass
3. St. Augustinegrass
4. Bahiagrass
5. Carpetgrass
6. Centipedegrass

In some cases, a species may have one cultivar that exhibits good wear tolerance and another with poor tolerance. For example, seashore paspalum cultivars 'Sea Isle 2000' and 'Sea Isle 1' both have excellent wear tolerance, while wear tolerance of the cultivar 'Adalayd' is poor. These differences exist as a result of genetic differences within a species and differences in rate of regrowth.

Factors that Enhance Wear Tolerance

Factors other than genetics that are important in imparting wear tolerance are:

- Amount of shoot tissue present to absorb the injury
- Proper hydration status. A lawn that is adequately irrigated (not over-irrigated) allows leaf tissue to better absorb the impact of the injury.
- Proper fertilization practices, which will impart greater overall stress tolerance and best allow the lawn to outgrow the injury. Potassium is particularly important in improving wear tolerance.

How You Can Improve the Wear Tolerance of Your Lawn

The first step to improving wear tolerance is to avoid the injury, if possible. If vehicular or foot traffic is to occur on an ongoing basis, pavement, bricks, or stone will provide a better ground cover than grass. Avoidance of repeated traffic paths will also alleviate injury, and will provide the grass with time to recover. Another tool is selection of wear-tolerant turfgrasses. Centipedegrass or bahiagrass are poor choices for high-traffic areas, while zoysiagrass or seashore paspalum are better suited to these locations.

Fertilization regimes can also strongly influence the ability of the grass to withstand injury as well as to outgrow it. Excess nitrogen fertilization (in amounts higher than indicated in this book) will reduce wear tolerance. This occurs because the nitrogen causes rapid growth of the grass, resulting in lush, succulent tissue that is less able to withstand injury. Proper nitrogen fertilization, however, will improve wear tolerance in two ways. First, it will promote greater shoot density (number of shoots per unit area) of the grass, thereby providing more shoot tissue to absorb the injury. Second, it will allow for faster regrowth following the injury and will promote new lateral growth to help the grass cover any bare ground resulting from the injury.

Potassium fertilization also strongly influences tolerance to many stresses, including wear injury. Adequate potassium fertilization will allow the grass to survive with less injury and to retain adequate carbohydrates for subsequent regrowth. Potassium should be applied to traffic-stressed turf in an amount ranging from one-half to equal amounts of potassium to nitrogen. For example, a 16-4-8 fertilizer would supply ½ pound of potassium for each pound of nitrogen applied, while a 12-2-12 would supply equal amounts of potassium to nitrogen. Refer to chapter 3, "Fertilizing Your Florida Lawn," for more information.

Proper mowing practices can also influence a lawn's wear tolerance. Higher mowing heights will improve tolerance because (1) this increases the amount of shoot tissue available to absorb the injury, and (2) this results in deeper rooting than you would find on a closely mowed turf, which provides greater stress resistance. Scalping, or low mowing, of a stressed turf will result in greater damage, slower recovery, and possible death of the turf.

Irrigation can also influence wear tolerance. Deep rooting is encouraged by infrequent, longer irrigations, applied only when the turf shows signs of wilt. Daily or frequent watering results in roots that remain in the top few inches of soil, and a grass plant with less capacity to withstand any environmental or biotic stress. It is important, however, to apply adequate irrigation to wear-stressed turf. As mentioned above, this allows the turf to better absorb the injury and results in less damage than would occur on dry turf.

If soil compaction is the primary problem, there are several steps to be taken. First, compaction can be alleviated by aeration of the soil, which helps loosen the soil and allows oxygen to reach the roots. Providing aeration can be as simple as using a small foot-press aerator in small areas, or a large-scale job requiring commercial equipment to drill holes in the soil. This procedure should be followed by topdressing, which is application of soil over the top of the turfgrass. Over time, topdressing may alleviate compaction, reduce thatch, and improve the drainage or water retention of the site. For more information, refer to chapter 4, "Cultural Practices for Your Florida Lawn."

7

Organic Lawn Care

There is a renewed interest today in organic lawn care and a trend among many homeowners to consider long-term environmental concerns in their lawn maintenance programs. The term "organic" can cover many different aspects of lawn care, including fertility and pest management. But there is also a certain amount of confusion and misunderstanding over the concept of organic lawn care and what it entails, and as to whether products are beneficial or fall into the "snake oil" category.

What Is Organic?

By definition, an organic compound must contain carbon. Other than that, organics may be naturally occurring or synthetic compounds, and they may be fertilizers, pest control products, or biostimulants. Generally, an organic care program would be expected to include integrated pest management (IPM) practices and recycling, and would emphasize a lower-input and less manicured environment.

Organic Fertilizers

Organic fertilizers fall into two categories: natural organics and synthetic organics. Natural organics are products such as manures, dried blood, bone meal, sludge, or other plant or animal products. These products generally contain between 3% and 10% nitrogen. Benefits from using natural organics are that they become available to plants slowly over time, as soil microorganisms break them down. Because of the slow-release properties of these materials, natural organics are less apt to leach from the soil, to burn turfgrass, or to cause rapid growth spurts than are water-soluble fertilizers. This may reduce the ground- or surface-water contamination sometimes seen with synthetic fertilizers.

However, there are also some drawbacks to the use of organic fertilizers. Because they are dependent on microbial activity, soil temperature and pH can play a large role in plant uptake of organics. Use in cool climates or seasons may result in reduced plant response, and because they are generally low-analysis fertilizers, they are often required in large quantities by plants. They may be bulky to handle and store, they may have an objectionable odor or appearance, and they are generally more expensive than synthetic fertilizers. Regardless of these pros and cons, a turfgrass plant is not concerned about the source of its fertilizer and will ultimately use the nitrogen and other nutrients for growth and metabolic functioning regardless of the fertilizer's origin.

Compost

Compost is an organic (carbon-containing) product that has undergone a period of decay. Compost may come from a variety of sources such as vegetative material, sewage sludge, cottonseed meal, peat, etc. When nutrients are contained in adequate supply, compost may be marketed as an organic fertilizer.

Applying organic matter such as compost to the soil will supply simple and complex sugars, proteins, and amino acids. This will provide a nutrient source for both the turf and the microbial population, will improve nutrient uptake through greater cation exchange capacity, and will reduce leaching. Compost may be added to the soil prior to planting, or, after some of the larger material is screened out, applied as a topdressing ½–1 inch deep over the top of existing lawns.

Nutrient content of compost will vary with the source of the substance. Further fertility, from either natural or synthetic sources, may be necessary for best health and vigor of your lawn. If buying commercial compost, look for the nutrient analysis label, which will tell you what nutrients are supplied. If you make and use your own compost, you may want to have it tested periodically to determine what nutrients are being provided. Compost will always supply carbon and nitrogen, but an additional source of nitrogen, as well as other required plant nutrients, may still be necessary.

Humic Substances

Another source of natural organic matter for soils is humic material. These are products similar to compost, in that they are decomposed organic matter, but generally they have been decomposing for thousands of years and may come from deposits of peat, lignite, coal, or marine algae. These all contain humic acids in addition to carbon and nitrogen, and often also contain plant hormones or biostimulants, which are substances not required of fertilizers, but which the plant itself produces. Sometimes the addition of supplemental hormones may provide benefits; for example, the plant hormone cytokinin is often found lacking in turfgrass that has suffered a root dieback or decline. Application of cytokinin can offset the stress resulting from the root decline.

Application of humic substances provides benefits beyond those offered by compost. In addition to supplying nutrients, increasing soil nutrient availability, and improving soil structure, humates have been shown to enhance photosynthesis, protein synthesis, root functioning, and seed germination. They are especially beneficial in soils that are low in organic matter, such as sandy Florida soils.

Organic Pest Control

Organic pest control may fall into various categories: use of natural, organic products such as corn gluten meal, use of natural predators and biocontrols, and use of proper cultural practices to relieve pest pressure (integrated pest management). Often a combination of these methods will provide the most effective pest control. In addition, the use of new cultivars developed for resistance to insects or diseases can greatly reduce the overall need for pest control.

Weed Control

The best way to combat weeds is to maintain a healthy, vigorous turf. This is best accomplished through combinations of proper fertility, mowing, and irrigation practices as described throughout the *Florida Lawn Handbook*. One new natural weed control product has been shown through university research to suppress growth of certain weeds: corn gluten meal, a substance commonly found in dog food and cooking oil. It is now commercially available through different companies and has been labeled for use on many warm-season grasses.

Insect Control

It has been shown that many insects that plague our lawns have natural enemies in harmless insects. The use of nonpest insects to reduce populations of problem insects is gaining favor in all sectors of the turfgrass industry. Examples of this include nematode species that have been shown to be predators of mole crickets and sod webworms. For more information, refer to "Insect Management" in chapter 5.

Disease Control

The primary factors needed for a disease to develop are a susceptible host, a pathogen, and a conducive environment. Use of species less prone to disease and proper cultural practices are two of the most effective ways to reduce disease on your lawn. As mentioned above, proper fertility, irrigation, and mowing are all essential to disease control. Use of compost or other organic fertilizers may offer disease suppression as well. For more information on this, refer to "Disease Management" section in chapter 5.

How Do You Know If a Product Will Work?

Before you buy a product that claims to be organic, natural, or effective against a particular problem, ask these questions to determine if the product will be useful to you:

1. Are independent (i.e., university) test results available? Many companies make claims that testing has been done on their product, but it's important to ask who did the testing (their in-house lab or a nonbiased university?) and what the test results showed. Merely indicating that testing has been done does not imply that the product showed a significant advantage over another product, but that fact may be omitted in advertising.
2. Are test results consistent? Are repeated tests validating the results being advertised? Will the product work under different environmental conditions?
3. Are there any problems with application of the product? For instance, if a product claims to provide natural control of a specific insect, are there any other characteristics that would deter your purchase of the product, such as toxicity to the lawn or strong odors?
4. Does this product address a problem that applies to your particular situation? For example, it's great to have an insect predator as a natural control agent, but only if its prey is the insect that is your particular pest. Does the predator naturally occur in Florida?
5. Are the costs justified? Is the response going to be worth the money spent on the product, or is there just a slight or short-lived improvement in the situation? Can you comfortably live with the problem, or use another type of control, rather than correcting it? An example of this would be manually pulling weeds or eliminating the environmental condition making the turf conducive to weed growth, rather than buying a product claiming to naturally eliminate weeds.

Appendix

Florida Extension Service Telephone Numbers

County	City	Telephone
Alachua	Gainesville	352-955-2402
Baker	Macclenny	904-259-3520
Bay	Panama City	850-784-6105
Bradford	Starke	904-966-6299
Brevard	Cocoa	321-633-1702
Broward	Davie	954-370-3725
Calhoun	Blountstown	850-674-8323
Charlotte	Punta Gorda	941-639-6255
Citrus	Inverness	352-726-2141
Clay	Green Cove Springs	904-284-6355
Collier	Naples	239-353-4244
Columbia	Lake City	386-758-1030
Desoto	Arcadia	863-993-4846
Dixie	Cross City	352-498-1237
Duval	Jacksonville	904-387-8850
Escambia	Pensacola	850-477-0953
Flagler	Bunnell	386-437-7464
Franklin	Apalachicola	850-653-9337
Gadsden	Quincy	850-627-6317
Gilchrist	Trenton	352-463-3174
Glades	Moore Haven	863-946-0244
Gulf	Wewahitchka	850-639-3200
Hamilton	Jasper	386-792-1276
Hardee	Wauchula	863-773-2164
Hendry	LaBelle	863-675-5261
Hernando	Brooksville	352-754-4433
Highlands	Sebring	863-386-6540
Hillsborough	Seffner	813-744-5519
Holmes	Bonifay	850-547-1108
Indian River	Vero Beach	772-770-5030
Jackson	Marianna	850-482-9620
Jefferson	Monticello	850-997-2986
Lafayette	Mayo	386-294-1279
Lake	Tavares	352-343-4101
Lee	Ft. Myers	239-338-3247

Leon	Tallahassee	850-487-3004
Levy	Bronson	352-486-2165
Liberty	Bristol	850-643-2229
Madison	Madison	850-973-4138
Manatee	Palmetto	941-722-4524
Marion	Ocala	352-620-3440
Martin	Stuart	561-288-5654
Miami-Dade	Homestead	305-248-3311
Monroe	Key West	305-292-4501
Nassau	Callahan	904-879-1019
Okaloosa	Crestview	850-689-5850
Okeechobee	Okeechobee	863-763-6469
Orange	Orlando	407-836-7570
Osceola	Kissimmee	321-846-4181
Palm Beach	West Palm Beach	561-233-1712
Pasco	Dade City	352-521-4288
Pinellas	Largo	727-582-2100
Polk	Bartow	863-533-0765
Putnam	East Palatka	386-329-0318
Santa Rosa	Milton	850-623-3868
Sarasota	Sarasota	941-793-2728
Seminole	Sanford	407-323-2500
St. Johns	St. Augustine	904-824-4564
St. Lucie	Fort Pierce	772-462-1660
Sumter	Bushnell	352-793-2728
Suwannee	Live Oak	386-362-2771
Taylor	Perry	850-584-4345
Union	Lake Butler	386-496-2321
Volusia	DeLand	386-822-5778
Wakulla	Crawfordville	850-926-3931
Walton	DeFuniak Springs	850-892-8172
Washington	Chipley	850-638-6180

Credits

Chapter 1. Grasses

Selection of a Turfgrass for Florida Lawns
    L. E. Trenholm, J. Bryan Unruh, and John L. Cisar
Bahiagrass for Florida Lawns; Bermudagrass for Florida Lawns; Carpetgrass
for Florida Lawns
    L. E. Trenholm, John L. Cisar, and J. Bryan Unruh
Centipedegrass for Florida Lawns
    L. E. Trenholm, J. Bryan Unruh, and John L. Cisar
Seashore Paspalum for Florida Lawns
    L. E. Trenholm and J. Bryan Unruh
St. Augustinegrass for Florida Lawns
    L. E. Trenholm, J. Bryan Unruh, and John L. Cisar
Zoysiagrass for Florida Lawns
    J. Bryan Unruh, L. E. Trenholm, and John L. Cisar

Chapter 2. Preparation and Establishment

    L. E. Trenholm

Chapter 3. Fertilizing Your Florida Lawn

Fertilizer Recommendations for Your Florida Lawn
    J. B. Sartain
The Florida Fertilizer Label
    J. B. Sartain and W. R. Cox
Spreader Calibration; Soil Testing
    J. B. Sartain

Chapter 4. Cultural Practices for Your Florida Lawn

Mowing Your Florida Lawn; Watering Your Florida Lawn; How to Calibrate
Your Sprinkler System
    L. E. Trenholm, J. Bryan Unruh, and John L. Cisar
Overseeding Your Florida Lawn
    L. E. Trenholm and J. Bryan Unruh
Thatch Control in Your Florida Lawn
    L. E. Trenholm, J. Bryan Unruh, and John L. Cisar

Chapter 5. Pest Management

Integrated Pest Management Strategies
    J. Bryan Unruh and L. E. Trenholm
Weed Management
    J. Bryan Unruh, Barry J. Brecke, and Laurie E. Trenholm
Insect Management
    Eileen A. Buss and J. Bryan Unruh
Disease Management
    M. L. Elliott
Nematode Management
    Billy T. Crow and Robert A. Dunn

Chapter 6. Environmental Stresses and Your Florida Lawn

L. E. Trenholm

Chapter 7. Organic Lawn Care

L. E. Trenholm

About the Editors

Laurie E. Trenholm heads statewide research and extension programming for the Urban Turfgrass Program for IFAS at the University of Florida. She specializes in Best Management Practices for home lawns, turfgrass stress physiology, and use of seashore paspalum.

J. Bryan Unruh joined the faculty at the University of Florida in 1996. He teaches courses in Turfgrass Culture, Landscape and Turfgrass Management, and Golf and Sports Turf Management. As an extension turfgrass specialist, he conducts extensive turfgrass research/demonstration trials focused on turf management. Unruh frequently speaks about his work in many different venues across the country.

Contributors

Brecke, B. J., weed scientist, University of Florida, WFREC, Jay

Buss, E. A., entomologist, University of Florida, IFAS, Gainesville

Cisar, J. L., turf specialist, University of Florida, FLREC, Ft. Lauderdale

Cox, W. R., environmental manager, FDACS, Tallahassee

Crow, W. T., nematologist, University of Florida, IFAS, Gainesville

Dunn, R. A., nematologist, University of Florida (retired)

Elliott, M. E., plant pathologist, University of Florida, FLREC, Ft. Lauderdale

Sartain, J. B., soil scientist, University of Florida, IFAS, Gainesville

Related-interest titles from University Press of Florida

Florida Butterfly Caterpillars and Their Host Plants
Marc C. Minno, Jerry F. Butler, and Donald W. Hall

Florida Butterfly Gardening: A Complete Guide to Attracting, Identifying, and Enjoying Butterflies of the Lower South
Marc C. and Maria Minno

Florida's Best Native Landscape Plants: 200 Readily Available Species for Homeowners and Professionals
Gil Nelson

Florida Landscape Plants: Native and Exotic, second revised edition
John V. Watkins, Thomas J. Sheehan, and Robert J. Black

A Gardener's Guide to Florida's Native Plants
Rufino Osorio

Landscape Plants for the Gulf and South Atlantic Coasts
Robert J. Black and Edward F. Gilman

Landscape Plants for Subtropical Climates
Bijan Dehgan

Landscaping for Florida's Wildlife: Re-creating Native Ecosystems in Your Yard
Joe Schaefer and George Tanner

Vegetable Gardening in Florida
James M. Stephens

Your Florida Garden, Fifth Edition Abridged
John V. Watkins and Herbert S. Wolfe

Your Florida Guide to Bedding Plants: Selection, Establishment, and Maintenance
Robert J. Black and Edward F. Gilman

Your Florida Guide to Shrubs: Selection, Establishment, and Maintenance
Edward F. Gilman and Robert J. Black

For more information on these and other books, visit our website at www.upf.com.